Kate

Kate Middleton:
Princess in Waiting

CLAUDIA JOSEPH

MAINSTREAM
PUBLISHING
EDINBURGH AND LONDON

First published in Great Britain in 2009 by
MAINSTREAM PUBLISHING COMPANY
(EDINBURGH) LTD
7 Albany Street
Edinburgh EH1 3UG

ISBN 9781845964207

A catalogue record for this book is available
from the British Library

Typeset in Adobe Garamond and Pouty

Printed in Great Britain by
CPI Mackays, Chatham ME5 8TD

To my parents, who gave me everything,
and the man who gives me nothing but trouble

Acknowledgements

There are so many people I would like to thank for helping me in the course of researching and writing this book, but a special thank you must go to journalist Simon Trump, without whose support I would never have got it written, and members of the Harrison, Goldsmith, Middleton, Lupton and Glassborow families who have been so kind and generous towards me in researching their family history.

I am extremely grateful to Sian James, the assistant editor of *The Mail on Sunday*, George Thwaites, the editor of the *Review* section and Marilyn Warnick, the books editor, whose advice has been invaluable and without whom I would never have got my first book published. I must also thank my solicitor, John Polsue, a partner at Alen-Buckley & Co., who has been incredibly supportive when I have needed legal advice.

I am also indebted to the journalists Laura Collins, Ian Gallagher, Jo Knowsley, Liz Sanderson, Daniel Townend and Edward Black, and the photographers Jason Buckner, Michael Wheeler, Paul Macnamara and Oscar Kornyei for their generous help.

And I would like to thank the following researchers, whose attention to detail is second to none: Andy Kyle; Peter Day; Patricia Irving; Tony Whitehead, author of *Mary Ann Cotton: Dead But Not Forgotten*; Vanda Hall, customer services assistant at Maidstone Library; Louise-Ann Hand, information librarian at Leeds Central Library; Michele Lefevre, local studies manager at Leeds Central Library; Richard High, team librarian in special collections at the Brotherton Library, Leeds; Leeds University archivist Liza Giffen; Adam Bull, webmaster at The Friends of Gledhow Valley Woods; Lyn Aspland, a historian at the Gledhow Valley Conservation Area Group; Neville Hurworth; Jane Powell, search room assistant at Berkshire Record Office; and Caroline Liggett, senior archives and local studies assistant at the Centre for Buckinghamshire Studies.

Finally, I would like to thank my publisher, Bill Campbell, editor Claire Rose, editorial coordinator Graeme Blaikie, marketing and rights executive Amy Mitchell, designer Emily Bland, publicity manager Fiona Atherton and publicity consultant Sharon Campbell.

To donate to the Children's Hospital, Oxford, home to Tom's Ward, referred to on p. 250, call 01865 743 444 or go to www.oxfordradcliffe.nhs.uk/getinvolved/charitablefunds/children/intro.aspx.

Contents

Preface

On 3 September 1660, in a mansion on The Strand overlooking the River Thames, a secret wedding ceremony took place between the Duke of York, the 27-year-old heir presumptive to the English throne, and his sister's lady's maid Anne Hyde. Performed during the night by the duke's chaplain at her father's home, Worcester House, and witnessed by only two people, the marriage of the future King James II and his heavily pregnant 23-year-old mistress scandalised the royal court, which could not accept that a blue blood had married a commoner. After Anne's death, on 31 March 1671, it was written that she 'indeed shew'd both her witt and her vertue in managing the affaire so dexterously, that the duke, overmaster'd by his passion, at last gave her a promise of marriage some time before the Restoration'. Anne had earned her place in history as the last commoner in this country to marry a king, and she had produced two daughters, Mary and Anne, who would rule the country.

Since that time, Britain's monarchs have rarely veered from the accepted convention of marrying into European royalty, although

there are two notable exceptions: the late Queen Mother, Lady Elizabeth Bowes-Lyon, and Prince William's mother, Lady Diana Spencer. However, both had aristocratic families, and Queen Elizabeth was never expected to become royal consort; it was only after the abdication of Edward VIII that her husband, George VI, became king.

Now, for the first time in 350 years, another commoner has won the heart of an heir to the throne. If, as widely predicted, Kate Middleton marries Prince William Arthur Philip Louis Windsor, after he qualifies as an RAF search-and-rescue pilot in 2010, she will become the first non-aristocrat to marry a future king of this country since the seventeenth century.

The marriage would breathe new life into the monarchy as the Queen enters the twilight of her reign, bringing new blood and a fresh perspective to an institution that faces criticism for being elitist and out of touch. William and Kate have a thoroughly modern relationship – they met as students at St Andrews, where they lived together, and have been dating for some five years.

It was on 7 April 2002 that Kate first graced the pages of a British newspaper, having modelled a diaphanous dress on the catwalk during a charity fashion show at St Andrews. Since then, she has become a permanent fixture in the society pages, a style icon – she regularly makes best-dressed lists both in this country and abroad – and one of the most photographed women in the country. The editors of magazines including *Vogue*, *Tatler* and *GQ* have waxed lyrical about her youth, fashion sense and appeal, and *Hello!* estimates that her image on the cover increases sales by 100,000.

Thousands of words have been written about her, hordes of paparazzi follow her every move, fans blog about her on the Internet and she is regularly discussed on radio and television. She even inspired author Peter York to update *The Official Sloane Ranger Handbook* and has her own unofficial fan club.

Yet, despite the reams of coverage, Britain's potential future queen remains something of a mystery, never having given an interview or spoken about her relationship with the second in line to the throne. So who is the woman who once so memorably retorted: 'He's so lucky to be going out with me!' And does she share the same gifts of 'witt' and 'vertue' as her predecessor?

CHAPTER I

The Harrisons 1837-98

*L*ying in her wooden and gilt bateau lit in her opulent bedroom below the state apartments at Kensington Palace, four weeks after her 18th birthday, Princess Victoria was woken by her mother, the Duchess of Kent, to be told that she was Queen of England. It was 6 a.m. on 20 June 1837 and her uncle King William IV – who had no legitimate children – had died of heart failure and pneumonia at the age of 71, leaving Prince William's great-great-great-great-grandmother to inherit the throne.

Queen Victoria went on to become the longest-reigning monarch in British history and head of a vast empire, marrying her cousin Prince Albert of Saxe-Coburg-Gotha and bearing nine children, from whom both Queen Elizabeth and Prince Philip are descended. The family split their time between Buckingham Palace (Victoria was the first monarch to live there), Windsor Castle, where heads of state were entertained, and their holiday homes, Osborne House on the Isle of Wight and Balmoral Castle in Aberdeenshire, both of which Victoria and Albert bought after their marriage.

At the other end of England, 290 miles from the royal court, in a cramped cottage in the Newcastle suburb of Byker Hill, life could not have been more different for Kate Middleton's great-great-great-great-grandmother Jane Harrison, a miner's wife.

While Queen Victoria was mistress of all she surveyed (and a great many parts of the world she had never even seen), Jane's husband James, 41 in the year of Victoria's accession, enjoyed a considerably narrower view. He earned a pittance working down the mines, while Jane juggled the demands of running a large household on a straitened income, bringing up four children and nursing a fifth. The eldest daughter, also Jane, sixteen, helped with her younger brothers (Thomas, nine, James, seven, two-year-old John and the baby, Septimus), but their mother would not have had any time for relaxation and the news of the King's death – which she would have learned about through word of mouth, because Jane, like so many of her peers, could not read or write – would have had little impact on her world.

By piecing together historical documents and records, it is possible to construct a picture of Jane's life during the early Victorian era. Her whole world would have revolved around the shift patterns of her husband, who worked as a shifter, or maintenance worker, repairing the horseways and other passages in the mine at Byker Colliery, then owned by Sir Henry Lawson.

James was employed under a bond by Sir Henry, which meant that he had been given two shillings and sixpence (about one hundred pounds in today's money) for promising not to work for another colliery. Despite this, he was not guaranteed employment, but at 41 years old he would have been considered well beyond his prime and would not have complained. He was lucky to have work at all, especially with so many mouths to feed.

Thomas followed his father into the mine as a trapper. Working for up to 18 hours a day, in solitude and complete darkness, he was

responsible for opening and shutting the mine traps, or doors, when the underground trams passed, in order to maintain ventilation. Later, Thomas became a driver, steering the horses that pulled the sledges and wagons from the crane to the shaft of the pit, and his younger brother James followed him into the mine. Despite the hardships – men and boys worked round the clock, except on Sundays, Christmas and Easter, and were liable for arrest, trial and imprisonment if they broke their bond – the family must have counted its blessings.

Life down the pit was brutal and dangerous, and in those days there was no sick pay or compensation for death or injury. While the owners supplied the pit ponies, the miners had to provide their own equipment, including picks, shovels, candles, ropes and explosives. The miners worked in gangs in order to protect themselves from thieving, and fights regularly broke out between rival groups.

Such skirmishes aside, the daily danger of mine working tended to unite the communities. Any report of an accident would mean that the women in the area would gather at the pithead, anxious for information about their men. It was a tradition that would last well into the twentieth century, when pit disasters, although much rarer, were by no means eradicated.

In James Harrison's time, though, the dangers of working underground were ever present. Records indicate that there were more than 30 mining disasters in Durham and Northumberland in the nineteenth century, in which 1,500 men and boys were killed. Of course, these were only the major incidents. Individual deaths were commonplace but are more difficult to quantify, as the death of a single collier barely merited an inquest. Not only were there fires, rockfalls and explosions in the mines, but many pitmen were crushed to death by the trams (four-wheel carriages that carried corves, or tubs, of coal), kicked to death by ponies, fell down shafts or were drowned.

Life was hard for women, too. In Victorian England, they were deemed chattels of their husbands and would have to behave as such. With no hope of contraception, Jane Harrison was almost constantly pregnant. Her sixth baby, a daughter Margaret, was born in 1839, the year after Victoria's glittering coronation at Westminster Abbey. Jane and her eldest daughter would have spent their days cleaning their sparse home, a tiny single-room cottage with an open fire and a ladder to the loft, where the children slept. They drew water at a street pump, washed, darned and mended ragged clothing, cooked for the family on the open fire and heated water in a tin bath for James and his sons when they finished a shift. The little food they bought came from the local 'tommy shop', the name deriving from the coarse bread that eighteenth-century soldiers received in their rations. Tommy shops were run by the owners of mines. Workers were often given some of their pay in tokens that could be used only in the shop, and the prices were inflated. Thus, mine owners made even more profit out of their employees, who often fell into debt. The family sometimes supplemented their meagre income by working in the fields, picking fruit, potatoes or turnips.

It was an unrelentingly tough existence for the Harrisons. Never would they have considered that one of their descendants would be poised to marry into the royal family. Indeed, it is a near-miracle that their line survived at all. Many mining villages were decimated by epidemics of tuberculosis, cholera, polio, scarlet fever and diphtheria, which raced through the densely populated communities, fuelled by the insanitary outside latrines that were shared by scores of people.

While Queen Victoria lived to the ripe old age of 81 – dying at Osborne House of a brain haemorrhage and being buried beside her beloved Albert at Windsor – Kate's great-great-great-great-grandmother had a pauper's death. Jane fell victim to

consumption, an infection of the lungs more commonly known today as tuberculosis, at her home in Byker Hill on 23 April 1845, shortly after her 50th birthday, leaving her husband a widower with four young children.

After his wife's death and the expiry of his bond, James joined thousands of families heading 20 miles south of Newcastle to the pit villages of County Durham. They may well have been amongst the first passengers on George Hudson's new Newcastle to Durham Junction Railway, which opened amidst great acclaim in 1844. Certainly, by 1850 they were living in a miner's cottage in Low Row, one of four streets in the tiny village of Low Moorsley, seven miles north-east of Durham.

There, Kate's great-great-great-grandfather John and his younger brother Septimus joined their father down the pit at North Hetton Colliery, owned by the 2nd Earl of Durham, George Lambton, whose father had been a prominent Whig politician and whose great-grandmother had been mistress to the Prince of Wales, later George IV. The Earl, who was the great-grandfather of former prime minister Sir Alec Douglas-Home, made his money from mining on the lands around his Lambton Castle and proved equally as hard a taskmaster as Sir Henry Lawson.

Although the 1842 Mines Act prevented children under ten from working in the mines, the two boys would have joined the workforce the moment they reached double figures. There was a hierarchy down the mines and they would have begun as trappers and drivers before graduating at the age of 17 to become putters, pushing the corves of coal on trams from the coalface to the crane or shaft. The work was just as dangerous as it had always been. In 1853, one of John and Septimus's colleagues, John Straughan, a 12-year-old driver, was killed when his head was crushed between two moving trams. At nearby Hetton Colliery, 23 stonemasons died in an underground explosion in 1860, and

all the horses and pit ponies in the stables perished as flames rampaged through the mine.

At the age of 21, the Harrison boys reached their physical prime and became hewers, the men who actually cut the coal at the face, in tunnels so small they had to work on their hands and knees. Although the job was dangerous, it was sought after, as hewers were the best-paid workers. Perhaps the extra money (the family also took in two lodgers, joiner George Dixon, 33, and William Mitcheson, a 36-year-old labourer) allowed the Harrisons to move on, because soon they had a new home two miles down the road, a miner's cottage in the village of Sherburn Hill.

John was by this time making his own way in the world: he had moved into a cottage just around the corner from his father's. On 7 April 1860, he married his girlfriend Jane Liddle, a 20-year-old miner's daughter from the village, who was already four months pregnant on their wedding day.

In August of the same year, Septimus, 23, wed a girl from the neighbouring village of Houghton-le-Spring, Elizabeth Jenkyns, 19, who was heavily pregnant, at the same church. Their son James was born the following month. They moved into another miner's cottage in Sherburn Hill, meaning that the three families were all within walking distance of each other.

John and Jane's first child, Jane Ann, was born in September, followed by a son, Anthony, in 1862, and another daughter, Margaret, in 1863. The family would have been far too busy to mourn the death of Queen Victoria's beloved Prince Albert in 1861, celebrate the wedding of William's great-great-great-grandfather the future Edward VII to Princess Alexandra in 1863 or follow his liaisons with society beauties such as actress Lillie Langtry or Camilla Parker Bowles' great-grandmother Alice Keppel.

By the 1860s, Kate's great-great-great-great-grandfather James had long since retired from the pit. It can be surmised that following

his retirement he spent a good deal of time in the local pubs, for he died of liver failure in 1866 at the age of 70. His illiterate daughter Jane, who cared for her father during his final two weeks, signed his death certificate with a cross.

After James's death, his family moved away from Sherburn Hill. While Septimus moved six miles down the road to the village of Brandon, John moved with Jane and their children to Hetton-le-Hole, four miles away. They were part of migration to the town: in 1801 there were just 212 people living in Hetton, but by 1861 the population had increased to 6,419. John worked at Hetton Colliery, once owned by former bankrupt and speculator Arthur Mowbray. In 1822, it had become the first colliery to have its own private railway, an eight-mile track from Hetton to the River Wear at Sunderland, designed by George Stephenson, the 'Father of Railways'. This was the first line in the country not to use horsepower.

Life at the coalface was hard, but John and his family, who lived on Downs New Houses in one of the 1,318 stone cottages in the town, had a better lifestyle than their parents, as the town had chapels, schools, pubs and shops, as well as a wide range of tradesmen, including blacksmiths, tinsmiths, stonemasons and joiners, printers and publishers, even a physician. Above all, the town had something that previous generations of the Harrison family had never experienced: a school. At least one of the children was registered in the 1871 census as a scholar, a tiny sign that the forces of social reform that would eventually change Britain for ever were beginning to make their presence felt.

On 25 July 1874, Kate's great-great-grandfather, named John like his father, was born. Within five years of his birth, the Harrisons' family had swollen to ten children, forcing them to move to a new home in the town's Lyons Street. Their happiness, however, was short-lived. On 23 December 1881, Jane died of tuberculosis

at just 42. Her husband, who was by her bedside when she died in their home, was left a widower with ten children aged between two and twenty-one.

The following year, John's eldest child, Jane Ann, left home, marrying a 21-year-old miner from the village, John Anderson, at the local parish church. Margaret, 19, became the woman of the home, caring for her father and younger siblings.

It was a hard life with very little reward for those on the bottom rung of the ladder, the antithesis of the luxurious lifestyle enjoyed by Queen Victoria and her children. In 1887, Victoria marked 50 years on the throne with a sumptuous banquet served on golden platters, a procession through London in a gilded carriage, a glittering ball and a thrilling firework display.

The following year, 18-year-old Isabella died of the same disease as her mother. There was still no treatment for tuberculosis and it cut a swathe through working-class homes. Once again, her father sat by the bedside of a dying loved one. He was grief-stricken at having lost his wife and a daughter within seven years of each other, and within five months he too was dead from the same disease, most probably caught at his daughter's bedside. The date was 29 January 1889 and he was just 54 years old. Before a year had passed, his 17-year-old son James, who worked as a coal putter, would become the family's fourth victim of tuberculosis within a decade.

Kate's great-great-grandfather John was an orphan at the tender age of 14. He and his two unmarried sisters were forced into lodgings. But the family's run of bad luck did not end there. At about 11.30 a.m. on 13 December 1895, John's eldest brother, Anthony, was killed in a mining accident. The father of two, who was a hewer at Hetton Coal Company's Eppleton Colliery, was hailed as a hero after trying to rescue two of his colleagues, deputy John Brown and putter Robert Lawns, but he paid with his life. He was commended in the 1895 Mines Inspection Report:

I should like here to say a word or two in appreciation of the courage and gallantry shown by the men who were amongst the rescuers. The three hewers, as well as the manager, under-manager, overman, and back-overman, all showed that they possessed the qualities which in the past made pitmen famous for heroism in the time of danger; such conduct as theirs should not go without commendation, and I am pleased to have the opportunity in this report, to show my appreciation of it, and I regret that one of them should have lost his life in the plucky attempt made to rescue Brown and Lawns.

Such a run of tragedy seems extraordinary by today's standards and would be enough to destroy lesser men. But John Harrison had lived a tough life in which illness and death were by no means unusual.

At the age of 22, on 23 February 1897, John married domestic servant Jane Hill, 21, the daughter of a joiner at the colliery, at Houghton-le-Spring Register Office. They moved into a miner's cottage on Chapel Street in the suburb of Hetton Downs. Eleven months later, they celebrated the birth of their first child, Jane, named after her mother and grandmother. For the young couple, it marked a new beginning. Another generation of the Harrison family had been born and it was the end of the nineteenth century, the dawn of a new era. The next century would bring terrible wars and extraordinary advances that could never have been foreseen. The Harrisons could not possibly have realised, either, how much their personal fortunes would change and how close they would come to the gilded world of royalty.

CHAPTER 2

The Harrisons 1901-53

*I*t was 2 February 1901. The weather was bitterly cold and snow was falling. Queen Victoria had died 11 days earlier. Prince William's great-great-great-grandfather Edward VII rode behind his mother's coffin as the cortège snaked its way through the streets of London. Its final destination was St George's Chapel at Windsor Castle. After a state funeral attended by the great and good of the Commonwealth, Victoria's body lay in state for two days before being laid to rest beside that of Prince Albert in the Royal Mausoleum at Frogmore House.

Queen Victoria's death heralded a new age. Eighteen months later, Edward VII and Alexandra were crowned king and queen by the Archbishop of Canterbury at Westminster Abbey – a little later than expected, as the 59-year-old monarch was diagnosed with appendicitis shortly before the date originally set for the coronation. The King donated Osborne House, where his mother had died, to the state and lived at Sandringham House in Norfolk, as he had done before his accession. His son George – Prince William's

great-great-grandfather – and his wife Mary, who by then had four children, including the future Edward VIII and George VI, lived in York Cottage on the estate.

John Harrison would have read about the coronation in the newspaper or heard the news at the local pub. But he would have given little thought to the lives of the royal family and could never have guessed that his great-great-granddaughter might one day be so close to the country's rulers. He had more pressing matters on his mind, such as raising enough money to make ends meet. John was not long married to Jane, and the couple lived in a cramped cottage in Chapel Street, Hetton Downs, with their three-year-old daughter Jane and baby son Ernest. Jane's sister Sarah Hill lived with the family and helped out with the daily chores, but it was still a tough existence and the couple hoped that their children would be able to make a more comfortable future for themselves.

When their third child – Kate's great-grandfather – was born on 23 June 1904, they named him Thomas after Jane and Sarah's father, who was a carpenter and joiner. A devoted grandfather, he spent many hours with the young boy and when his grandson was barely out of short trousers, he began to teach him the rudimentary skills of his profession.

Thomas was just five years old when King Edward VII collapsed, suffering from bronchitis, while on holiday in Biarritz. A heavy smoker – he is reputed to have smoked 20 cigarettes and 12 cigars a day – he then suffered several heart attacks following his return to Britain. He died on 6 May 1910, his wife Alexandra and mistress Alice Keppel at his bedside. He had just been told by his son George, Prince of Wales, that his horse Witch of the Air had won that afternoon at Kempton Park. 'I'm very glad,' the King replied. They were his final words. George V and Queen Mary were crowned

at Westminster Abbey on 22 June 1911. Afterwards, the King and Queen travelled to India, visiting their subjects. During the trip, the King indulged his hobby of hunting, shooting 21 tigers.

Three years later, on 28 June 1914, Archduke Franz Ferdinand, the heir to the throne of Austria–Hungary, was assassinated by a Bosnian Serb named Gavrilo Princip. The event sparked the beginning of the Great War. Life would never be the same again. Thomas Harrison was too young to fight in the First World War, but it had a major impact on his formative years, as Hetton-le-Hole, which had a population of 13,673 at the turn of the century, became a shadow of its former self. Hundreds of miners from the area volunteered for the Northumberland Fusiliers and the Durham Light Infantry, while the women and children had to adapt to life without them.

At first, Thomas's father John, who had just celebrated his 40th birthday when war broke out, remained at home, looking after his young family, but eventually he was forced to enlist. In March 1916, the British government, in response to the rising losses on the Western Front – Britain lost 75,000 men at Ypres and 60,000 at Loos – and the dwindling number of volunteers, introduced conscription for single men between the ages of 18 and 41. By May, the order had been extended to married men. It was just two months before John Harrison's 42nd birthday, an accident of birth that would change the course of his descendants' lives.

John enlisted with the Duke of Cambridge's Own Middlesex Regiment in the neighbouring town of Houghton-le-Spring. The 43-year-old corporal was killed in the trenches just three months before armistice, on 24 August 1918, one of 201 soldiers from Hetton-le-Hole not to return from the battlefields. His name is inscribed on a war memorial outside the working men's club in the town – a granite plinth and statue of a soldier resting on a reverse rifle with his head bowed. It bears the inscription: 'Erected by the

members of Hetton and District Working Men's Club in memory
of fellow members who died for their country in the Great War
1914–1918'.

The conflict finally drew to a close at 11 a.m. on 11 November
1918. That day, a declaration of peace was read to the community of
Hetton-le-Hole. Thomas was 14 years old. His world had changed
irrevocably. Spurred on by his father's death, he was apprenticed
to his maternal grandfather – now the only male role model in
his beleaguered family – and became the first Harrison to learn
a trade.

Not long after the war's end, the royal family suffered a
bereavement of their own. While Thomas lost his father, George
V lost his son. Prince John, his sixth and youngest child, died of
an epileptic seizure on 18 January 1919. He was a year younger
than Thomas. The Queen wrote to her husband: 'The first break
in the family circle is hard to bear but people have been so kind
and sympathetic and this has helped us much.'

The interwar years were not good ones for the North-east. The
war had damaged Britain's trading position with regard to exports
such as textiles, steel and coal. Heavy industry went into decline
and mining bore the brunt of the slump. In 1923, 170,000 miners
were employed in Durham alone. Over the 16 years before the
outbreak of the Second World War, many of them lost their jobs as
demand for coal decreased. A series of strikes crippled the country
and Britain slumped into a depression. Miners concerned about
dangerous working conditions, reduced pay and longer hours took
part in the 1926 General Strike in support of the Trades Union
Congress, as well as holding two national coal strikes. Finally, the
1929 stock market crash brought the Great Depression. Demand
for British products collapsed and levels of unemployment increased

from 1 million to 2.5 million. The industrial areas of the North were hardest hit, especially the collieries. Mining was no longer a job for life.

However, there was a huge building boom after the war – a third of all houses built before 1939 were erected in the previous two decades – and tradesmen were much in demand. Grateful for his grandfather's carpentry training, Kate's great-grandfather Thomas spent the years between the wars moving around the north of England to find work. By 1934, the 29-year-old house joiner was living in the village of Easington Lane, a few miles away from Hetton-le-Hole, and going out with a girl from Tudhoe, a village just south of Durham. Elizabeth Temple, who was a year older than Thomas, was the daughter of a farm worker who had turned his hand to gardening after the war. A 'fallen woman', she had an illegitimate daughter, Ruth, from a previous relationship.

Even so, times had changed and the young couple would have enjoyed a very different romance from their parents and grandparents before them, travelling to Durham and Sunderland for dates, going to dance halls and jazz clubs, spending the evening at the pictures, listening to the wireless or gramophone. Within months, they had fallen in love and both their families were delighted when they got engaged. They were married on 12 May 1934 at the parish church in Tudhoe, with Thomas's brother Albert and Elizabeth's sister Maggie as witnesses. Ruth was barely a year old.

After their wedding, the couple moved back to Thomas's home village of Hetton-le-Hole, where a year later, on 26 June 1935, Kate's grandmother Dorothy was born. It was Dorothy's pursuit of property, prosperity and respectability that would lead Kate to the throne of England. But she was helped by a number of political events that drove her family south, towards the royal family.

Dorothy was barely six months old when King George V died at Sandringham at 11.55 p.m. on 20 January 1936. A heavy smoker, he had suffered from a series of persistent breathing problems, including emphysema, bronchitis and pleurisy. According to the diary of the royal physician, Lord Dawson, the King's final words were 'God damn you', mumbled to a nurse as she administered a sedative. Dawson admitted giving him a lethal injection of cocaine and morphine that night to hasten his death and relieve his suffering.

The Harrison family would have been glued to the wireless again at the end of the year, when George V's son Edward VIII, having caused a constitutional crisis by becoming engaged to Wallis Simpson, an American divorcee, decided to renounce his right to the throne. On 11 December 1936, his abdication speech was broadcast throughout Britain and the Empire: 'You must believe me when I tell you that I have found it impossible to carry the heavy burden of responsibility and to discharge my duties as King as I would wish to do without the help and support of the woman I love,' he said.

That burden of responsibility was passed to his brother, King George VI, who had never expected to inherit the crown. His wife Elizabeth, the late Queen Mother, never forgave her brother-in-law for removing her family from their peaceful existence at 145 Piccadilly and throwing her daughters Elizabeth, ten, and Margaret, six, into the limelight.

Kate's grandmother was a toddler when William's great-grandfather ascended the throne and just four years old when Hitler invaded Poland. But her parents would have listened with a sense of impending doom to Neville Chamberlain's broadcast at 11.15 a.m. on 3 September 1939, stating that 'this country is at war with Germany'. Like his father before him, Thomas could not avoid service; unlike his father, though, he survived the war. Ironically,

those who worked in reserved occupations, including coal miners, were exempt from military service on the grounds that they were essential to the war effort at home. How Thomas must have rued his step up the social ladder.

While the men of Hetton-le-Hole went off to war, many of the women became 'Aycliffe Angels', taking a 25-mile bus journey for 12-hour shifts in the ammunitions factories in Newton Aycliffe.

Sunderland was one of the most heavily bombed areas in England during the war because it was the largest shipbuilding centre in the world. Family life in the region was thrown into chaos as air-raid shelters were dug, blackout curtains fitted, beaches closed and railings removed and melted down to build ships and tanks. Families were issued with gas masks and ration books of coupons. They huddled around the radio in the early evening to listen to the BBC Home Service and were enthralled to read about the morale-boosting visit of King George VI and Queen Elizabeth to a Sunderland shipyard after a series of heavy bombings in 1943.

For once, the Harrisons' lives mirrored those of the royal family, who insisted on staying in Britain during the war. The King and Queen split their time between Buckingham Palace and Windsor. On one occasion, they narrowly escaped death when two German bombs exploded in one of the courtyards while they were in residence at Buckingham Palace. Afterwards, the Queen memorably stated: 'I'm glad we have been bombed. Now I can look the East End in the face.' In total, the palace suffered nine direct hits during the war, and one of their loyal policemen died as a result. PC Steve Robertson, who was on duty at the palace on 8 March 1941, was killed by flying debris when the north side of the building was struck by a bomb. The royals insisted on adhering to the limits imposed on their subjects by rationing, to the extent that when Eleanor Roosevelt, the First Lady, stayed at Buckingham Palace, she remarked on the restrictions on hot water.

After the war, Thomas and Elizabeth Harrison moved down from the North-east to the outskirts of London with their children Ruth and Dorothy. Kate's grandmother was now within easy travelling distance of both Windsor Castle and Buckingham Palace, but the family certainly did not have the money to enjoy the lifestyle the capital had to offer. That would come to the next generation.

Now, having reached an era when we can learn about the Harrisons from first-hand information, we have a more detailed picture of just how impoverished they were. Virtually penniless, they lived in a run-down house on Bankside, on the edge of the Grand Union Canal, in Southall, west London.

Ann Terry, who is the couple's great-niece – the niece of Dorothy's husband Ronald – would go and stay with them when she was a child during the '50s. She and her cousins Harry Jones and Pat Charman have keen memories of the poverty in the Harrisons' household.

'Thomas was a very dapper little man with a moustache,' Ann recalls. 'He and his wife Elizabeth were just ordinary people. They had nothing to be snobbish about. They had a smallholding where they kept chickens. But Dorothy always thought she was one above everybody else. I don't know where she got her airs and graces from.'

'They came from nothing,' adds Harry. 'They were complete commoners, as poor as poor can be.'

Pat remembers feeling intimidated by Dorothy, despite going to a grammar school herself. 'She lived in one of the most scruffy streets you could imagine, on a canal bank,' she says, 'and went to an ordinary secondary modern school. But she had a way of making you feel uneasy.'

Kate's grandmother Dorothy was a 12-year-old schoolgirl when William's grandmother Princess Elizabeth married Lieutenant Philip Mountbatten in a glittering ceremony at Westminster Abbey

on 20 November 1947. Dorothy had yet to even meet her own Prince Charming, but a couple of miles down the road lived the man who was destined to be her future husband.

George VI died in his sleep on the night of 6 February 1952, after 16 years on the throne. He was just 56 years old and was battling lung cancer when he suffered a coronary thrombosis. His daughter Elizabeth, who was about to embark on a tour of Australia, flew back from Kenya for the funeral ten days later. Her coronation took place at Westminster Abbey in June of the following year. Crowds lined the streets of London to catch a glimpse of the new monarch as she made her way to and from Buckingham Palace in the golden state coach. Others listened to live coverage of the event on the radio or watched it on television.

Thomas Harrison had now lived under five monarchs – remarkable when you consider that his grandfather had been born, lived and died under Queen Victoria. Thomas, though, had more pressing matters on his mind than princes and princesses. He had to earn the money to pay for two weddings. His eldest daughter Ruth was 19 and working as a shop assistant when she married machinist Ivor Pritchard, 25, at the Holy Trinity Church in Southall on 4 April 1953. Four months later, it was the turn of his other daughter, Dorothy; she married Ronald Goldsmith. And it was her ambitions and aspirations that would ultimately lead the family to the gilded gates of Buckingham Palace.

CHAPTER 3

The Goldsmiths 1837–1918

Working from dawn to dusk as a carpenter to feed his wife and five children, John Goldsmith would have greeted the dawn of 28 July 1837 as any other, by getting ready for work. Waking early in his tiny terraced house in Maidstone, he dressed in a hurry, downed a mug of tea and rushed out of the door, barely glancing at the headlines in the local newspaper, which on that day pronounced the election of the town's new MP, Benjamin Disraeli, a notorious and debt-ridden philanderer who was one day to be Prime Minister and a great friend and ally of Queen Victoria.

Kate Middleton's great-great-great-great-grandfather John Goldsmith would have been too busy earning a crust to pay much attention to the political events of the day. Like Kate's other maternal great-great-great-great-grandfather, Goldsmith came from an impoverished working-class background. However, their experiences of life were light years apart. While John Harrison lived in a mining community in Durham, John Goldsmith had

grown up in the county town of Kent. Maidstone, on the banks of the River Medway, was in 1837 a dirty and insanitary town. Although it had gas lighting, it was yet to have modern drains or sewers. The town was, however, prosperous, supplying the capital with hops, linen, paper, ragstone and gin. The brewing and paper-manufacturing industries boomed and others grew up, including food processing and bottling mineral water. As a result, the population was growing rapidly – it increased from 8,000 people at the turn of the nineteenth century to 20,000 half a century later – and Maidstone had its own police force and a corn exchange, where grain was bought and sold. As the population increased, the roads between the main thoroughfares became crammed with houses for the working class and the town expanded towards the county jail as the upper classes moved into the suburbs on the estates of the 2nd Earl of Romney, a landowner and parliamentarian who lived in the stately home Mote House. According to an edition of *Gardener's Chronicle* that appeared towards the end of the nineteenth century, Mote House's impressive gardens employed 25 staff members, were home to exotic plants and included a kitchen garden that supplied the house with oranges, peaches and grapes.

In contrast, John, who was 56 in 1837, lived in a cramped tenement in Wheeler Street, near the prison walls, with his wife Rebecca, 14 years his junior, and their five children. The street was also home to The Greyhound pub, which had a pleasure garden. There, John and his two elder sons, Charles, 19, and Richard, 17, who were both labourers, surely enjoyed many a pint while Rebecca cared for the younger children – two daughters, Mary Ann, twelve, and Sophia, eight, and a son, also named John, ten, who was Kate's great-great-great-grandfather. There was a British School for 200 boys in the street, where youngsters were taught to 'reverence the scriptures', 'respect their parents and instructors' and be 'honest, sober and useful in society'. These schools, the

brainchild of Quaker Joseph Lancaster, were run by the British and Foreign School Society and were intended to provide an affordable elementary education for the children of the poor. It is unlikely, however, that the Goldsmiths would have been able to afford even the penny a week for their sons to learn to read, write and do arithmetic.

It was a tough existence and the family mixed with people who had no qualms about breaking the law, becoming close friends with one family in particular, the Hickmotts, who were no strangers to prison. A builder's labourer and thief, Samuel Hickmott and his older brother Thomas gained notoriety in 1837 when they went on the run after being indicted for stealing three lambs from a Sussex farmer called Samuel Pix. They were finally arrested two years later at Brighton railway station, were tried at Maidstone Assizes in January 1840 and transported to Australia that April.

Samuel's son Edward was, like his father before him, an inmate of the new Maidstone jail, which had been opened on the north of the town in 1819. After being released, he met the Goldsmith brothers on a building site where he was working as a bricklayer. He soon captured the heart of their sister Mary Ann, by now a pretty teenager. They tied the knot at Trinity Church, Maidstone, on 30 May 1842. She was just sixteen years old and he was five years her senior. The following year, she gave birth to the first of her six children, Mary Ann. Some years later, however, her husband was working on the other side of the world, in India, leaving her to bring up their children.

Sadly, John Goldsmith did not live to see any of his grandchildren grow up. After a long battle against stomach cancer, he died on 7 June 1847, at the age of 66. His wife Rebecca was at his bedside.

The following year, it was the turn of the couple's youngest daughter, Sophia, to marry into the Hickmott family. She would

have been deemed a scarlet woman in those days; the 21-year-old was living in sin with her brickmaker fiancé, Henry Hickmott, in Hackney, east London, and was heavily pregnant with their second child when they tied the knot at the parish church on 18 June 1848. Within a year, the couple followed in the footsteps of Henry's convict father and emigrated to Australia with their two daughters, Emma, a toddler, and baby Eliza. They boarded the ship *Emily* at the Port of London on 4 May 1849 and arrived at Port Adelaide three months later on 8 August.

Perhaps John Goldsmith travelled to London to wave his sister off on her voyage. We know that before long the lure of the capital would prove too great. By the time John had turned 21, in 1848, he was the only one of his siblings still living at home. His two brothers, Charles and Richard, had made their way to London to find work as brickies and his sisters, Mary Ann and Sophia, had married and moved far away from home. To the impressionable young labourer, the bright lights beckoned. While his widowed mother Rebecca, who was now working as a charwoman, moved to nearby Tovil and took in a lodger, John moved up to London, taking a room in a house in Green Man's Lane, Hounslow, close to his elder brothers.

In the capital, John met laundress Esther Jones, who was the daughter of a workmate and five years younger than him. They fell in love and got married on 23 September 1850, at the Parish Church of St John the Baptist in Hoxton in the East End of London. Both were illiterate and signed the register with a cross. They moved in with her parents. Within weeks of the wedding, Esther was pregnant with their first child and Kate's great-great-grandfather, named John after his father and grandfather, was born at Esther's parents' home on 6 July 1851. There was to be a nine-year gap before they had another child, but then another five came along. Due to their expanding brood, they moved into their own

Kate

home in Triangle Place, Islington, and their happiness seems to have been complete. The only sadness to blight their life together was the death of John's mother, Rebecca, on 29 December 1869, as a result of bronchitis.

Although life expectancy was short, both John and Esther lived long enough to bring up all their children and see them leave home. They were still alive on 18 September 1882, when their eldest son John, a general labourer like his father and grandfather before him, tied the knot with his common-law wife Jane Dorset, four years his junior, at St Mary's Church, Paddington, and for the birth of their daughter Eliza two years later. Sadly, however, on 19 December 1885, Esther succumbed to bronchitis at the age of 53. In 1888, the year after Victoria's golden jubilee, Esther's widower husband John died of a strangulated hernia at the age of 61.

So, unlike Kate's other great-great-grandfather John Harrison, orphaned at the tender age of 14, John Goldsmith was 37 and married with three children when his father died. His third child – Kate's great-grandfather – was born at home in Priory Road, Acton, on 6 November 1886, a cause of great celebration for the family. He was christened Stephen Charles but known as Charlie to his family. The couple went on to have another six children – in those days, large families were the norm among the working classes – although several died. The couple eventually settled in a run-down house in Featherstone Terrace, Southall, shortly before the turn of the century. It was there that they heard about the death of Queen Victoria on 22 January 1901, and the coronation of Edward VII and Queen Alexandra. Little did the Goldsmiths realise how different from the Victorian age the dawning twentieth century would be for them and their descendants.

Within a few years, Charlie had moved to Villier Street in Uxbridge, where he worked as a mechanic. It was there that he would meet his future wife, Edith, who lived with her family

two streets away in Chiltern View Road. Although Edith had grown up with her father Benjamin, an ornamental plasterer, and mother Amelia in a large house in the village of Denham, Buckinghamshire, her family had fallen on hard times and been forced to sell up and move three miles to the less salubrious town of Uxbridge, known for its flour production and breweries. However, it seems they soon became part of the community, as Benjamin became a bell ringer at St Margaret's Church in the heart of the town.

Their daughter Alice Tomlinson, now 97, and the only one of her siblings still alive, recalls her mother telling her about her background. 'My mum was the baby of the family,' she says. 'She grew up in a big house in Denham. Her parents were both quite well off. Their families had had a baker's shop and a butcher's shop opposite one another and that's how they came together. Somehow or other, along the line, they lost all their money. It was held in chancery and somebody signed the wrong documents or something.'

Edith was a tiny woman, under 5 ft tall and weighing 7 st. She was disfigured by a huge scar on her torso, which she had got during a narrow escape from death when she was a toddler. 'Grandad used to light his cigar in his big oil stove in the hall of the big house where they lived,' says Alice. 'He would roll a piece of paper up and put it in the stove and light his cigar. Of course, when he went out, my mum copied. She had a go doing the same thing and nearly burned herself to death.'

Charlie and Edith got married at Uxbridge Register Office on 27 March 1909. He was 22 years old and she was a year younger. The ceremony may have been brought forward because she was four months pregnant with their first child. They moved into their first home, just streets away from his parents, at 16 Spencer Street, Southall. Their eldest son, Stephen Charles, also nicknamed Charlie,

was born on 20 August 1909, followed by Alice, nicknamed Minnie, in 1911, and Edith, known as Ede, in 1913.

However, within a year of Ede's birth, war had broken out. Charlie signed up on 19 May 1915 and served in France with the Royal Fusiliers, initially in the trenches and afterwards in the cookhouse. He was one of Kitchener's 'shilling men', having signed up in the wake of Secretary of State for War Lord Kitchener's campaign for men between 19 and 30 to join the army. 'My dad used to work on the coal carts when we were little,' recalls Alice, 'but then he went to war. All the lads joined up together to get the King's shilling to get some beer.'

Just ten days after Charlie arrived in France, he discovered that his elder brother John, a private in the 3/8th battalion of the Middlesex Regiment, had been taken into South Western Hospital in Stockwell, which cared for people with fevers, smallpox and other infectious diseases. He died at the age of 30, one of 2,343 civilians and 1,136 soldiers who succumbed to cerebrospinal fever, or meningitis, in England and Wales during 1915 alone. There were numerous outbreaks of the disease during the Great War because of the overcrowded conditions experienced by young recruits in army barracks, depots, camps and billets.

The boys' father was heartbroken. He soon lost the will to live, dying of exhaustion, melancholia and vascular disease at the age of 68, shortly after the war ended. The war spelled the end of another generation of the Goldsmith family, but it was the dawn of a new era for Kate's great-grandparents Charlie and Edith and their children.

CHAPTER 4

The Goldsmiths 1918-53

*I*t was just before Christmas 1918, six weeks after Armistice Day, and thousands of soldiers were still in France while their leaders wrangled over the terms of the peace. But others, more fortunate, were on their way home. Kate's great-grandfather Private Charlie Goldsmith arrived back from France shortly after his 32nd birthday. There was great excitement at 57 Clarence Street, Southall. His wife Edith greeted him with their three small children, Charlie, nine, Alice, seven, and Ede, five. But there was also a new addition to the clan, one whom Charlie had yet to meet: six-month-old baby Annie, known as Hetty, who had been conceived when he was on leave.

After welcoming Charlie home, the young family joined the other local veterans and their children for a Christmas party and then a tea in the white-brick Southall Town Hall. Alice, now 97, still remembers the occasion. She recalls: 'I was only a little girl but I remember him coming home in his soldier's clothes. I remember the children's party and celebrations. It was in a hall at the bottom

of the station, which used to be the old billiard hall. We marched from there to the town hall for tea and a present from Father Christmas. I got a skipping rope.'

The joyous occasion was a welcome break for the family, who found life between the wars a constant struggle. While Southall is now a predominantly Asian area, in those days it was a white working-class suburb, providing labour for the sprawling brick factories, flour mills and chemical plants, the railway depots and engineering works that had sprung up around the Grand Junction Canal (once the main freight route between London and Birmingham), Brunel's Great Western Railway and the Uxbridge Road. Unfortunately, life did not become much easier for the family when Charlie, who was nicknamed 'Putty' by his mates, returned home, as he was suffering from emphysema. He had to abandon his manual work shifting household coal in favour of factory work, landing a job at the Maypole Dairy, owned by a Danish margarine manufacturer. Opened in 1894, it had grown to become one of the largest such plants in the world and was serviced by a specially constructed railway siding and branch of the canal.

'When my dad came home, he wasn't really well,' says Alice. 'I don't know whether he got emphysema from the trenches or from smoking. He never talked about the war or told us anything about it. But after he came home from France, he would always tell us, "Never volunteer for anything. You never know what you are letting yourself in for." We were allowed to run free and do as we liked. We weren't restricted or anything. But I suppose all children were like that then. Everybody was hard up and nobody had anything.'

Despite their straitened circumstances, Charlie and Edith had two more children, Joyce in 1924 and Kate's grandfather Ronald on 25 April 1931. Both were born in Clarence Street, which in those days was one of the most impoverished streets in the neighbourhood. It was crammed with large working-class families who earned a

living in the nearby factories and gasworks, working all the hours they could. The hardship brought with it a sense of community, with neighbours rallying round to look after the latchkey children, keeping a watchful eye over them as they played in the streets. The Goldsmiths' neighbours included the family of jazz singer Cleo Laine, who was three and a half years older than Ronald. Her father, Alexander Campbell, was an itinerant labourer from Jamaica, who busked to make a living, while her mother, Minnie, ran a boarding house in the street, renting out rooms to Irish labourers.

By the time Ronald was born, his father had given up working at the factory and returned to manual work as a builder's labourer. Alice, then 20, had already left home, having got married two years earlier to Bill Tomlinson, a Welsh miner who had moved to London and was employed at Rockwell Glassworks. 'I left school at 14 and did various jobs in factories before marrying Bill when I was 18,' says Alice. 'We met in Southall Park. We were glad to get married and get away from home, really.'

Ronald was eight months old when his elder brother Charlie, then 22 years old and a master plasterer, married labourer's daughter Emma Neal on Boxing Day 1931. The couple wed at the Parish Church of St John in Southall. 'Charlie was a clever boy but remote,' says Alice, who went to the wedding with her husband. 'He couldn't do wrong as far as my mother was concerned. She was one for the lads and spoiled both the boys. She idolised Ron and butter wouldn't melt in Charlie's mouth.

'He learned to plaster as a child. My grandad Ben was an ornamental plasterer and worked in grand houses like Osterley Park. He did all the cherubs and bunches of grapes and cornicing. He had a workshop where he used to make plaster casts. I remember playing in there as a child. He taught Charlie how to plaster right from when he started school. He could get out the tools and plaster a wall even when he was quite a tiny little boy. As he got older,

he worked for the best local builder before he started working for himself. He did really well. He was the only man in Clarence Street who had a car. I think it cost him £300 brand new.

'He had a posh wedding in a church with bridesmaids and then hired the Co-op Hall. Emma was always the heart and soul of the party. But she never had any children. I don't know whether they couldn't or didn't want them. They were much in love, always together. They had a good life. They were always comfortably off and had a little bit of dosh.'

Alice's daughter Pat Charman, now 75, was very fond of them both. 'Aunty Em was a bit eccentric,' she remembers. 'She was the sort of person you would bump into in the high street during the daytime wearing a taffeta dress and a fur coat. But I loved her to bits. She was very kind and always smiling. She always made you welcome. When she saw you, her face would light up.'

A year later, Ronald's sister Ede, a shop assistant, followed her siblings down the aisle, marrying labourer Henry 'Titch' Jones, also at the Parish Church of St John, although it was a much smaller occasion than Charlie and Emma's wedding. Both Alice and Ede immediately had children – Alice's daughter Pat was born in 1933 and Ede's son Harry in 1935 – and Ronald spent a lot of time with his niece and nephew.

'As the eldest daughter, I helped look after the others,' recalls Alice. 'I was already married when Ron was born, was there at the birth and had quite a lot to do with him. I always had him with me. I used to have my daughter Pat at one end of the pram and Ron at the other. I used to take the two out and people would say, "Oh, you've got two children," but of course Ron was my brother and Pat was my daughter. Nobody could have disliked my Ron. He was a lovely little blond boy. We were all blond; we were like fairies, all of us. He was a lovely child and a lovely man. I loved every hair on him.'

The family's life was sadly changed on 5 January 1938, when Charlie Goldsmith senior died of asthma and acute bronchitis, most likely a legacy of the war, leaving his wife Edith to bring up their two youngest children alone. Kate's grandfather Ronald was just six years old.

Edith was less than 5 ft tall but a tough, bird-like woman who smoked 20 Woodbines a day and used to send her daughters to the local pub in the evening for a jug of stout and 10 cigarettes. She never really managed to escape her impoverished roots, but she ruled her family with a rod of iron and instilled in her children a resourcefulness and a refusal to be defeated.

After her husband's death, she was forced by penury to move with her daughter Joyce, then 13, and Ronald to a condemned flat in Dudley Road, a scruffier street in the neighbourhood, parallel to Clarence Street. As she had to go out to work – she was on the production line at Keeley & Toms, making mincemeat, during the war and then worked at the Tickler's factory, producing jams, jellies and pickles – she farmed her children out to her parents, who lived in nearby Spencer Street, and her elder daughters.

'My mum had to work hard to bring us all up,' says Alice. 'She did not like leaving her children; she had no choice. She wasn't a bad lady, but she had a temper. You only had to say one word and she would take her shoes off and throw them at you. She would take the odd swipe at her kids herself, but woe betide anyone else who said or did anything to hurt them. She would defend them to the death. She liked a drink and smoked, and who could blame her with what she had to put up with. In those days, everybody was hard up.'

Alice's daughter Pat still remembers visiting the Dudley Road flat. 'In the corner of the kitchenette, there was one of those old-fashioned boilers, like a three-corner bath, which had a fire underneath to warm the water,' she recalls. 'Granny Edith used to

put coal in it. All the washing went in the boiler and she used to do the Christmas puddings there as well. She was the star for making Christmas puddings in the whole family. They were beautiful. The lavatory was next door to the boiler, in the same room. She loved her drink. She used to send my mother with a jug to the Havelock Arms to get some ale. The jug was orange with a pearly sheen and a picture of tulips on the side. I can remember seeing that throughout my childhood.'

On 26 February 1938, less than two months after her husband's death, Edith's third daughter and fourth child, Hetty, got married to bricklayer George Clark at Uxbridge Register Office. She was seven months pregnant with the first of their eleven children, all of whom were brought up on benefits in a council house. 'She had a lovely nature, Hetty,' says Alice. 'She would give you anything. Her husband was one of these fellers who never worked. I don't know how she managed to look after all those children.'

A year after Hetty left home, life was to change again for the Goldsmith family. The Second World War loomed and the menfolk were off to fight. Ronald was eight years old when England declared war on Germany at 11.15 a.m. on 3 September 1939. Although his father was already dead, his brothers-in-law Bill Tomlinson and Henry Jones, who were the main male influences in his life, were stationed away from home. While Bill worked on Operation Pluto, in which a team of scientists, oil engineers and army officers constructed a giant oil pipeline under the English Channel, Henry was stationed in Rochester, Kent, looking after prisoners of war.

Their wives, Alice and Ede, worked at Hoover's munitions factory, making caps for shells, and looked after their brother Ronald and their own children, Pat, who was five when war broke out, and Harry, who was three. 'During the war, if women only had one child, they had to go out to work,' recalls Pat. 'They had to do so many hours a week. So both my mum and Aunt Ede worked

at the factory and took it in turns to look after us. Mum would die for you. She'd give up her last slice of bread. I remember her during the war telling my dad that she had already eaten so that he would let her give him her meat ration. But she was very strict. My dad was about 6 ft tall and Mum is about 5 ft 4 in., yet she ruled him with a rod of iron.

'Ron was living in that terrible, decrepit flat, but he was the loveliest person. He had a very hard time of it – he was never even taken to the dentist – but he was very popular because he had a lovely nature and sense of humour. Everybody loved him. He was a real softie.'

During the war, many children in towns and cities were evacuated to the countryside for their own safety. Pat was one of the nearly three million people, the majority of them children, who were moved away from home under Operation Pied Piper, which began two days before the declaration of war. She left London at the beginning of 1940 but was so homesick that her mother took her back to Southall with her just before the Blitz. 'I was staying in a miner's cottage in Wales,' she says, 'and I would see all the miners come down the valley singing. I can remember seeing all these black faces because there were no baths in the mines then. I remember my dad saying, "Yes, that used to be me." My mum came to visit me after I had been there about nine months. I cried so much when she was leaving that she took me back home with her. Neither Ronnie nor Harry was evacuated.'

In fact, Ede's son Harry stayed with Edith and Ronald during the war. 'My mother did night work when dad was in the army,' he remembers, 'so I stayed the night with my nan, was taken home in the morning to go to school and went back to Dudley Road every night to sleep, except weekends. Ronald and I would often have to get up in the middle of the night and go to the air-raid shelter.'

'We all grew up together through the rest of the war, bombs and

all,' says Pat. 'One night when Mum was working at the Hoover factory, Dad and I were in the shelter in the garden when our front door was blown in by a bomb that dropped nearby.' Southall was struck by German bombs several times. In August 1944, for example, a V-1 flying doodlebug destroyed several houses in Regina Road, a few streets away from Dudley Road, littering the area with rubble and broken glass and killing the occupants.

Edith's youngest daughter, Joyce, had left school and begun working at the factory with her mother, juggling this with looking after her younger brother and helping out with the other children. 'Ronald and my mum were very close,' says Joyce's daughter Ann. 'She used to look after him quite a bit. They were quite often hungry as kids, so they used to go to Mitchell's, the grocer's shop opposite, and they would give them food and help them out. It was sometimes hard for Edith to make ends meet. She would pawn things on the Tuesday and take them back out another day. I remember my mum telling me she bought Ronald his first pair of long trousers. He must have been about ten. He was really excited.'

The family spent all the holiday festivals together. 'We were a very close family,' says Pat. 'At Christmas, when the men were in the army, we had nothing. We used to get together at Aunt Ede's house or my mum's house and they would pool whatever food they had. We used to play charades. Ede was great at playing the piano. I can see her now in my mind's eye playing "Roll Out the Barrel".'

In 1943 – at the height of the war – Joyce left home, leaving Ronald alone in the condemned flat with his mother. When she turned 18, she married George Plummer, a year her senior, who was a 'Desert Rat' in the 7th Armoured Division, fighting in most of the major battles in North Africa, including El Alamein in 1942. After the war, he became a herdsman at Osterley Park, a stately home in nearby Hounslow, living in a cottage on the estate and doing the

milk round. 'They met on a blind date during the war,' recounts Ann. 'It was love at first sight. He had four days' leave and then went back to Africa. She went back to work at the factory. She also did fire-watching and worked on the telephones at night.'

Ronald was 14 years old when the war ended and his brothers-in-law returned home. The family was fortunate to avoid the dreaded telegram announcing that a loved one had died. Like his brother and sisters before him, Ronald left school at 14, and he began dabbling in a series of jobs to make ends meet.

On 1 January 1949, the National Service Act came onto the statute books, obliging all men between the ages of 17 and 21 to enlist in the armed forces for 18 months, remaining on the reserve list for the following four years. Ronald was 17 years old and was sent to Aqaba in Jordan. It was during his time in the army that he worked as a baker, a skill that his grandson James, Kate's brother, would inherit.

When he came out of the army, he had just turned 18, and he went to work for his brother-in-law Bill Tomlinson as a haulage driver. 'I have an image of sitting opposite him when I came home from school for lunch,' says Pat. 'I can still see him there, looking up at me and laughing. He was the nicest man you could ever meet. Nobody ever had a bad word to say about him.'

'He was a smashing guy, a top boy,' adds Harry. 'We worked together in the '50s for Alice's husband Bill, who had set up his own haulage business. He was a good lad. I remember he would always take his hat off whenever a hearse went past. He was a real gentleman, a diamond guy.'

It was those good manners that attracted the attention of Kate's grandmother Dorothy Harrison, leading to a love match that would change the fortunes of the two families for good.

CHAPTER 5

Dorothy Harrison and Ronald Goldsmith

Wearing a white satin Norman Hartnell dress embroidered with gold and silver thread and encrusted with pearls and crystals, Princess Elizabeth stepped into the horse-drawn gold state coach in the courtyard of Buckingham Palace. Escorted by the Duke of Edinburgh, who was wearing full naval uniform, and carrying a bouquet of orchids, lilies of the valley, stephanotis and carnations grown in England, Scotland, Northern Ireland and Wales, Prince William's grandmother was on her way to Westminster Abbey for her coronation.

Prince Charles, who was four at the time, watched the glittering ceremony, which took place at 11.15 a.m. on 2 June 1953, alongside 8,251 guests from around the Commonwealth. Princess Anne was considered too young to attend the service.

It was the very public start of a new age for the royals, but elsewhere, much more quietly, the Harrisons and the Goldsmiths

were also about to enter a new era, one that would show how the circumstances of a family can reverse within a couple of generations.

It was the year when Joseph Stalin died after 31 years in control of the Soviet Union, Hussein was proclaimed King of Jordan and the Korean war came to an end. Sir Edmund Hillary and Tenzing Norgay conquered Everest, the first issue of *Playboy* appeared on news-stands and Ian Fleming published the first James Bond novel, *Casino Royale*. It was also the year when Dorothy Harrison and Ronald Goldsmith got married.

Kate Middleton's grandparents had met at the wedding of a close friend and were instantly attracted. At the time, Dorothy was working as a sales assistant in Dorothy Perkins and Ronald was employed in his brother-in-law Bill's haulage company. On 8 August 1953, within two months of watching the royal coronation on their black-and-white television, they walked up the aisle at Holy Trinity Church, Southall. The wedding was simple and traditional. Dorothy, 18, walked down the aisle in a demure ivory dress, accompanied by her two matrons of honour and two bridesmaids, Ronald's nieces Ann, daughter of his sister Joyce, and Linda, the youngest child of Bill and Alice Tomlinson. Afterwards, the couple were photographed on the steps of the church.

The family celebrated at the Hamborough Tavern in Southall, a pub that later became notorious as a haunt of racist skinheads. In 1981, two years after teacher Blair Peach had been killed during clashes between police and anti-fascist protestors, the Hamborough Tavern was burned down by Asian youths during a skinhead gig.

Happy as the two families were, it was hardly a fairy-tale wedding. Neither Dorothy nor Ronald had a penny to their name. Indeed, the bride was so poor that she had to borrow her going-away outfit from Ronald's sister Joyce, and instead of moving into their

own home, they had to squeeze into the Dudley Road flat with Ronald's mother Edith.

Nonetheless, the couple soon would prove a formidable match. Although both came from working-class families with little money or education, Dorothy had drive and ambition, while Ronald was artistic. He was a talented painter, carpenter and baker. Together, they climbed the social ladder while other members of their families remained in relative poverty. In a sense, Kate's family history mirrors those of millions of British people who have aunts, uncles and cousins whom they have never met. When one branch of a family thrives, it is not uncommon for them to lose contact with others.

'Dorothy was the domineering one,' says their niece Ann, daughter of Ronald's sister Joyce. 'She always wanted to better herself. My nan used to call her Dot and it really wound her up. She used to go quite mad. Ronald was a very quiet man, but he worshipped her. He would do anything she wanted. I've seen her walk into a newly decorated room and say she didn't like it and he would strip the wallpaper off and start again. She was never satisfied. She always wanted better. Luckily, Ronald could do it all himself. That's why she got away with so much. He was brilliant with his hands. He made Dorothy a violin at night school out of wood. He carved it all out and you could play it. He was very, very talented.'

Kate's mother, Carole, was born at Perivale Maternity Hospital on 31 January 1955, by which time Dorothy's aspirations were evident. 'After she and Ronald got married, they lived with my granny Edith until my dad helped them get a deposit for their first home,' recalls Pat, Alice Tomlinson's daughter. 'Dorothy had the biggest Silver Cross pram you have ever seen, and it had to be carried up and down the stairs. My grandmother used to grumble about Dorothy to my mother because she thought she henpecked

her Ronald. She thought Dorothy always wanted more and more money. She wanted to be the top brick in the chimney. You got the feeling that she thought she was too good for the rest of us.'

Over the next decade, Dorothy and Ron began to make their way in the world, first moving out of the condemned flat into a council flat in nearby Newlands Close and then buying their own home. With a little financial help from Ron's successful brother-in-law Bill, who lent them the deposit, they were soon the proud owners of a small house in Arlington Road, a short distance to the north. Pat reveals that it was while they were living there that there was 'a family kerfuffle'. 'Dad owned two lorries,' she says, 'and used to let Ron take one home with him. But he was doing private jobs with the lorry to get money for Dorothy to buy whatever she wanted. That caused a bit of a row. Mum went absolutely ape. But Dad was more pragmatic. He said to Mum, "It's nothing I wouldn't be doing if I needed money. It's not as if he's stealing from anybody. I would do it as well." He was a lovely bloke, my dad.' Ronald's sister Joyce also gave the young couple a leg-up. 'My mum lent them money to buy their first car,' says Ann. 'They would ask in a way you couldn't refuse.'

In 1966, when Carole was 11 – a year after the birth of her brother Gary – Ronald and Dorothy moved into a larger house in Kingsbridge Road, Norwood Green, bought from the General Housing Corporation for £4,950, the equivalent of £135,000 today. The new-build semi-detached house, which had three bedrooms, was in the middle of a council estate on a plot of land that had been bombed during the war.

'Ron wasn't an ambitious man,' says Pat. 'He went to work, got his wages, came home and got changed. He was contented. Dorothy was the mover and shaker in the family. I think Ron would have been quite happy to stay in Arlington Road, but it was the wrong side of Southall and Norwood Green was more posh.'

'Dorothy was always immaculately turned out. That was another reason why she seemed so intimidating. You couldn't imagine knocking on her door and finding her in hair curlers. But if she hadn't been so aspirational, maybe Kate would not be where she is now. She certainly had her priorities right for her own family.'

Ronald and Dorothy stayed in Kingsbridge Road for the next 25 years, until Carole got married and Gary left home. They were very much part of the community. 'We would go to dances at the local hall,' remembers Ann, 'and they would make a great play of being the ones to pay for the band. Once my husband Brian paid to wind them up. Dorothy was apparently beside herself that somebody had stolen her thunder. She always wanted to have one up on somebody. We used to tease her about it, but nobody took it too seriously. We knew what she was like. Everybody in the family was overshadowed by her, but she was always good fun. We used to enjoy dancing and mucking around.'

By the time they moved to Kingsbridge Road, Ron had plucked up the courage to leave Bill's haulage firm to set up in business as a builder. Although he made a success of it, he was not affluent enough to send his children to a private school – that would come in the next generation. The couple made up for any lack of material things by giving Carole and Gary a loving childhood. Dorothy gave up work when each of the children was little, taking a job at an estate agent in between their births.

'She was a good mother,' says Ann. 'She was very proud of both of them. She played with them a lot and was into their education. She wasn't well educated herself, but she wanted them to do well, better than she had done. They were two nice kids. Carole loved dancing. If *Top of The Pops* was on, she would stand in front of the telly and dance her heart out. She was a proper girlie girl. She loved pink and was very fair-headed. Gary was a terror when he was little. He painted the sideboard, shook talcum powder everywhere

and dug up Dorothy's pot plant on the stairs. He was a bugger. If he was quiet, you knew he was getting into trouble. When he was older, he was very good-looking. I remember he could take Michael Jackson off brilliantly; he was better than Jackson himself. He and Carole got on very well.'

During the '70s and '80s, Dorothy, who was always slim and beautifully dressed, earned pin money at Collingwood Jewellers in Hounslow High Street, where Ann was the manager. 'She learned her trade from me,' says Ann. 'I needed a part-timer and she was looking for work. She was a good saleswoman, but she was a bit of a snob. The whole family used to call her "Lady Dorothy".' In years to come, Gary would also work in the jewellery shop on Saturdays. Meanwhile, Carole, eight years younger than Ann, took a job as a Saturday girl at C&A while she was at secondary school.

It was on New Year's Day 1971, just weeks before Carole's 16th birthday, that her grandmother Edith, the powerful matriarch of the Goldsmith family, passed away. The indomitable widow, who had brought up six children virtually single-handed, died of a stroke at the age of 81 in a council flat in Havelock Road. It was she who had instilled in her children a sense of the importance of hard work.

Kate's mother Carole celebrated her 21st birthday on 31 January 1976. By then, she had begun working, perhaps lured by the glamour of the position, as an air stewardess at British Airways. It was a job that fulfilled her love of foreign travel and would ultimately lead her to her husband.

Sadly, later that year, on 24 August 1976, her grandfather Thomas – Dorothy's carpenter father – died of pancreatic cancer at home in North Road, Southall. It was a tremendous loss for the family, who were deeply indebted to him. It was he who had broken with family tradition, learning a trade instead of going down the mines, and moving the family down south. He had lived under

five monarchs and survived two world wars, and that wealth of experience was now lost to the family for good.

Dorothy was 41 years old when her father succumbed to cancer. Within four years, her daughter's wedding – to a middle-class British Airways flight dispatcher called Michael Middleton – would finally fulfil Dorothy's dreams of prosperity and respectability, cement the family's precarious social status and lead to the birth of a possible royal bride. Over the previous decades, there had been hard times and moments of triumph. Yet, looking at Kate now, it is hard to believe that just 50 years ago her grandmother was struggling to make ends meet in a condemned flat on the outskirts of London.

CHAPTER 6

The Middletons 1838–1914

*S*tanding on the balcony of Buckingham Palace in the dwindling hours of the balmy evening of 28 June 1838, Queen Victoria watched the fireworks in Green Park and reflected on her day. She had been woken at 4 a.m. by the sounds of guns in the park, crowds gathering, soldiers marching and bands setting up in anticipation of her long-awaited coronation at Westminster Abbey, which was greeted by deafening cheers from the crowds.

Wearing an 8-ft velvet and ermine train and holding an orb in her left hand and a sceptre in her right, she walked regally out of the abbey at 4.30 p.m., having been crowned Queen of the United Kingdom of Great Britain and Ireland, for the procession back to the palace. 'I really cannot say how proud I feel to be the Queen of such a nation,' the 19-year-old monarch wrote in her diary afterwards. 'The enthusiasm, affection and loyalty were really touching. I shall ever remember this day as the proudest day of my life.'

Two hundred miles north of the palace, in the industrial town of Leeds, Kate's great-great-great-grandfather William Middleton, a solicitor, probably read about the coronation in the local newspaper while having breakfast with his new wife, Mary. The couple had been married for four months and had set up home in a terraced house on the outskirts of the town, where they brought up their large family. On Coronation Day, Mary was already pregnant with their eldest son, Kate's great-great-grandfather John, although it is unlikely that she would have known yet that she was with child. Her son would grow up in very different surroundings from the Harrisons and the Goldsmiths.

Unlike Kate's other ancestors, William, the 30-year-old son of a joiner and cabinetmaker from Wakefield, a small town 15 miles south of Leeds, was educated and trained in a profession. He had moved to the larger town after qualifying as a solicitor and was now wealthy enough to provide for a family.

It was in Leeds that he had met and fallen in love with 27-year-old Mary Ward. William would have been considered her social better – she was the daughter of a milliner who lived on Briggate, the town's main thoroughfare, running from the newly opened Corn Exchange to the River Aire – but she was a young woman who seems to have been determined to make something of herself.

In those days, Leeds was a thriving town. It had flourished from the beginning of the Industrial Revolution and workers poured into the factories, mills and workshops. Coal was brought into the town centre by steam trains from Middleton Colliery and the streets were lit with gas lamps. There was a courthouse, a prison and a bank. But behind the elegant timber-fronted façade of Briggate, which was one of the oldest streets in Leeds, home to rich merchants and coaching inns, were narrow alleyways and courtyards crowded with back-to-back cottages and workshops. Conditions were squalid and insanitary, as there was no proper drainage or sewerage, and

there was terrible pollution. Cholera was rife and there was a high death rate. Body snatchers ransacked cemeteries and rioting was common. Dickens described it as 'the beastliest place, one of the nastiest I know'.

While Mary was well acquainted with the less salubrious areas of Leeds, her husband could afford to offer her a better lifestyle than her father had been able to provide. So, after they got married, they moved northwards, settling in a house in St George's Terrace, a street on the outskirts of the town.

It was there that John – Kate's great-great-grandfather – was born on Valentine's Day 1839, almost a year to the day since his parents had got married. Over the next decade, the couple went on to have another seven children – Edwin, Anne, Leonard, Arthur, Robert, Charles and Margaret. All their children were scholars, a rarity in Victorian England, where most people were uneducated and illiterate, but not surprising for the offspring of a professional man.

As he became more successful, William craved a house that befitted his new social status and decided to move to the wealthy suburb of Gledhow, just east of the village of Chapel Allerton, which was fast becoming a popular retreat for the middle classes. Gledhow Valley, a strip of unspoiled woodland through which a stream runs into a lake, is now a conservation area. By 1851, the family had moved into Gledhow Grange, a substantial house in Lidgett Lane, which ran northwards out of the heart of the village.

Down the road was the magnificent seventeenth-century Gledhow Hall, now a listed building, which was built on monastic land once owned by Elizabeth I and was the subject of a painting by J.M.W. Turner. When the Middletons moved to the area, Gledhow Hall was owned by Thomas Benyon, 50, a flax mill proprietor who employed 652 flax spinners and linen, canvas and sailcloth manufacturers. He and his wife Anne, 36, lived in great luxury, with 13 servants

including a butler, housekeeper, lady's maid, two housemaids, cook, kitchen maid, laundry maid, footman, coachman, governess and two nursery maids. The couple had bought the Hall after their marriage in 1835, a lavish affair for which Anne wore a £140 dress – a staggering £11,000 in today's money – and the cake weighed 335 lb. They had five sons and daughters – Jane, thirteen in 1851, Anne, twelve, Mary, nine, William, eight, and Joseph, seven – who were roughly the same age as the Middleton children, and the families became close friends. They were devastated when Mary died as a result of a perforated stomach ulcer in 1854.

Four years later, there was great excitement in the village when Queen Victoria came to Leeds to open the new town hall, designed by Cuthbert Broderick, the architect of a series of imposing public buildings in the city centre. Little did William Middleton realise how closely the paths of his and the Queen's descendants would one day cross.

Sadly, the Middleton siblings' idyllic childhood was brought to an end on 15 June 1859, when their mother Mary died at the age of 48 after a short illness that left her with an obstructed bowel and peritonitis, a blood infection that was untreatable in the days before penicillin. John had yet to reach his 21st birthday; his youngest sister, Margaret, was just nine. Mary was buried three days after her death in the graveyard of St Matthew's Church, Chapel Allerton, leaving the family bereft and rudderless.

Unable to care for eight children on his own, William cast around for another wife. Within two years, he had married his sister-in-law, Sarah Ward, who was twelve years younger than him, and she had moved into the family home, becoming stepmother to his brood. The couple were comfortable enough to have two servants: a cook and a housemaid.

Two years later, his eldest son John, who was 24 years old and, like his father before him, had qualified as a solicitor, found

himself a wife and moved out of home. A chip off the old block, he too married a woman of a lower social class, Mary Asquith, 23, the daughter of a cloth finisher who had been brought up, as his mother had been, in the crowded workshops off Briggate. The couple wed on 27 August 1863, at the parish church in Leeds, and moved to their own home in Potternewton, two miles south of Gledhow. In 1865, their happiness was crowned by the birth of their first child, Gilbert. Having given birth to their son and heir, Mary went on to have two daughters, Olive, in 1870, and Ellen, in 1872.

The union of the Middleton and Asquith families was compounded the following year when John's younger sister Anne, by then 31 years old, a spinster by the standards of the age and unlikely to find a husband, fell in love with Mary's younger brother John, a cloth finisher like his father. They got married at the same church as their siblings on 22 October 1873. But the family's wealth and stature could not shield them from tragedy, and less than five months after they got married, on 16 March 1874, John, Anne's husband and Mary's brother, died of scarlet fever at home in Cumberland Road, Headingley, and she was forced to move back home to her father and stepmother.

By then, William and Sarah had moved down the road to Hawkhills, a sprawling mansion in Gledhow Lane, Chapel Allerton. Sadly, it has since been demolished, although the gateposts and lodge still remain. They socialised with the upper echelons of Leeds society, people such as Sir John Barran, an innovative entrepreneur in the fabric industry, who introduced the use of the bandsaw in fabric cutting, having been inspired by its use in the manufacture of wood veneers. A Justice of the Peace, Lord Mayor of Leeds and later Liberal MP, he lived 500 yards down the road in Chapel Allerton Hall, set in 41 acres of parkland, which he mortgaged to buy Roundhay Park for the

people of Leeds. He is commemorated by a drinking fountain, presented by him, in the centre of the park.

The Middletons also knew James Kitson, who ran the Monkbridge Iron and Steel Company with his brother Frederick. He moved into Gledhow Hall in 1878. There was great excitement in the village when he married his second wife, Mary, in 1881. James, who was president of the Leeds Liberal Association, organised the campaign for Gladstone's re-election to Parliament in 1880, and Sarah and William may well have met the Prime Minister at the Hall. Husband and wife were both dead by the time of James's greatest triumphs. He was created a baronet in 1886, elected as a Liberal MP in 1892 and became Lord Mayor of Leeds in 1896. The Middletons would no doubt have been thrilled to hear about the visit Kitson received in 1902 from the former prime minister the Earl of Rosebery, who was escorted to Gledhow Hall by 200 torchbearers.

While the couple enjoyed their retirement, their son John was working his way up the career ladder. He and his wife Mary moved into a house on the Leeds Road in Far Headingley, a village three miles west of Potternewton. The road ran from Leeds to Otley, where the furniture maker Thomas Chippendale grew up, and in Victorian times the area was a magnet for prosperous, middle-class families. It was there that John and Mary brought up their increasing brood. William, named after his grandfather, was born in 1874; twins Caroline and Gertrude arrived in 1876; and Kate's great-grandfather Richard Noel, known as Noel, was born on Christmas Day 1878. Their eighth child and youngest daughter, Margaret, was born in 1880.

A gifted solicitor, John handled all the legal work for the flourishing Leeds Permanent Benefit Building Society, and his hard work was soon rewarded. In 1881, he was appointed vice president of the Leeds Law Society, becoming president in 1882, a role he

held for two years. In 1883, he was also elected an extraordinary member of the council of the Incorporated Law Society.

William lived just long enough to see his son's achievements but spent the last months of his life paralysed as a result of a brain disorder. He died on 21 December 1884, at the age of 77 – a good age in those days – leaving his family to celebrate Christmas without him. After what must have been a miserable winter, his widow Sarah followed him to the grave just three months later, fracturing her skull when she was thrown from her carriage. She died of a brain bleed at home at Hawkhills on 3 April 1885, having suffered from concussion.

Despite his father and stepmother's deaths, John did not ease up on the workload. As well as becoming head of the family firm, he began to develop into a leading figure in Leeds society, founding the Leeds and County Conservative Club and acting as an election agent for Tory parliamentary candidate Richard Dawson in 1885 and 1886. He and Mary split their time between their four-storey bow-fronted townhouse in Hyde Terrace, Leeds, near the family firm, and their new country home, Fairfield, in Far Headingley. Both houses were crammed full of antiques, oil paintings, silver and crystal.

Less than three years after his father's death, John too was summoned to a higher bar. He had been suffering from angina, probably brought on by the stress of work and his parents' deaths. He died at home in Far Headingley on 16 July 1887, a month after Queen Victoria's golden jubilee, at 48 years of age. He is buried in the family vault at Chapel Allerton cemetery. His obituary in the *Law Times*, dated 6 August 1887, stated: 'His death, which was comparatively sudden, was hastened, if not occasioned by the strain of a five days' trial in London on a matter concerning the Leeds estate.'

After John's death, his widow Mary and her children moved

into Hyde Terrace, but their mother barely outlived their father. She died two years later, on 22 September 1889, of typhoid fever and a pulmonary embolism, while staying in a cottage in the fishing village of Filey, near Scarborough, 70 miles away. Thus, two generations of the same family were extinguished within seven years.

Kate's great-grandfather Noel was only ten years old when he became an orphan, but he was not penniless. His mother Mary, having inherited nearly £5,000 from her husband, left £13,627 in her will – the equivalent of £6.7 million today – meaning that her children would be able to be educated privately and live the lifestyle to which they had become accustomed. Noel also inherited a family heirloom, a sapphire ring, which he cherished.

In the 1891 census, his oldest brother, Gilbert, by then a 24-year-old solicitor, was listed as resident in a boarding house in Filey, with William, an engineering student, and his sisters. Noel, who would have been 12, was in lodgings in Bilton-cum-Harrogate, 15 miles north of Leeds. It is not known whether the rest of the family was living in Filey while Noel attended school in Harrogate or if they were just on holiday.

At that time, the spa town of Harrogate was one of the fashionable places to be seen. It was popular with the English aristocracy, and nobility from across Europe came to bathe in its waters. Samson Fox, the great-grandfather of actor Edward Fox, was mayor of the town for three successive years, 1889–92 (a feat not achieved since), and one of its great philanthropists. He lived in the magnificent Grove House estate, where Queen Victoria's eldest son, the Prince of Wales, was a regular visitor. During the period, the future Edward VII's mistress Lillie Langtry

performed in *The School for Scandal* at the Promenade Inn theatre, the D'Oyly Carte Opera Company had a season there and Oscar Wilde gave a lecture on dress.

On 26 January 1892, the family came together when Gilbert got married to Alice Margaret Joy, a spinster two years his senior, but the reunion was short-lived. By now 13 years old, Noel was sent to the boys' public school Clifton College, in Bristol, as a boarder. Alumni included Field Marshal Haig and artist Roger Fry, and Noel was in the same year as Edwin Samuel Montagu, the Jewish Liberal politician who was appointed Secretary of State for India towards the end of the First World War.

After Clifton, the lure of home proved great and Noel moved back to the North, going to Leeds University before, following in the family tradition, he became an articled clerk. He lived with his four older unmarried sisters, Olive, Ellen, and twins Caroline and Gertrude, and three servants, in the family home they had inherited from their parents in Hyde Terrace. Gertrude was very religious and artistically gifted; she drew illuminated manuscripts and embroidered altar cloths.

The family spent many holidays together in Filey, where tragedy struck once again. One summer, when Noel was 20, they went for a walk along Filey Brigg, a rocky promontory that juts out 1,600 metres into the sea. When they got back to the shore, they were devastated to discover that Margaret, the youngest, who was 18 at the time, had disappeared. Her body was never discovered and the family returned to Leeds haunted by her death.

Like his father and grandfather before him, Noel worked his way up from articled clerk to solicitor (he qualified in 1903 when he was 25 years old) and began to mingle with the great and good of Leeds. He moved out of his sisters' home and down to London, where he practised law and shared a home in Mayfair with six other professional men, including an architect and an

army officer. He moved back to Leeds just before the start of the First World War, buying a house in the village of Roundhay. There, his path crossed that of the beautiful Olive Lupton, who came from one of Leeds' richest and most illustrious families. It was a union that would bring Noel untold success and riches, and lead his descendants to the gates of Buckingham Palace.

CHAPTER 7

The Luptons 1847–1930

*I*t was a bitter winter's day, 6 January 1914, and the great and good of Leeds were gathered at the Mill Hill Unitarian Chapel in the city centre for the wedding of the daughter of one of its most illustrious families.

Alderman Francis Martineau Lupton – one of four brothers who held office in the town during the nineteenth century – was giving away his eldest daughter Olive, 32, a society beauty, to Noel Middleton, 35, who came from a line of successful and affluent lawyers. They made a handsome couple. Olive was dark, with defined features; Noel had brown hair and hazel eyes. Watched by friends and family, Kate's great-grandparents made their vows in the Gothic chapel, with its stone pulpit and stained-glass windows, remembering those who could not be with them. Both shared the pain of loss – Noel was an orphan by the age of ten and Olive lost her mother when she was still a child – and were bound together by the experience.

Their Nonconformist wedding – the Unitarian Church is

Presbyterian in structure and at variance with the Church of England in several of its teachings – was one of the last to be held at the chapel before the outbreak of war six months later.

Olive Lupton came from an illustrious, aristocratic Leeds family who had made their name as wool merchants in the eighteenth century and mixed with the upper echelons of society. Her paternal grandmother Fanny was directly descended from Sir Thomas Fairfax, a leading Parliamentarian general in the English Civil War. Prince William is also descended from Fairfax, through the Spencer line, which means that Kate and William are distantly related – they are in fact 15th cousins.

The daughter of surgeon Thomas Greenhow and his wife Elizabeth Martineau, Fanny had links to many of the great philanthropists and thinkers of the day. She was the niece of the author, philosopher and feminist Harriet Martineau, who herself was a devout Unitarian and mixed in a circle that included Florence Nightingale, Charlotte Brontë, George Eliot and Charles Darwin. She was also the second cousin of Guy Ritchie's great-great-grandfather William Martineau. His granddaughter Doris McLaughlin married the war hero Major Stewart Ritchie, a Seaforth Highlander who won a Military Cross during the First World War, meaning that not only does Kate have aristocratic blood, but she also has connections to Hollywood royalty.

The family business, William Lupton & Co., founded in 1773, was the oldest firm in the city when it closed in 1958. Fanny's husband, Frank Lupton, expanded the company, buying an old cloth mill (against his wife's wishes) and letting it out to weavers who brought their cloth to his warehouse every Friday for him to inspect. Gradually, he expanded into making fancy tweeds, livery tweeds and police uniform fabrics, and he bought a finishing plant, which

meant that he was involved in every stage of the manufacturing process. It was a decision that would benefit the entire family, including his great-great-great-granddaughter Kate, as he slowly became a very rich man.

Family life for Frank and Fanny, who got married in 1847, revolved around their five sons, of whom Olive's father Francis was the oldest. He was born on 21 July 1848, followed by Arthur in 1850, Herbert in 1853, Charles in 1855 and Hugh in 1861. By then, the family was living at Beechwood, a sprawling Victorian mansion down a winding carriage lane in the village of Roundhay, seven miles north of Leeds, which they had bought from Sir George Goodman, who had served as the city's mayor. They were wealthy enough to employ six servants to cater for their every whim. Sadly, Herbert died when Hugh was a baby, but the other four sons grew up to make their parents proud, doing well at school and becoming model citizens. The family socialised with the city's elite, involving themselves in the politics of the day, worshipping in the same churches and walking in the same parks.

Like his father before him, Olive's father Francis was sent to grammar school. He was a bright boy and became the first member of the family to go up to Trinity College, Cambridge, which had just opened to Nonconformists. This soon became a traditional route for Lupton sons: his brother Charles and three sons all followed him there. Charles was the first Lupton son to go to the boys' public school Rugby, which had just opened its prep school, setting a tradition of private education that would carry right down through the family to Kate. Francis took a degree and an MA in history before returning to Leeds. He joined the family firm as a cashier – which, his mother noted in her diary, 'he likes fairly' – and was given a commission in the Leeds Rifles. The family was delighted when he fell in love with Harriet Davis, the daughter of the vicar at their local church, St John's. She lived with her parents and four

sisters in the vicarage in Roundhay, and the two families were close friends. The couple got married at St John's on 6 April 1880, when Francis was 31 and Harriet 29, and they moved to their own home, Rockland, in Newton Park, a hamlet between Chapel Allerton and Potternewton. Olive was born on April Fool's Day 1881.

On 20 May 1884, when Olive was barely three years old, her grandfather Frank died of heart disease at the age of 70, the first of a series of deaths that would rip the heart out of the family, proving that even the wealthy could not guard against illness and disease in Victorian times. It was Frank who built up the family fortune, leaving his four sons wealthy enough to become leading members of the Establishment. He left a staggering £64,650 in his will – the equivalent of £32.6 million today – meaning that his family would be handsomely provided for.

After his death, Francis and Harriet went on to have another four children – Francis, known as Fran, in 1886, Maurice in 1887, Anne in 1888 and Lionel in 1892 – but Harriet's immune system was low after giving birth to her fifth child and she caught influenza. She died at home at Rockland on 9 January 1892, leaving her distraught husband, paralysed with grief, having to care for five children under the age of ten. Two months later to the day, Francis's mother Fanny died of diabetes and exhaustion. Francis had lost his wife and both his parents in the space of eight years and the joy went out of his life.

'The birth of the youngest boy took place when a severe epidemic of influenza was at its worst,' his nephew Charles Athelstane Lupton, known to the family as 'Athel', wrote later in a family history, *The Lupton Family in Leeds*.

> The confinement was normal but Harriet was attacked by the infection and died a fortnight later. Frank never really recovered from the blow. He kept his grief entirely to himself. For many years

he never talked about her to the children. He rarely took holidays.
It was some 30 years before he would go abroad again. And we
remember what a joy such holidays were to him in his young days.
He devoted himself to the business and to civic work.

Devastated by his wife's death, Francis threw himself into work
and local politics. As well as running the family firm with his
brother Arthur, he became a prominent figure in Leeds public
life. Beginning as a Liberal Unionist, opposing Home Rule for
Ireland, by 1895 he had gained a seat as a Conservative alderman,
or councillor, a post he held for the next 21 years. It was during
that time that he found his calling. As the first chairman of the
Leeds Unhealthy Areas Committee, he cleared inner-city slums and
replaced them with affordable homes.

He is also remembered as one of the 'Big Five' council members
who negotiated with the workers during the 1913 strike by council
labourers over wages. Athel Lupton recorded:

> The attitude of the five great men was moderate and patient but
> they remained completely firm, and in two or three weeks the
> strike collapsed. There was no serious violence. Electricity and
> water were maintained throughout and there was always some
> gas available. Other large towns watched with keen interest the
> course of the strike in Leeds and the attitude of the Big Five.
> They showed their admiration and gratitude to Frank by the
> presentation of a vast silver tray and a 'huge and abnormally
> ugly china flower pot on a china leg'.

Not content to limit himself to his council work, Francis was
also a magistrate on the West Riding Bench, was involved with
Cookridge Hospital and regularly attended Mill Hill Chapel,
despite his deceased wife's Anglican sympathies.

Yet despite being the eldest son, incredibly successful and philanthropic, Francis remained humble and unsure of himself, possibly as a result of his wife Harriet's death. He remained close to his younger brothers – Arthur, with whom he ran the family business, Charles, who was head of the legal firm Dibb Lupton, and Hugh, who was chairman of Hathorn Davey & Co., a hydraulic engineering company – and would consult them regularly. Together, the tentacles of their influence reached across the city.

Arthur, who was pro-vice-chancellor of Leeds University, must particularly have been able to empathise with Francis's loss, having himself been widowed four years earlier. His wife Harriot, who was a cousin of Beatrix Potter's mother Helen, had died in childbirth in 1888, before her famous cousin published her first children's book *The Tale of Peter Rabbit*. Charles, a renowned art collector, was treasurer and chairman of the General Infirmary and later, in 1915, became Lord Mayor. He left his extensive art collection to the city. Hugh was chairman of the Board of Guardians, an organisation that aimed to protect the poor and needy, served as a councillor for many years and became Mayor himself in 1926. '"I must consult my brothers" was his reaction to doubt,' recalled Athel of his uncle Francis in his history. 'His three brothers played a great part in his life.'

In those days, it was not the done thing for a gentleman to look after his children, so Francis employed a Scottish Presbyterian nanny called Miss Cadell to look after Rockland and bring up his young family. Olive, who was the eldest, went to Roedean boarding school. Athel writes:

> Miss Cadell was not really fitted for the care of children. Poor
> Frank seems to have left household affairs very much in her hands.
> And while no doubt she was well meaning and scrupulously
> honest in her dealings, she was soon the dominant figure in the

house. It is recorded that on one occasion she had the house painted without any request to Frank for his permission. On another occasion she renewed the drawing room cretonnes [draperies] with her own lamentable choice. Frank paid the bills without complaint. Vanity in the young must be crushed. It appeared that Anne aged ten was afflicted with that vice; her hair was promptly cut short. It may certainly be claimed that in later years vanity was not a family failing. The boys perhaps suffered less regimentation than the girls as they were often away at school. But eventually things came to a crisis. Miss Cadell departed. The drawing room cretonnes were ripped off. And so ended an unfortunate episode.

By this time, the three boys, Fran, Maurice and Lionel, had gone off to Rugby School, while Olive had left Roedean and was old enough to become her father's housekeeper, caring for him and her younger sister Anne. She must have been jealous of her brothers' freedom as they went up to Trinity College, like their father before them. It was during his time at Cambridge that Maurice became something of a legend for his love of motor cars. He had a yellow steam car, which blew up and had to be towed back from Cambridge to Leeds by his friend Leonard Schuster, who owned a Rolls-Royce, a sight that apparently caused quite a sensation.

After leaving university, Fran and Lionel joined the family firm, while Maurice became an apprentice engineer at Hathorn Davey in Hunslet, where his uncle Hugh was managing director. Fran and Maurice both moved back into the family home, where they were looked after by Olive and five servants – a cook, waiting maid, housemaid, kitchen maid and sewing maid.

Olive did not get her own freedom until 1914, when she married Noel Middleton and her sister Anne, by then 25 years old, took over the running of Rockland. That summer, their eldest brother,

Fran, 28, was married to Dorothy Davison, the daughter of a mathematics master at King Edward's School, Birmingham, who specialised in seismology. But war was looming and it would be the last time the large family would be together.

When the Great War broke out, Olive's brothers Fran, Maurice and Lionel were all in the Territorial Army, along with two of their cousins, Michael, son of their uncle Arthur, and Hugo, son of their uncle Hugh. Fran and Maurice joined the Leeds Rifles. While Fran remained in England as the adjutant of a training brigade, Maurice became a captain in the 7th battalion of the West Yorkshire Regiment, the Prince of Wales' regiment, and was shipped to the support trenches in Belgium as part of the all-territorial 49th (1st West Riding) Infantry Division. He arrived on 19 April 1915, and died exactly two months later, at the age of only 28, one of 2,050 members of the Leeds Rifles to be killed on active service in France and Flanders during the war. He is buried at the Rue-Pétillon Military Cemetery in Fleurbaix, northern France.

His letters to his family, which are published in *The Next Generation*, a sequel to *The Lupton Family in Leeds*, edited by Athel's nephew Francis Lupton with contributions from various family members and local historians, seem strangely naive in retrospect. 'I would not have missed coming out here for worlds,' he wrote on 28 April. 'We have done no actual fighting yet but only moved about at very short notice, which is great fun.' 'I am sitting in a little mud and wood shelter for all the world like playing Indians,' he said the following day. 'Now and then we hear an occasional rifle crack or a shell going over like a wild duck, but not aimed at us, at least I don't think so.'

Gradually, though, Maurice became more aware of the dangers. On 6 June, he wrote:

Into trenches for six days. I am going to try fitting the field glasses sent by Father onto a periscope so as to see more details of the German trench line because one cannot point a telescope directly at them. They are sometimes extraordinarily quick at picking off little things like periscopes.

And on 15 June:

One afternoon the Germans suddenly started shelling our end of the trench with shrapnel. By sheer mischance, one of these shells did not burst in the air but hit a sand bag wall against which our billet policeman was standing and cut off his leg a little below the knee. He was a tremendously strong chap and chloroform did not seem to have any effect on him, at least not for ages, but sadly he died the next day. All the other deaths we have had in the company have been practically instantaneous, shot through the head while firing over the parapet.

Four days later, he himself was killed.

Lionel set off with his Royal Field Artillery unit around the same time as his brother and had made his way to the front, riding in cattle trucks and marching on foot, when he found out that his brother had died. He wrote to his sister Anne:

I like your letters about Maurice. They make me feel much happier. I thought at first that it was an absolute waste him being killed so soon, before he had done anything really good in life but it is lovely to think that he is really having a nice time now.

He survived the Battle of Loos at the end of August and returned home for a week on leave, but he was wounded on 1 December and sent to a London hospital to recuperate. He then travelled

to Rockland for Christmas, where he found his family in mixed spirits – mourning the death of Maurice but celebrating the birth of Olive and Noel's first child, a son Christopher, who was born on Christmas Eve that year.

Lionel returned to the front in April and was killed on 16 July 1916 at the Battle of the Somme. He was just 24 years old and had been mentioned twice in dispatches. He is buried at Bouzincourt Communal Cemetery. In *The Next Generation*, his nephew Peter – Kate's grandfather – records:

> Lionel's battery took part in seven days of continuous bombardment of German lines, which was supposed to destroy all their defences and communications. But the Germans had dug themselves in so deeply that they were not dislodged by the barrage and were able to mow down the British infantry 'like ripe corn' when they attempted to advance. The British guns, including Lionel's battery, just went on firing, with occasional rests to allow the guns to cool. He was passing behind a gun pit shortly after midnight on 16 July when a German shell landed, wounding three men and killing Lionel instantly.

Olive's husband Noel was stationed at Bulford Camp on Salisbury Plain when he heard about Lionel's death. He had spent the early part of the war as chief administrator of the Leeds Special Constabulary's Motor Transport Section – responsible for traffic control during air raids – and had had to seek the permission of the chief constable to enlist. He joined the Royal Army Service Corps in November 1915, when his wife Olive was eight months pregnant with their first child, and became a private in the Officer Training Corps. He was on a temporary commission as second lieutenant with the 152nd siege battery, Royal Garrison Artillery, when Lionel died. A month later, on 31 August 1916, he was sent

to France, where he worked as a driver, supporting the front-line troops at the Somme. Olive must have been terrified that he would never return. Two of her three brothers had already died and she was all alone, coping with an eight-month-old baby.

Noel was later attached to 406 Company's transport depot, where drivers were assigned to deliver munitions to the front, move artillery or transport men and equipment, and to 611 Company. His personnel file records his conduct as 'very good' and his driving as 'competent'. He may well have been one of the 1,400 lorry drivers with 406 Company's siege park at Poperinghe, near Ypres, who were delivering 1,000 tons of ammunition to the front each night under heavy shellfire. Their commanding officer, Major A. Cowan, remarked: 'The new gas masks are very effective but it is not possible to drive at night without lights with them on and in some cases the drivers removed their masks too soon with fatal results.' He could also have been among the 85 officers and 2,933 men of 611 Company who supplied ammunition to 41 siege batteries and 11 heavy artillery groups at the Arras front, working with extreme difficulty because of the poor conditions – the terrible roads and badly maintained lorries – around the Somme.

Fortunately, Noel survived the war, being released on 5 June 1919 with the rank of lieutenant and officially demobbed on 5 October. His third brother-in-law, Fran, was not so lucky. Fran was still in England when he found out about the deaths of his younger brothers, so he must have felt a certain amount of trepidation when he went out to France in January 1917 with the Leeds Rifles to serve with the all-territorial 62nd (2nd West Riding) Infantry Division. He had been married for less than three years and his daughter Ruth had just started toddling when he was posted as missing after just six weeks. According to *The Next Generation*:

Despite thorough searching at the time, no trace of his body could be found and it was thought that he might have been taken prisoner. But some two months later his body was found near that of the man with whom he had been on patrol. Apparently both men had been blown up by a hand grenade and killed instantly.

He was buried in Bucquoy, not far from Arras. The eldest of the three brothers, he was still only thirty when he died.

Already a widower, the death of his three sons proved too much for Francis Lupton to bear. Even the birth of his third grandchild – Olive's second son Anthony – on 27 April 1917 failed to stem his grief. He let Rockland to the Pensions Committee at a token fee of one pound per year for use as a home for the orphans of soldiers and sailors, and, with his daughter Anne, took a smaller house in Lidgett Park Road on the outskirts of the village. He later moved to another house, Low Gables, across the fields from Hawkhills, the grand house once owned by William Middleton, but he found it hard to settle down. 'He never recovered from his triple blow,' wrote Peter Middleton in *The Next Generation*. 'He never broke down. And at times he could be induced to talk about his sons and his wife too. But the light had gone out of his life.'

He died of chronic kidney failure at Low Gables on 5 February 1921, at the age of 72, and was buried four days later at St John's Church, Roundhay, where he had got married and where his wife was buried. He left a sum equivalent to almost £10 million today in trust to his two daughters and their descendants, making Olive Middleton a very wealthy woman. At his funeral, the minister said that Francis was 'a member of a family which for generations has been associated with the commercial, municipal, educational and religious life of Leeds' and that he brought 'sunshine to the fetid slum . . . it was largely due to him that men, women and children

can now all live in surroundings essential to health and decency
. . . We, his fellow worshippers, honour him for his simplicity, his
sincerity, his integrity – for himself.'

The First World War had a devastating effect on the Lupton family,
wiping out nearly an entire generation of men and plunging the
whole family into mourning. Only three out of seven male cousins
survived – Arthur's son Arthur and Hugh's sons Hugo and Athel
– leaving the family businesses short of young men to follow in
their fathers' footsteps. But the war also had a great effect on the
women of the family, as they were left to fend for themselves. Many
hundreds of thousands of men were killed or maimed during the
war, and it has been estimated that in the interwar years there
were some two million 'surplus women' who could not hope to
find a husband. The Lupton women were no different. Although
Olive was already married at the start of the war, her sister Anne
died a spinster and the majority of her female cousins did not
find husbands.

Robbed of the chance to find a husband, Anne also found
it difficult to get work after the war, despite having dedicated
herself to good causes. In 1914, she had become secretary to
the Leeds General Hospital Committee, raising funds for men
in military hospitals, and later she had worked on the local
Pensions Committee, advising disabled soldiers. It was she who
had persuaded her father to rent the house to them. But, despite
having been presented to King George V and Queen Mary twice,
in 1916 and 1918, and getting a mention for her war work in the
London Gazette in 1920, her application for a post as Inspector
of Local Committees was rejected because she was a woman. She
later had to endure the ignominy of being rejected by the family
firm because she was female.

Fran's widow Dorothy, nicknamed Dort, was one of the more fortunate. Despite having a four-year-old daughter, Ruth, she soon managed to find herself a second husband, her late husband's cousin Arthur. The couple married in 1919 and their son Tom was born the following year. They moved into a house on the edge of Chapel Allerton, and Arthur split his time between supervising the farm at Beechwood, where he had grown up, playing polo and hunting. On 14 December 1928, while riding with the Bramham Hunt, he was involved in a horrific accident. After failing to take a fence, his horse threw him and rolled on top of him, fracturing his pelvis. He died eleven months later, when his son Tom was only nine years old, leaving Dorothy a widow for the second time. Within a year, his father Arthur had died, his end hastened by grief.

CHAPTER 8

Noel Middleton and Olive Lupton

L ying in bed after giving birth at her home, Fieldhead House, in the Yorkshire village of Roundhay, Kate's great-grandmother Olive Middleton cradled her newborn son Peter and prayed for a new dawn.

Married for six years to solicitor Noel Middleton and approaching her fortieth birthday, the mother of three wanted to give her sons Christopher, four, Anthony, three, and now Peter the idyllic upbringing she had been denied. It was 3 September 1920 – two years after the end of the Great War – and Olive had already suffered more pain than most people experience in a lifetime. Her mother Harriet had died when she was ten, leaving her in the care of a succession of housekeepers, nannies and governesses, and her brothers Fran, Maurice and Lionel had been killed in the war. Now she was watching with sadness as her father faded away before her eyes, overwhelmed with the grief of losing his wife and three sons.

He died five months later, as much of a broken heart, it seems, as of any other cause, leaving his daughter a wealthy woman but a saddened one.

Despite being dealt such a terrible hand, Olive was stoical about her experiences. After all, she was fortunate. Not only was she wealthy in her own right and married – quite a feat in those post-war days – but her husband Noel had returned from the battlefields of France, where he had worked as a driver for the Royal Army Service Corps.

The only other member of the family to have been so lucky was her cousin Hugo, a Wellington School and Trinity College alumnus, who had won a Military Cross for his service in France. On 17 July 1920, he married Joyce Ransome, the daughter of a family friend, Leeds University professor Cyril Ransome, who came from Far Headingley. Her brother Arthur would find fame a decade later when *Swallows and Amazons*, the first of his series of children's novels, was published.

After the war, Noel gave up his partnership at solicitors W.H. Clarke, Middleton & Co. in South Parade, Leeds, to join Olive's family business, William Lupton & Co., as a cashier. Olive's sister Anne, who was single, had hoped to fulfil her brothers' role at the company but was rebuffed because she was a woman.

When Olive gave birth to her and Noel's fourth child, a daughter Margaret, known as Moggy, on 29 June 1923, the couple's happiness was complete. Together, they created a carefree family home. Fairfield – a substantial Edwardian villa at 12 Park Avenue, an exclusive tree-lined street in the suburb of Oakwood by Roundhay Park – was full of voices and laughter. Gentle and kind, with a relaxed temperament, Olive was a natural mother, and the children thrived in their surroundings. They had a governess, who taught them with their second cousin Francis, the eldest son of Hugo Lupton and Joyce Ransome. In *The Next Generation*, Francis remembered:

When I reached school age, my mother taught me for a while, but I later shared a governess with my cousins, Peter and Margaret Middleton. They lived at Oakwood, some three miles away, and I clearly remember that I used to start out each morning with a lift on a horse-drawn milk float which took me for a mile or so along the way, while my mother caught me up on a bicycle.

Noel, who had a keen interest in music, was chairman of the Northern Philharmonic Orchestra and organised many musical soirées in Leeds between the wars. He was also interested in photography and shared with his wife a love of painting. In *The Next Generation*, Kate's grandfather Peter wrote:

My mother was an adequate pianist and a very talented painter of watercolours. One of my fondest memories is of her playing the piano in my father's home orchestra. My father played first fiddle, Margaret second fiddle, Tony viola, myself cello and Christopher double bass. I particularly remember rehearsing Handel one afternoon when my father called a halt for some reason and we all stopped playing except for Tony, who had not seen the stop signal. He continued happily scraping away at 'The Vicar of Bray', which he apparently found easier than Handel, and anyway it fitted in quite well. Cousin Tom used to join us occasionally with his fiddle, accompanied by his mother Dort. He says today that the whole prospect terrified him.

The whole family used to gather at Beechwood, the Lupton family's old seat, where Olive's father Francis had been brought up with his brothers Arthur, Charles and Hugh, and which was now home to Arthur's daughters Elinor and Bessie, two spinster sisters. Peter remembered:

We were somewhat in awe of our cousins Elinor and Bessie. Visits to them at Beechwood were always rather special occasions before which my mother held careful inspections for dirt behind the ears, clean hankies etc. An even greater ordeal was the annual 'Beechwood Party', for which I still remember the horrors of trying to tie a black bow tie for my first dinner jacket. Nor will I forget my terror of Elinor and Bessie's aunt, Lady Bryce, and my admiration for Reggie Skinner [married to Charles's daughter Frances], who organised the after-dinner charades.

The family spent a lot of time outdoors in the countryside and summer holidays were spent camping in the Lake District or staying in their holiday house in Kettlewell, one of the prettiest villages in the Yorkshire Dales, which overlooks the Wharfedale Valley to the north of Skipton. Of these idyllic trips, Peter wrote:

My mother was a superb maker of picnics to be carried up Lake District mountains or the hills of upper Wharfedale . . . As well as the Kettlewell cottage, we had a wooden camping hut in the Lake District, where we went as a family to learn self-reliance and what would now be known as 'survival techniques'. My mother must have already learned the latter as, during the summer holidays and in primitive conditions, she catered for parties of up to ten youngsters, sleeping in tents, cooking on two Primus stoves and drawing water from a stream.

It was while they were in the Lake District during the summer of 1936 that Olive was taken to hospital with peritonitis, a blood infection, after her appendix burst. There were complications and, on 27 September, at the age of 55, she died, ripping the heart out of the family. She left £52,031 in trust for her children. It was a fortune in those days, but the money could not make up for the loss to the

Middleton siblings. Peter was only 16 years old when his mother died and Margaret was barely a teenager. Yet another generation of Lupton children was left to make their way in the world without a mother. Olive's sister Anne, who was seven years younger than her and the only one of her brothers and sisters still alive, became a shoulder for Noel to lean on and a good friend to the children.

After the First World War, following the deaths of her father and three brothers, Anne, unmarried and with no ties, had decided to go travelling, visiting Asia and South America. Her adventures enthralled her nieces and nephews. When she returned to England, she set up home at 7 Mallord Street, Chelsea, with Enid Moberly Bell, an equally inspiring and inexhaustible woman, who was not only a prolific author but also the founder and first headmistress of Lady Margaret School in Fulham and a vice chairwoman of the Lyceum Club for female writers and artists. It was in Mallord Street that Anne found out about the death of her sister.

In those days, Chelsea was not an exclusive, well-heeled haven for investment bankers and celebrities but a quarter of London inhabited by artists, writers and poets. One of the women's neighbours was the artist Augustus John, who commissioned the Dutch architect Robert van t'Hoff to design a cottage for him at No. 28 after a chance encounter in a pub. The painter Cecil Hunt, whose wife was a leading figure in the suffrage movement, resided in Mallord House, and author A.A. Milne, a former journalist and assistant editor at *Punch*, who created the children's stories about Winnie the Pooh for his son Christopher, lived at No. 13, a red-brick house with a wrought-iron fence and leaded windows.

Anne fitted well into the progressive, bohemian milieu of Mallord Street. She had inherited her father's social conscience and worked on improving housing conditions in Fulham, for which she was

awarded an MBE. She was also involved in the creation of the Quarry Hill estate in inner-city Leeds, which opened in 1938 as the country's largest municipal housing scheme, to replace the back-to-back housing of the Victorian era, a cause that had been close to her father's heart. The new flats became iconic and were modern and well equipped, with solid-fuel ranges, electric lighting and state-of-the-art refuse collection, but the buildings were demolished in 1978 because of structural defects.

In *The Next Generation*, Peter wrote:

> Anne was brilliant and vivacious. A school report of 1906 reports: 'Such gifts as hers should be given every opportunity for development for the sake of her own happiness and that of others.'
>
> She undertook the role of mother figure to our family. She visited us frequently and took a lively interest in her nephews and niece, urging us to work harder and achieve more.
>
> She was a marvellous teller of travellers' tales, enthralling her nephews and niece, who called her 'Nantanne', with accounts of her many travels. She told how she had been surrounded by bandits in South America; been importuned by a Portuguese man while travelling on an open flat car on an Argentine train, escaping his attentions by drilling a hole in his neck with the corner of a biscuit tin; and of the time when she was on board a ship anchored in Tokyo harbour during the horrific 1923 earthquake. Until she was in her 50s she ran, and usually won, an annual race with my brother Tony.

Three years after Olive's death, the family faced another challenge, the outbreak of the Second World War, and another generation of Luptons went off to fight for their country. It was on Peter

Middleton's 19th birthday, 3 September 1939, that war was declared. While his older brother Christopher joined the Royal Artillery and Anthony went into the army, Peter joined the RAF. He got his wings in Canada, where many pilots were trained because it was not safe to conduct exercises over Britain during wartime.

It was another anxious time for Noel, who had seen his wife's family almost wiped out by the First World War, but ultimately a kinder one, as the family celebrated a marriage, a birth and political honour.

On 6 December 1941, the family was reunited at Christ Church, Chelsea, when Christopher, by then a lieutenant in the Royal Artillery, got married to Dorothy Martin, the daughter of a builder, who was three years older than him. His aunt Anne signed the marriage certificate in his mother's place. Once again, she was holding the family together, keeping her home in Chelsea open for friends and relatives passing through London. She was eventually driven out by the bombing and set up home in a rented house in Midhurst, Kent, where she continued to get involved in war relief work. 'When I visited her there she was furiously sterilising fruit and putting it into cans to feed children evacuated from London to escape the bombing,' recalled Peter.

A year later, on 18 November 1942, the family celebrated again when Jessie Kitson, great-niece of the 1st Baron Airedale, who had been a close friend of Peter Middleton's great-grandfather William, became the first female Lord Mayor of Leeds. She was a lifelong friend of Arthur Lupton's daughter and Anne's cousin Elinor, who once joked that she and Jessie were 'the two worst-dressed ladies in Leeds'. The family were delighted that Elinor, a Cambridge graduate in classics who lived in the family home, Beechwood, became her Lady Mayoress.

Then, in 1943, Noel became a grandfather for the first time when his daughter-in-law Dorothy gave birth to Philippa. The first

member of the Middleton family to be born outside Leeds, she arrived into the world at the Fulmer Chase Maternity Hospital in Berkshire, where many wives of junior officers gave birth.

Despite being a leading centre for manufacturing, Leeds survived the war largely unscathed. Local legend had it that the thick black smoke produced by the city's industries prevented enemy planes from spotting their targets. Nevertheless, some 70 people were killed during attacks, the worst of which happened in March 1941, when the town hall, the station, the Quarry Hill estate and Leeds City Museum were all bombed, the museum suffering the loss of an ancient Egyptian mummy. Meanwhile, Waddingtons, the local board game and playing card manufacturers, rose to the challenge by supplying British servicemen held in prisoner of war camps in Germany with games in which they had secreted maps to aid them in their attempts at escaping.

None of the Middleton brothers was killed during the war, and the family must have breathed a huge sigh of relief when the end came. In Leeds, thousands danced in the streets, clambering up on top of the lions in front of the town hall to celebrate VE Day. On 13 May 1945 there was a victory parade through the town, attended by thousands despite the pouring rain.

The end of the war spelled the beginning for a new generation of Middletons as they celebrated their new-found freedom. Both Kate's grandfather Peter and his brother Anthony fell in love in those heady post-war days, with two ravishing sisters.

Peter, who became a civilian pilot after being demobbed, was the first brother to take the plunge, getting married at the respectable age of 26. He tied the knot with Valerie Glassborow, 22, the daughter of bank manager Frederick Glassborow, on 7 December 1946 at the Norman parish church in Adel, the oldest church in Leeds. The marriage proved the foundation for another love affair, between Peter's older brother Anthony, a 29-year-old cloth

manufacturer, and Valerie's sister Mary, 23. They got married on 5 April the following year at the parish church of St John in Moor Allerton, cementing the warm relationship between the two families.

Sadly, Noel did not live long enough to walk his youngest daughter Margaret down the aisle when she wed musician James Barton eight years later. He died suddenly of a heart attack at the age of 72 on 2 July 1951, leaving in his will the equivalent of £1.3 million, which was split between his four children. Kate's grandfather Peter, who was 30 when his father died, also inherited a bronze bust by Jacob Epstein, an oil painting by local artist George Graham and a picture of himself by Edward Neatby, an accomplished Leeds-born painter of landscapes and portraits.

Noel's sister-in-law Anne, who had played such a major role in his children's lives, outlived him by 16 years, but after the death of Enid Moberly Bell in 1966 she seemed to wilt. Crippled by arthritis, she died the following year of leukaemia and tuberculosis, contracted during the First World War. She was 79.

CHAPTER 9

The Glassborows 1881-1954

*D*ressed in her traditional black mourning gown trimmed with white lace, with tears falling down her cheeks, Queen Victoria sat at her bureau in Windsor Castle and penned a letter to Lord Rowton, private secretary to Benjamin Disraeli. Once again plunged into grief, this time after the death of her favourite prime minister, Prince William's great-great-great-great-grandmother wrote that day: 'I can scarcely see for my fast falling tears . . . Never had I as kind and devoted a Minister and very few such devoted friends.'

The date was 19 April 1881 – nearly 20 years after Victoria had withdrawn from public life following the death of her beloved Albert – and the former Conservative prime minister, a favourite of the Queen, had succumbed to bronchitis.

His death, which came a year after he had lost a general election to Gladstone's Liberal Party, spelled the end of a friendship between the Queen and her minister that had begun in 1868 when he replaced Lord Derby as Prime Minister and was cemented when he

won a second term in power in 1874. Disraeli lured Victoria out of seclusion, proclaiming her Empress of India, charming her by kissing her hand, calling her 'the Faery Queen' and sending her witty letters. 'Everyone likes flattery,' he told the poet Matthew Arnold, 'and when you come to royalty, you should lay it on with a trowel.' In return, the Queen made him Earl of Beaconsfield and Viscount Hughenden, sending him bunches of spring flowers and nicknaming him 'Dizzy'. She sent bouquets of primroses to his funeral. Afterwards, she paid a visit to Hughenden to lay a wreath on his tomb and later had a memorial erected to him in her name.

While Victoria suffered the pain of grief, 30 miles away, in the depths of Holloway Prison, Kate Middleton's great-great-great-grandfather Edward Glassborow was enduring an altogether different ordeal. Incarcerated in a cramped cell – 13 ft by 7 ft – on one of three wings for male inmates in the jail, the 55-year-old was one of 436 prisoners from the city of London and Middlesex to be held in Holloway when the 1881 census was taken.

Prison records have not survived from that era, so it is impossible to know why the father of seven, who worked as a messenger for an insurance company, was jailed. The most likely explanation is that he was sent down for a short period for a minor offence such as being drunk and disorderly. In those days, Holloway, previously known as the City of London House of Correction or City Prison, was the jail for male and female prisoners sentenced at the Old Bailey, the Mansion House or Guildhall Justice Rooms. It also housed debtors; although imprisonment for unpaid debts officially ceased in 1862, debtors were sometimes jailed for contempt of court or non-payment of fines.

Whatever the crime, Edward's father Thomas would have turned in his grave. He volunteered as a parish constable when he was in

his early 20s and arrested dozens of criminals like his son. He was a witness at the Old Bailey many times in cases of stealing and pocket-picking, and his evidence condemned many convicts to be transported to Australia and Tasmania. But he gave up that job before his marriage to Edward's mother Amy on 18 February 1823 and became an insurance company's messenger. The couple lived at 1 Bartholomew Lane, which at that time was the headquarters of the Alliance Marine Insurance Company, founded by Nathan Rothschild, so it appears that Thomas was such a model employee that he lived on the premises.

By that time, Sir Robert Peel had been appointed Home Secretary and the first rumblings about forming a modern salaried police force for the capital were under way. Law and order had become a major headache for the authorities as people flocked to London during the Industrial Revolution. Australia and Tasmania refused to allow more convicts into the country, and Britain had to find another way of dealing with its criminals. The obvious solution was to reform the police force and build more prisons. The Metropolitan Police Act of 1829 replaced volunteer constables and night watchmen with a centralised police force of 3,000 men responsible for policing the entire metropolitan area with the exception of the City of London. Clad in blue uniforms and carrying truncheons, they were nicknamed 'bobbies' after Peel.

Ninety prisons were built between 1842 and 1877. Holloway Prison alone cost £91,547 10s 8d. It was opened in 1852. Each prison was run by a jailer who essentially made up the rules as he went along, doling out privileges to convicts who could afford to pay for books and letters, more visitors and better food. Many prisoners had to pay the jailer to be released after their sentences were served, being required to purchase a 'ticket of leave', the day's equivalent of the parole system. Those who could not afford to improve their lot ended up sleeping on comfortless wooden beds,

eating monotonous food and doing hard labour: walking treadmills and picking oakum – separating strands of old rope to be sold on for use in shipbuilding – were the most common activities, more punishment than purposeful work. Conditions were damp, unhealthy, insanitary and overcrowded, and many prisoners died before they could be released.

Perhaps luckily, neither of Edward's parents lived long enough to see him jailed. Thomas died at 65 of consumption on 29 December 1860, and Amy followed her husband to the grave four years later, dying of 'natural decay' and jaundice. Edward moved into 1 Bartholomew Lane, taking over his father's job, but things appear to have gone awry, as he ended up on the wrong side of the law.

He would likely have been taken to prison in a Black Maria. There he would have been photographed and examined for distinguishing marks, have had to hand over his personal property and remove his clothes. He would have had his head shaved and been bathed in filthy water before being dressed in prison garb, with the number of his cell stitched on the back of his shirt.

Meanwhile, his beleaguered wife Charlotte, 55, to whom he had been married for 33 years and with whom he had five sons and two daughters, was left at the family home in the East End of London to care for their four youngest children, Amy, 24, Kate's great-great-grandfather Frederick, a 22-year-old commercial clerk, 16-year-old Charles and Herbert, 14, who was still at school. Their two eldest sons, Edward, 32, and William, 26, had long since left home. Their daughter Charlotte, a milliner, had died of typhoid fever at home five years earlier at the age of 25. The family had moved from Bartholomew Lane, in the heart of the City, to a run-down house in Nelson Terrace, Trafalgar Road, Haggerston, in the parish of the ancient church of St Leonard's, Shoreditch, made famous by the line from the children's nursery rhyme 'Oranges and Lemons': 'When I grow rich, say the bells of Shoreditch.'

Fourteen years after Edward Glassborow's spell in Holloway, the renowned playwright and novelist Oscar Wilde would follow him through the portcullis gate. It was in Holloway that he was held on remand, awaiting trial for gross indecency. The author of *The Picture of Dorian Gray* and *The Importance of Being Earnest* had issued a writ for libel against the Marquess of Queensberry, the father of his lover, Lord Alfred 'Bosie' Douglas, after he accused him of being homosexual. Although Wilde withdrew the case when it became clear that he could not win, he was arrested in the wake of the trial and spent several months on remand at Holloway before being sentenced to two years' hard labour in Reading Gaol.

By then, of course, Kate's great-great-great-grandfather had long been released, and he had moved to Leyton, Essex, to build a new life. By the time his third son, Frederick, 27, got married on 1 June 1886 to 23-year-old Emily Elliott at the parish church in Leyton, he was describing himself as a 'gentleman', an extraordinary turnaround for a former crook. Edward lived long enough to see all his children settled, quite a feat in those days, although it is not known whether he was invited to their weddings or whether he was ostracised by the family as a result of his past.

His son Charles, 23 years old and a stockbroker's clerk, married Florence Alderton, who was five years his senior, at Hackney Parish Church on 13 August 1887, but chose his younger brother Herbert to be his witness. Five years later, it was the turn of Edward's only daughter, Amy, who married a widower twice her age. She was 36 years old and would have been deemed to be on the shelf in those days when she tied the knot with Samuel Alderton, a 65-year-old ivory turner, at Hackney Register Office. Again, it was Herbert who witnessed the ceremony. Finally, Herbert himself, a stockbroker of 29 years of age, tied the knot in 1896 at St Andrew's Church, Leytonstone, with local manufacturer's daughter Catherine Monahan, 28.

Edward and Charlotte must have been delighted that all their children were married, but they lived barely long enough to meet their grandchildren. On 11 August 1898, Edward died of apoplexy, in other words, following a sudden loss of consciousness, at home in Vicarage Road, Leyton, having suffered from chronic rheumatism. His son Frederick – Kate's great-great-grandfather – was at his bedside, so the family was certainly reconciled at his death. Less than two years later, on 21 July 1900, Charlotte died peacefully at home of natural causes, at the age of 75. Her daughter-in-law Emily, who was married to her second-eldest son, William, another stockbroker's clerk, was holding her hand.

After his mother's death, Frederick, 41 years old and a shipowner's clerk, moved into his parents' home in Vicarage Road with his wife Emily and their two children, Amy, 14, and Frederick, 11. Their third child, a son Wilfred, was born in 1905.

Kate's great-grandfather Frederick Glassborow, a 24-year-old banker at the London and Westminster Bank, 5 ft 9 in. tall with brown hair and brown eyes, was conscripted into the Royal Navy as an ordinary seaman on 12 August 1914 and attached to Benbow battalion ten days later. The battalion formed part of the First Royal Naval Brigade in the Royal Naval Division, known as 'Winston's Little Army' and created when the navy formed a division of surplus sailors to fight alongside the army.

Military records state that Frederick was one of 2,000 raw recruits to be sent to a training camp in Walmer, Kent – at most he had two days' musketry training – before being dispatched to Belgium to support the Belgian army in their defence of Antwerp, a cause close to Churchill's heart. Churchill himself was at the city's Hotel de Ville, not far from the front line at Vieux Dieu, on 6 October 1914, when he ordered the Naval Division to hold the line of

forts forming the inner defences of the city. But while the Belgian troops manned the forts, the British were positioned in shallow, flooded trenches, with 500 yards of cleared land in front of them, making them perfect targets for German gunfire. After two days, Churchill gave the order to withdraw, but it failed to reach the division commander, Commodore Wilfred Henderson, and the brigade was bombarded by heavy shelling. In the confusion, some battalions withdrew by train. Others, including Benbow, were left stranded, without transport, unable to cross the bridge over the River Schelde because it had been destroyed by the retreating Belgians and unable to catch a train as the line had been cut by the Germans. In order to evade capture, Commodore Henderson decided to take his exhausted men across the border into Holland, which was neutral.

Frederick was one of 545 men and officers from Benbow battalion, led by Commander Fargus, to be interned by the Dutch at the English Camp in the city of Groningen, after making it into the Netherlands. This proved to be his saviour. Billeted in a purpose-built wooden hut in the place he and his fellow soldiers dubbed 'Timbertown', he was able to use a gym, recreation hall, library, classroom and post office. A football pavilion was converted into a bar, where the men could entertain visitors. They produced their own newspaper, had sports teams who played against local clubs, an orchestra and a theatre company named Timberland Follies, and they were even allowed out of camp on the strict condition they did not try to escape.

Two weeks after he and his men had been forced to flee to Holland, Commodore Henderson sent a letter to the adjutant general of the Royal Marines, Sir William Nicholls, describing the fiasco. He reported that the men arrived at the front on 6 October and had begun digging trenches but were hampered by lack of equipment, the fact that some of the men had never handled a

pick or shovel, and the absence of food, water, communications and orders. Two of the battalions had suffered without water for 24 hours in the trenches and four battalions had no food for 36 hours other than a quarter-pound ration of meat. The men had been issued with charger-loading rifles three days before leaving Britain but had never been trained to use them. There was no organised transport, no signalling equipment apart from a few semaphore flags, one bicycle per battalion for messengers and no horses for the officers. 'The men had not received their khaki clothing and were still in their blue jumpers, and therefore without pockets in which to carry food and ammunition,' he added. 'Only a small proportion had received greatcoats . . . and [the men] suffered very considerably from the cold. The absence of haversacks, mess tins and water bottles proved a great disadvantage.'

Frederick was granted leave from Holland on 22 March 1917, which was extended until 26 May 1918. His file notes: 'Appreciation for the excellent work done at Consulate General, Rotterdam.' He arrived back in England on 4 March 1919 and was demobbed six days later, remaining with the 2nd reserve battalion.

Frederick survived the war but some of his cousins were not so fortunate. Herbert, a clerk and father of two from Leytonstone, who enlisted at the age of 36 on 2 December 1915 as gunner No. 86318 in the Royal Garrison Artillery and was sent to France, was disciplined for neglect of duty at the end of the war. He was sentenced to 14 days' field punishment No. 2, and was shackled in irons for up to two hours a day, a penalty generally considered harsh and humiliating by the men. His record states: 'While on active service. Neglect to the prejudice of good order and military discipline.'

Another cousin, James, who was a gunner in the Royal Horse Artillery, was only 21 years old when he was wounded in a mustard gas attack on 6 October 1917. He was treated at Bradford War Hospital and the injury affected the rest of his life. He was awarded

a temporary pension on discharge because of his general weakness, having been categorised as '20 per cent disabled'. James's older brother Charles, a 24-year-old corporal in the 11th Australian Light Trench Mortar Battery, was killed on 14 March 1917, and is remembered with honour at the cemetery in Armentières where he is buried.

After the end of the Great War, Frederick returned to his job as a manager with the London and Westminster Bank, where he met Constance Robison, a bank manager's daughter from Leytonstone. The couple, both 30, sealed their union on 24 June 1920 at Holy Trinity Church, Marylebone, an Anglican church built by Sir John Soane. They shared a love of travelling and when a job came up managing the bank's Valencia branch, Frederick was the first to volunteer. It was there that their son Maurice was born on 16 April 1922. Nearly two years later, on 5 January 1924, the family was completed with the birth of Kate's grandmother Valerie and her twin sister Mary. By then, Frederick was the sub-manager of the bank in Marseilles, on the south-east coast of France. It was an idyllic place in which to bring up children, but, as was traditional, Maurice was sent to prep school and public school in England. His second wife, Helen, remembers him telling her that the tour operator Thomas Cook used to make sure he arrived safely at his destination. 'He was sent off with a label with his name on it round his neck,' she recalls. 'That wouldn't happen nowadays.'

On 21 December 1932, when Valerie was just eight years old, Frederick senior died at the age of 73 while his son and his family were visiting. Frederick suffered a brain haemorrhage at his home in Lismore Road, Herne Bay, Kent. His son was at his bedside. He left £1,000 to his three children, a reasonable sum in those days but not one that made their fortune. It was the next generation of Glassborows who would gain real financial security when they married into one of Leeds' wealthiest families.

It was two months before Frederick Glassborow's 50th birthday when England declared war on Germany and he faced the prospect of living through another world war. While he was too old to fight, Maurice, who was just 17, was desperate to join the navy. Too young to join the British Royal Navy, he signed up to the French navy, where he would have taken part in the Battle of the Atlantic against the Axis powers, later transferring to the Royal Navy when the family returned from Marseilles to Britain. Frederick escaped on a ship, with the bank's records stuffed into sacks, shortly before Marseilles was occupied by enemy forces in November 1942. As his ship was waiting to leave the port, it was heavily bombed by German aircraft. It must have been a terrifying experience, but he coped with it with typical composure.

On his return to Britain, Frederick was transferred to the North, where he became manager of the Leeds branch of the Westminster Bank, in Park Row. He was active in the life of the city, being appointed chairman of the Institute of Bankers and of the Banking Advisory Committee of the Leeds College of Commerce, a member of the Council of the Leeds Chamber of Commerce, treasurer of the Economic League in the West Yorkshire region, as well as a Freeman of the City of London. These networking skills would eventually have beneficial repercussions for all his children.

While Maurice married into one of the country's most illustrious theatrical dynasties, Valerie and Mary landed the sons of one of Leeds' richest and most influential families. Frederick saw all three of his children happily settled and retired to Folkestone, Kent, where he died suddenly on 10 June 1954, at the age of 64, from a stroke caused by high blood pressure. He left his wife the equivalent of £323,000 – comfortably off but a widow in her 60s. She lived another two decades, long enough to see all her grandchildren grow up but not long enough to see her pilot grandson Michael marry air hostess Carole Goldsmith, or to meet her great-granddaughter Kate.

CHAPTER 10

Peter Middleton
and Valerie Glassborow

*D*escribed by Sir Winston Churchill as the 'first splash of colour' after the long years of war, the wedding of Princess Elizabeth to the Duke of Edinburgh on 20 November 1947 heralded a new age of peace and optimism for Britain in the aftermath of the conflict.

The 21-year-old princess had saved up her clothing coupons to buy the fabric for her dress: ivory duchesse satin woven from silk created by Chinese silkworms. Designed by couturier Norman Hartnell, it was embroidered with seed pearls in patterns inspired by the Botticelli masterpiece *Primavera*. Wearing a silk-tulle veil and diamond tiara lent to her by her mother, Queen Elizabeth, she walked down the aisle of Westminster Abbey in front of 2,000 dignitaries and guests on the arm of her father, King George VI.

Afterwards, the young couple, who received 2,500 wedding presents from across the globe, moved into their first home, a

five-bedroom house in Sunningdale, Ascot, which they leased until they moved into Clarence House in London two years later. Their new home, Windlesham Moor, was set in 58-acre grounds, and had four reception rooms, including a dining room, a 50-ft drawing room and a Chinese room. This was where they were living when Prince Charles was born on 14 November 1948.

The royal wedding ushered in a new dawn for Britain as it emerged from the hardship of the Second World War. The lives of all British citizens, whether they had fought abroad or on the home front, had been turned upside down, and everyone was looking forward to a time of peace.

French couturier Christian Dior's ultra-feminine 1947 collection echoed the turnaround as men returned to their old jobs and women were sent back to the traditional sphere of the home. Dubbed 'the New Look', after the term was used of the style in a *Harper's Bazaar* editorial, Dior's dresses and suits with soft shoulders, tiny waists and flowing skirts epitomised the mood of the post-war era. Scandalously extravagant and yet perfectly in tune with the times, the New Look caught the world's imagination. Rita Hayworth wore one of the new dresses to the premiere of *Gilda* and Margot Fonteyn bought a Dior suit. Such was the furore surrounding the clothes that, although George VI would not allow his daughters to wear the luxurious new style while times were tough, the designer was nonetheless asked to give them a private view of his next collection.

The year 1947 was a time of great change. It spelled the end of the Commonwealth – the partition of India resulting in the creation of the sovereign states of India and Pakistan – the Paris Peace treaties were signed and the International Monetary Fund was launched. Cambridge University voted to allow women full

membership for the first time and the French author André Gide won the Nobel Prize for Literature. The year also saw the deaths of Al Capone, car manufacturer Henry Ford and former prime minister Stanley Baldwin. It was an age of new technology: the first instant Polaroid camera appeared, Kalashnikov finalised the design of the AK-47 assault rifle, Hollywood mogul Howard Hughes piloted the enormous 'Spruce Goose' on its first and only flight – and there was the mysterious recovery by the US army of a crashed 'flying disc' from a ranch in Roswell, Texas.

It was also a year of celebrations for Kate's grandparents Peter Middleton, 27, and his wife Valerie, 23, in Leeds. Virtually the same age as the royal couple – Peter nine months older than the Duke of Edinburgh and Valerie two years older than the Queen – they themselves had got married a year earlier, on 7 December 1946, and were coming up to their first anniversary when Princess Elizabeth walked down the aisle. Their own wedding, of course, was not in the same league as that of Prince William's grandparents, but it was a very happy occasion. Peter's father Noel watched proudly as the young couple said their vows in front of friends and family at the Norman parish church in Adel, the oldest in Leeds, which rivals Westminster Abbey for beauty, and then witnessed their wedding signatures. He must have been sad that his wife Olive, who had died of peritonitis before the war, could not be at his side. Still, his sister-in-law Anne took her place and three of his other children, Christopher (already married to builder's daughter Dorothy), Anthony and Anne, were in the congregation along with Valerie's parents, Frederick and Constance Glassborow, who were close family friends.

The Glassborow twins, Valerie and Mary, had been brought up in Marseilles, where their father was sub-manager of the Westminster Foreign Bank, between the wars, and they were both bilingual. They met the Middleton boys in their home town of Leeds after

Frederick was transferred there in 1943, having fled the German invasion of France.

In an unusual twist, six months later, on 5 April 1947, when Valerie was four months pregnant with her first child, the two families were reunited once more for another wedding, this time that of Peter's older brother Anthony and Valerie's twin sister Mary. Tony, 29, who worked with his father Noel and brother Christopher at the family firm, William Lupton & Co., walked down the aisle with Mary, 23, at the Parish Church of St John in Moor Allerton, making them double brothers- and sisters-in-law.

The newly wed couple moved into one of two flats in Stanley Drive, Roundhay, belonging to Anthony's father Noel, just streets away from Valerie and Peter (who were living in the family home, Fieldhead), and Christopher, who lived in Oakwood Park with his wife Dorothy, four-year-old daughter Philippa and two-year-old son Stephen. Their younger sister Margaret had moved down to London and was living a more bohemian and glamorous lifestyle in Carlyle Square, an exclusive enclave off the Kings Road.

In another six months, on 21 September 1947, Valerie and Peter celebrated the birth of their first child, a son Richard, who was born at the Willows Nursing Home in Broad Lane on 21 September 1947, making him a year older than Prince Charles. By then, Peter had left the RAF, where he had been promoted to the rank of flight lieutenant, and was working as a commercial pilot for a charter company. He and his young family continued to live at Fieldhead with his ageing father while they searched for a home of their own.

The Glassborow girls' older brother Maurice, 25, having come out of the navy, was working temporarily as an asbestos manufacturer's representative. He was married to Monica Neilson-Terry and the couple lived a simple lifestyle in Primley Park Mount, to the east of Moortown Golf Club and three miles north-east of Roundhay, where his twin sisters lived. All four young families spent a lot of time together, especially after the birth of Maurice and Monica's daughter Matita at Chapel Allerton Nursing Home on 12 December 1947. She was just three months younger than her cousin Richard, and the two sisters-in-law must have appreciated each other's help and companionship.

Monica Neilson-Terry was descended from the great theatrical dynasty of the day, which numbered John Gielgud among its members. Gielgud's biographer Jonathan Croall described the family as having 'large appetites, gracious manners, fine voices and beautiful diction but also a flamboyant temperament, great stamina and an enormous capacity for hard work'. Monica's great-aunt was the legendary Shakespearean actress Dame Ellen Terry, who made her theatrical debut in front of Prince William's great-great-great-great-grandmother Queen Victoria at the age of eight – as Mamillius in *The Winter's Tale* – and was created a dame by his great-great-grandfather George V. A legend on the stage, she and the actor Sir Henry Irving, with whom she worked for 23 years, transformed British theatre. Offstage, her personal life caused scandal after Victorian scandal. She married three times, was pursued by George Bernard Shaw and eloped with an architect, Edward Godwin, by whom she had two children, a daughter named Edith, and a son, Edward Gordon Craig, who was the lover of Isadora Duncan and father of her ill-fated daughter Deirdre, who drowned in the River Seine at the age of seven.

Dame Ellen was the sister of Gielgud's grandmother Kate and Monica's grandfather Fred, a renowned actor-manager, making them second cousins. Monica's father was the esteemed actor Dennis Neilson-Terry, who died of double pneumonia at the age of 36, when she was just 10 years old. Her aunt was Phyllis Neilson-Terry, a successful stage actress who appeared in the film of John Osborne's play *Look Back in Anger*. Her sister Hazel, who had a role in Joseph Losey's acclaimed film *The Servant*, starring Dirk Bogarde,

was married to actor Geoffrey Keen, who played Frederick Gray, the Minister of Defence, in six James Bond films. So Kate's lineage includes famous authors, Hollywood actors and stage legends.

Towards the end of the '40s, Maurice moved down to London with his wife and daughter, leaving his twin sisters up north, where their lives remained as intertwined as ever. By the time Prince Charles was born on 14 November 1948, both Kate's grandmother Valerie and her great-aunt Mary were pregnant, Valerie with her second child and Mary with her first, a son John, who was born on 10 May 1949. Six weeks later, on 23 June, Valerie gave birth to her second son – Kate's father, Michael – at Chapel Allerton Nursing Home – an apt location, it would seem. Although its name has since changed, the building would appear to be the same one that backs onto Hawkhills, the house in Allerton Park where Michael's great-great-grandfather William lived a century beforehand. By this time, Valerie's husband Peter was a pilot instructor at the Air Service Training flying school, living with his young family in King Lane, west of Moortown Golf Club, and thinking of leaving Leeds and moving south. His father Noel, the patriarch of the family, died suddenly of a heart attack on 2 July 1951, and shortly afterwards the family did move south. At just 30 years old, Peter had lost both his parents. Perhaps it was easier for him to leave his home town behind when his father was no longer there.

Peter landed a job as a pilot instructor at the recently formed British European Airways, which was based at Heathrow Airport and flew to destinations in Europe and North Africa. He became a highly respected pilot and instructor and worked there until BEA merged with the British Overseas Airways Corporation in 1974, when he joined the newly created British Airways. In order to be near the airport, Peter moved his young family 200 miles south to the market town of Beaconsfield, Buckinghamshire, set in the Chiltern Hills, an Area of Outstanding Natural Beauty. The young couple

moved with their two sons, Richard, four, and Michael, two, to Silverthorne, a house in peaceful Grenfell Road, where homes now sell for around £1 million. It was there that they brought up their four children. Their third boy, Simon, was born on 24 August 1952 in Beaconsfield and their fourth, Nicholas, in nearby Chalfont St Giles on 11 September 1956.

Between their births, the family had to cope with a sad loss when, on 10 June 1954, Valerie's father Frederick suddenly died of a stroke at the age of 64. His wife Constance, and indeed the whole family, was devastated. There was also sad news on the business front: William Lupton & Co., the family firm that had been founded in 1773, the oldest company in Leeds, finally closed its doors in 1958, leaving Christopher and Tony without a job. The closure prompted Tony and his wife Mary to follow Peter and Valerie down south, the first generation of the Middleton family to leave behind their northern roots, with Christopher the only one of the siblings remaining in Leeds. Tony began working for the textile company Courtaulds, and he and Mary, who had four children – John, Gillian, who was born in 1951, Timothy, born in 1959, and Elizabeth, 1962 – settled in the same town as their siblings, in a house named Beechlawn in leafy Eghams Wood Road, just a mile away from Peter and Valerie. So the eight cousins, who were all similar ages, were brought up together.

By this time, the rest of the family was spread around the world: Christopher and his family were in Leeds; Maurice, now a wine merchant, was managing Saccone & Speed in Nairobi, where his daughter Matita went to Loreto Convent School; and Margaret was living in Barnet, north London, with her husband Jim Barton, a talented violinist who played chamber music, and their daughters Penny, who was born in 1957, and Sarah, who was the same age as Timothy.

The Middletons mourned when Peter's aunt Anne, Olive's younger

sister, died in 1967, from leukaemia and tuberculosis, at the age of 79. She was the last remaining member of his parents' generation of the family, most of whom had fallen during the First World War, and the woman they had turned to after their mother died. But it was the sudden death of Mary Middleton on 19 November 1975 that sent shock waves through the family. She died of breast cancer at the age of 51, leaving her husband Anthony, her elderly mother Constance, who was at that time living in a nursing home in the village of Penn, Buckinghamshire, and sister Valerie totally bereft. Her two elder children, John, 26, and Gillian, 24, had not yet married and the younger ones, Timothy, 16, and Elizabeth, 13, were both still at school. Less than two years later, on 19 July 1977, Constance died of coronary artery disease, leaving Valerie to mourn both her sister and her mother, who had been staying with her. Constance might have reached the grand old age of 90, but her loss was still keenly felt. Within a year, though, Valerie's sadness was supplanted by joy when she found out she was about to become a grandmother herself.

Kate's grandparents were living in a detached house in Vernham Dean, a pretty village nestled in the North Wessex Downs, in Hampshire, when their eldest son, Richard, told them that they were going to become grandparents. His wife Susan, the daughter of a journalist, whom he had married in 1976 – the year after his aunt Mary's death – was expecting her first child. That child, Lucy, who was born in 1978, brought a welcome ray of sunshine to disperse the dark clouds that surrounded them. But it would be their third grandchild, Kate, who would in time move the family to the very top of the social ladder.

CHAPTER II

Michael Middleton and Carole Goldsmith

Having arrived in a glass coach at St Paul's Cathedral, Lady Diana Spencer walked down the aisle on the arm of her father, Earl Spencer, in a £9,000 ivory taffeta and antique lace gown with a 25-ft train, designed by David and Elizabeth Emmanuel. Watched by 3,500 guests, the 20-year-old aristocrat took 3½ minutes to walk up to the altar to marry Prince Charles, 32, dressed in the uniform of a naval commander, at 11.20 a.m. on 29 July 1981.

The royal couple pledged their troth in a traditional Church of England service conducted by the Archbishop of Canterbury, Dr Robert Runcie, before walking out of the cathedral to the sound of Elgar's 'Pomp and Circumstance'. The streets were lined with 600,000 people – and another 750 million watched on television – as Prince William's parents travelled back to Buckingham Palace in an open-topped landau, emerging on the balcony shortly afterwards for the long-awaited kiss.

The marriage took place in a week when Shakin' Stevens was riding high in the charts with 'Green Door', in the year Bucks Fizz won the Eurovision Song Contest with 'Making Your Mind Up'. The film *Chariots of Fire* was pulling in vast audiences and thousands had lined the streets to watch the first London Marathon. The royal wedding was welcomed by a Britain in the grip of a recession and reeling from a series of assassination attempts on world leaders, including America's new president Ronald Reagan, Pope John Paul II and the Queen: teenager Marcus Sergeant fired six blank shots at the monarch from a starting revolver at that summer's Trooping of the Colour ceremony. Also that year, Peter Sutcliffe had been found guilty of the Yorkshire Ripper murders, Bobby Sands had died whilst on hunger strike in the Maze prison and race riots had broken out in Brixton, Toxteth and Chapeltown. The country needed a reason to party.

By the time Britain was celebrating its fairy-tale wedding, Kate's parents Michael and Carole Middleton had been married for 13 months and were living in the village of Bradfield, 30 miles from Windsor in the Royal County of Berkshire. Although Michael was virtually the same age as Prince Charles – he is seven months younger – his wife was six years older than Diana. Already expecting their first baby, the newly-weds could not have anticipated the high-profile lifestyle their eldest child would lead.

Carole, a glamorous air stewardess, in her tailored blue jacket with a scarf around her neck, an A-line skirt and a pillbox hat, had met her future husband during the '70s when she was working at British Airways. The daughter of a working-class couple, Ronald and Dorothy Goldsmith, who had climbed up the social ladder through hard graft, she came from a humble background. Her looks, however, were far from ordinary.

'Carole wasn't a girl for make-up,' remembers her cousin Ann Terry. 'She was a very natural girl who was happy in jeans and a sloppy jumper, more of a country girl. But she was very pretty. While our cousin Linda was the brains of the family, Carole was the beauty.'

In those days, working as an air hostess at British Airways, the national flag carrier formed in 1974 when BEA merged with BOAC, was a coveted job. Kim Sullivan, daughter of Carole's cousin Pat Tomlinson, worked with Carole at Terminal 1. 'British Airways was very exciting in those days,' she says. 'It was on the cusp when flying was for a privileged few with money but was opening up to the masses. It was a good job, there were lots of good-looking young people there and it felt like you belonged to a large club. It had a feeling of being glamorous – a bit like in the Leonardo DiCaprio film *Catch Me If You Can*.'

Carole soon attracted the attention of Michael, a flight dispatcher at the new company. He became her first serious boyfriend. Staunchly middle class, Michael was able to trace his lineage back through his blue-blooded grandmother Olive Lupton to the seventeenth-century aristocrat Sir Thomas Fairfax. It was a match made in heaven as far as Carole's mother Dorothy was concerned. 'Carole had one or two boyfriends, like anybody else, but nothing serious,' says Ann. 'Mike was her first proper love. He came from a good family and was very quiet and unassuming. In those days, when she was young, Carole was unassuming too. They seemed right together. They were good for one another. Dorothy was very happy about it. I think it was all her dreams come true. She would die to be alive today to see what's going on.'

Michael had followed in the footsteps of his father Peter, a pilot instructor at British European Airlines, in the hope of

flying high, but he switched from pilot training to ground crew. He did six months' training in which he learned how to use the computer system, before undertaking on-the-job training. By the time he met Carole, he was responsible for coordinating aircraft between arrival and departure and at the same grade as a captain. The job entailed working both in the terminal and airside, managing the loading of cargo and luggage, working out how much fuel was needed, dealing with awkward passengers, authorising take-off and ensuring aircraft were away on schedule. One of around 130 dispatchers earning the equivalent of about £35,000 today, he was quite a catch in his blue uniform, with its brass buttons, red hat and four gold stripes to denote his rank.

Colleague Dave Gunner, who joined BEA in 1960, remembers both Michael and his father Peter and describes them as being very different personalities. 'Peter was a captain and I was a lowly dispatcher,' he says. 'I met him on several occasions and he came across as very autocratic and aloof. He seemed disdainful of us and didn't talk to us. I think Mike joined as a graduate trainee. He was quite young when he came to us. I was surprised when I met him because he was so pleasant.

'He was quite a high-flying bloke but he was disenchanted because he had to work with us plebs on the ground,' jokes Dave. 'But everyone on the ground aspired to be a dispatcher. It was still a management-grade job. My last memory of him is from when I went to Malta in 1975. He dispatched our Trident 3 aircraft and he blocked off the forward Pullman seats for our family.'

Carole and Michael dated for a few years before moving into a modern flat eight miles from Heathrow, in Arborfield Close, just north of the M4 in Slough. In those days, Slough was a sprawling industrial suburb dotted with factories; the

headquarters of Mars and Citroën were there and it was home to Dulux paint. It was not the ideal place to bring up a young family, so the couple started looking for a home in the countryside, eventually settling on the tiny red-brick village of Bradfield Southend.

Eight months after moving into their new home, on 21 June 1980, the couple got married 27 miles down the road at the Parish Church of St James the Less in the village of Dorney on the banks of the River Thames in Buckinghamshire. Not, naturally, as grand as St Paul's, St James the Less was nonetheless an idyllic venue for the marriage of the woman now widely expected to become Prince William's mother-in-law. The church is picturesque and typically English; large parts of the building date from the twelfth century and it is decorated with restored medieval paintings. Carole, 25, arrived in a horse and carriage with her father Ronald, then 49 years old, who walked her down the aisle. Her proud mother Dorothy, 44, sat on the left in the front row. Across the aisle were Michael's parents Valerie, 56, and Peter, 59, who was a witness.

Ronald's sister Joyce and Carole's cousin Ann were her only relatives to be invited to the wedding apart from immediate family. 'Carole had everything that it was possible to have,' Ann recalls. 'A beautiful white dress, four bridesmaids and lovely flowers. They even had a horse and carriage. Afterwards, they had their reception at a local manor house. There was a big posh dinner and a band. They went abroad on honeymoon, I can't remember where. You wouldn't have expected them to have done anything else.'

It was Carole's marriage to Michael that made a reality her family's aspirations for her and moved her up the social ladder. Although his family was not in *Debrett's* or *Who's Who* – or on the *Sunday Times* Rich List – they were more educated and

affluent than her own. A totally different affair to her parents' wedding – the reception had been held in the local pub, with Dorothy borrowing a going-away outfit – Carole's big day was fit for a princess.

Catherine Elizabeth Middleton was born, with a mop of dark hair, at the Royal Berkshire Hospital in Reading on 9 January 1982 – five months before Princess Diana gave birth to Kate's future boyfriend Prince William. On 20 June that year, she was christened at the local church, St Andrew's, a flint-and-chalk building on the banks of the River Pang that still has its graceful fourteenth-century north aisle. At the ceremony, Michael wore a traditional dark suit with a striped tie and Carole wore a floral Laura Ashley dress. 'The christening was somewhere posh as well,' remembers Ann. 'Catherine was dressed in a full-length white christening gown and we moved on to the manor afterwards. Catherine was a little bit dumpy, with a cheeky round face.'

Twenty months later, on 6 September 1983, her sister Philippa, known as Pippa, was born at the same hospital. The two girls later snootily nicknamed 'the Wisteria Sisters' in society circles because they were 'highly decorative, terribly fragrant and with a ferocious ability to climb' had arrived in the world. Pippa was baptised in March 1984 at the same church where her sister's christening had taken place.

With two young children, Carole immersed herself in village life, making friends with the other locals and taking the two girls to the mothers-and-toddlers playgroup that was held on Tuesday mornings at St Peter's Church Hall. 'It was a chance for the mums to meet other mums and chat,' says Lindsey Bishop, who started the group in 1980, 'and for the children to meet other children and play.'

Later, Kate – known as Catherine in those days – and Pippa went on with the other local children to St Peter's Preschool, which was chaired by Audrey Needham, wife of the churchwarden, on the other weekday mornings. 'Her mother used to come along with the other mums and the children would play together,' she says. 'They would walk down along the footpath to the church hall. Every year, we would have a nativity play and the children would dress up and sing Christmas songs and rhymes. Afterwards, we would have a fair to raise money for the school.'

In those days, Carole had yet to launch her party-planning empire Party Pieces, but she was already showing the business acumen that would make it a roaring success: she'd begun making up party bags to sell to other mothers. Lesley Scutter, who lived opposite the family, remembers encountering her in the village. Her daughters Lindsey and Helene went to the same toddlers group and preschool. 'Carole would take her turn, like everybody else at the toddlers group, as mothers' helper, making teas, coffees and squash, washing children's hands and mopping up puddles on the floor. I remember her bringing her party bags in for us to see and make orders. It was something she felt she could do at the same time as having children.

'She would bring the kids to school herself and pick them up afterwards. I don't think she had any help at the time. She was always very pleasant when I spoke to her. If you passed her in the street she would stop and chat. I remember going to parties with the Twomeys, who lived next door, and Carole and Mike would be there. They were just a normal family – a really nice couple with well-behaved kids.'

In those days, on his British Airways salary, Michael and Carole could only dream of sending their children to private school. When Kate was four, at the start of the autumn term in

1986, she started at the local village school, Bradfield Church of England Primary School, which was next door to the Middletons' home. Pippa followed two years later. The school was a hub of the community and both girls thrived, visiting friends for tea and playing in each other's gardens. Carole would take them swimming in the school's outdoor pool during the summer holidays. Lindsey Reeves, a fellow pupil, remembers how keen the school was on sport, a subject at which Kate excelled. 'We had a school field where we played rounders and athletics,' she says. 'The outdoor pool was really cold. We also did our cycling proficiency test.'

Shortly after Kate's fifth birthday, there was a new addition to the family. James was born on 15 April 1987 at the Royal Berkshire Hospital. He remembers an idyllic childhood, playing with his elder sisters, baking cakes and sliding down the stairs on a tray. 'I have great childhood memories of my mother baking cakes,' he told *Tatler* recently, 'and I was always willing to participate, especially if it meant I could lick the bowl and revarnish the kitchen floor with treacle.'

It was around the time of James's birth that Carole established the family business, Party Pieces, aiming, according to the company's website, to 'inspire other mothers to create magical parties at home and to make party organising a little easier'. She rented a small unit in Yattendon, four miles from home, where she stored her merchandise. Yvonne Cowdrey, who did the family's housework at the time, recalls: 'Carole was fed up making up bags full of little gifts for the kids to take away from parties, and she realised other mums must feel the same, so she thought it would be a good idea to start a company that sold ready-made party bags. She used to send out little catalogues with her children modelling some of the things they sold. I remember Pippa and Kate being in them, wearing T-

shirts with their ages on them and holding cupcakes.'

Ultimately, it was Carole's business brains that would change the course of their lives, earning enough money for the couple to send their children to private schools, where they mingled with the cream of society.

CHAPTER 12

A Little Princess

Wearing a yellow sweatshirt, khaki skirt and yellow necktie, Kate Middleton ventured nervously into St Peter's Church Hall with her younger sister Pippa one Monday night in September 1990 to join the Brownies. After being enrolled in the 1st St Andrew's pack of twenty-four Brownies, the eight-year-old schoolgirl vowed: 'I promise that I will do my best to do my duty to God, to serve the Queen, help other people and keep the Brownie Guide Law.' She and Pippa, who had just turned seven, were then allocated to their respective sixes, with whom they would work on earning badges.

It was an exciting time for the sisters, who loved Brownies so much that they begged their parents to let them go on the pack holiday the following Easter, to a summer camp based in three old RAF buildings in seventeen acres of woodland at Macaroni Wood in the Cotswolds. There they fed chickens, collected eggs, watched chicks hatch, bottle-fed lambs and kid goats, rode horses and went for horse-and-cart rides. There was also a playground with rope swings, a slide, a sandpit, a playhouse and a barbecue.

Brown Owl June Scutter ran the pack for twenty-five years and remembers the two sisters joining together. She took them by coach to Macaroni Wood, where the Brownies slept in sleeping bags on camp bunk beds in two dormitories. 'When we went there it was more like a shed,' she recalls. 'It was very basic in those days. Now, apparently, they have showers, but in our day there were just washbasins, placed on a board across a bath. We had a big room where everyone congregated, which was pretty comfortable, and a crafts room behind it, which was easy to sweep up. There was a cook but the girls had to help around the place with the housework and make their own beds. They had to follow an itinerary and spend a couple of days washing up or wiping up or sweeping in order to get their house orderly badge. They would peel potatoes and onions, which would make them cry. Some of them had never even done the washing up before. On other days, they made puppets and Easter chicks for their toymakers' badge, and they would do sports. They had a special uniform for pack holidays – brown trousers and cardigans and yellow shirts – so that they didn't ruin their normal uniform, and they had overalls for craftwork.'

During the holiday, Kate and Pippa visited Cogges Manor Farm Museum, a traditional Victorian farmstead set in rural Oxfordshire. There they talked to the farm hands and dairymaids as they milked the cows, fed the pigs and made butter, visited the old milking parlour for an ice cream and watched maids cooking on the kitchen range. They also played with replica toys and games and dressed up in Victorian costumes. 'We would go on a couple of outings to villages in the Cotswolds,' says Mrs Scutter. 'I took Kate and Pippa to Cogges Farm, where they played with the animals. All the girls were allowed so much pocket money for shopping and souvenirs when they were out and about.'

By the time Kate joined Brownies, her parents' business had

begun to thrive and they were able to afford the fees to send their children to a private prep school, St Andrew's School in Pangbourne, four miles away from Bradfield Southend. Today, the annual fees are upwards of £10,000. Wearing her green blazer, kilt, white shirt and crested tie, Kate walked up the stone steps for the first time and into the coeducational school, housed in a Victorian mansion and set in 54-acre grounds, at 8.25 a.m. at the start of the autumn term in 1989.

The school motto, '*Altiora Petimus*', which translates as 'We Seek Higher Things', is echoed by the current headmaster Jeremy Snow, who writes on the school's website:

> We hope that the children in our care will leave us with a well-established set of values which will stay with them for life. We want them to gain confidence from their achievements in this school and move on to great future success and fulfilment.

It was at St Andrew's that Kate, a gangly seven-year-old, first showed the promise that would attract a prince. Above average height, she excelled at sport, winning swimming races and playing goal defence in netball. She was a natural athlete, gaining the school record in her age group for high jump and spending many Saturdays playing sport: netball and hockey during the winter, tennis and rounders in the summer, and basketball, volleyball and badminton whenever the opportunity arose. There were also skiing trips during the holidays. Sport is an interest that she has in common with William, who is a keen rugby player and footballer and enjoys water polo. 'Kate was very sporty,' remembers former pupil Samantha Garland, who was in her year. 'I don't think there was a sport she couldn't turn her hand to. She was very good at the high jump.'

As well as being a natural at sport, Kate loved drama and

took part in the school's public-speaking competitions, debates and poetry recitals. She was involved in many of the school pantomimes and plays – they staged three productions each year – and did drama workshops during the summer holidays. She also learned ballet and tap and had recorder lessons after school.

One parent whose daughter was at the school says: 'Kate was very well brought up. She never put a foot wrong when she came for tea and had beautiful manners. She was a credit to her mother. Her parents were lovely people. Carole was very hard-working; I just applaud her. I was of the same opinion as her: we wanted our daughters to learn everything.'

In 1992, at the age of ten, Kate starred as Eliza Doolittle in a production of *My Fair Lady*. Her leading man was Andrew Alexander, now a singer in the vocal group Teatro. 'Kate was enchanting,' he gushed in an interview. 'She played the role with passion and a steely conviction. I always like to think that, although I'll never be King, I was at least her first prince.' He mentioned that his most recent encounter with Kate had been at a party where he was serving hors d'oeuvres. After the play, Kate asked Andrew to go out with her, but he regretted that he was too shy to say yes. 'I was only ten years old and Kate was so mature at the time,' he told the *Daily Mail* later. When she asked him out, he recounted: 'I remember being flushed all of a sudden and getting tongue-tied. I think I caused myself more embarrassment than I caused her. If she asked me now, I wouldn't hesitate to say yes.'

Kate was also one of the students in the school's production of the Tchaikovsky ballet *The Nutcracker* and performed in a musical called *Rats!*, an adaptation of the Robert Browning poem *The Pied Piper of Hamelin*. In her final year at St Andrew's School, she appeared in an end-of-term play, a Victorian melodrama with an interesting twist – her leading man was called William. In a

scene that now has a certain irony, bearing in mind that she is still waiting for the prince to propose, William drops onto one knee and asks Kate's character to marry him. She replies, 'Yes, it's all I've ever longed for. Yes, oh yes, dear William . . . Ah, to think I am loved by such a splendid gentleman.' Later in the play, she proclaims, 'I feel there is someone waiting to take me away into a life that's full, bright and alive.' When a fortune teller reveals that she will meet a good-looking and wealthy man, she asks, 'Will he fall in love with me and marry me? Oh, how my heart flutters!' At the end of the play, Kate's character is abandoned with her child, as William turns out not to be such a splendid gentleman after all.

Kingsley Glover, another former classmate, interviewed for the *Daily Mirror* about a video of the play obtained by the paper, recalled: 'Back then, she was completely different. Shy, skinny and lanky. But just look how confident and beautiful she is now.' During her later years at the school, Kate would spend the occasional night at St Andrew's, which was a flexi-boarding school. Kingsley, who was a boarder, described being embarrassed after Kate and her friends witnessed his dressing gown being blown open by a gust of wind in the corridor. 'It made me cringe,' he told the *Mirror*, 'but now I laugh when I think that the girl who might be the future Queen of England has seen my crown jewels.'

While Kate and Pippa were at school, Carole juggled her mail-order company with looking after her youngest child, James. Sadly, on 1 December 1991, when Carole was 36 years old and her brother Gary, 26, their grandmother Elizabeth Harrison died of bronchopneumonia in a nursing home in Southall. Aged 88, she was their only surviving grandparent and the one they both knew the best. Their grandfather Charlie Goldsmith had died before they were born and both of their other grandparents, Thomas

Harrison and Edith Goldsmith, had died by the time Carole was 21. It was a difficult time for the siblings, whose mother was understandably devastated.

Around this time, Party Pieces began to blossom after Carole and Michael decided to create a website on the fledgling Internet. In an astute move, they registered the name with Companies House in order to prevent it being stolen by another firm. As Party Pieces flourished, the business outgrew its premises – today, it claims to be 'the UK's leading online and catalogue party company' – and in April 1995 it moved into larger premises, a collection of farm buildings a mile down the road in Ashampstead Common, Berkshire. Eight customer service staff now work in the 200-year-old barn, answering calls and taking orders, while packers work in the picking room, based in a converted cowshed, and the warehouse, a converted hayloft stacked to the roof with themed tableware, decorations, party bags and games.

The money began to roll in, and Michael and Carole set their sights on moving out of the village of Bradfield Southend and into the countryside. They sold their house in July 1995 and moved two miles down the road, to the outskirts of Chapel Row, a genteel place with a village green, a butcher's, a tea shop and a pub named the Blade Inn. Set in the well-heeled parish of Bucklebury, where neighbours include John Madejski, the multimillionaire owner of Reading Football Club, DJ Chris Tarrant, singer Kate Bush and TV personality Melinda Messenger, it is the quintessential English village, one that would not be out of place in *Midsomer Murders*. Over the past 13 years, the Middletons have become well-known faces in the village and regulars at its traditional August Bank Holiday fair, with its displays of wolves and birds of prey, sheep and duck races, vintage cars and hog roasts. 'They are a very jolly family and have been here a long time,' butcher

Kate's great-grandfather Charlie Goldsmith (bottom left) during the First World War. (Courtesy of Kim Sullivan)

Kate's grandfather Ronald Goldsmith (front) with (l–r) his brother-in-law Henry 'Titch' Jones, his sister-in-law Emma Goldsmith, his sister Ede Jones, his brother Charlie Goldsmith, his mother, Edith Goldsmith, and his sister Joyce Plummer.

Kate's great aunts, Ronald Goldsmith's sisters (l–r): Hetty, Ede, carrying Joyce, and Alice.

Kate's grandmother Dorothy Harrison and grandfather Ronald Goldsmith on their wedding day, 8 August 1953, at Holy Trinity Church, Southall.

Kate's great-great-great-grandfather Frank Lupton. (Courtesy of Arthur Lupton)

Kate's great-grandmother Olive Lupton. (Courtesy of Arthur Lupton)

Kate and Fergus Boyd at the Don't Walk charity fashion show
in St Andrews, 2002. (© Getty Images)

Kate on the catwalk in St Andrews.
(© Getty Images)

Kate at the wedding of Hugh van
Cutsem and Rose Astor in June
2005. It was the first time she and
Prince William had attended a high-
profile social event together.
(© Getty Images)

Kate at her graduation ceremony, St Andrews, 2005. (© Getty Images)

Kate and William photographed kissing for the first time, Klosters, 2006. (© David Parker)

Kate at the Cheltenham Gold Cup,
2006. (© Getty Images)

Kate wearing BCBG Max Azria
at the Boodles Boxing Ball,
2006. (© Alan Davidson)

The look of love: Kate and William gaze adoringly
at each other as the leave Boujis, 2006.
(© Matrix Syndication)

Kate, with her father, attends William's graduation from Sandhurst in December 2006. (© Getty Images)

Kate and William at the 2007 Cheltenham Festival, shortly before their split. (© Getty Images)

Kate (third row, far right) and William at the Concert for Diana in July 2007. (© Getty Images)

Kate and Chelsy Davy at the wedding of Peter Phillips and Autumn Kelly in May 2008. (© Goff Photos)

Kate in an Issa dress at the 2008
Boodles Boxing Ball.
(© Davidson/O'Neill/Rex Features)

Kate watches Prince William's
investiture into the Order of the
Garter in June 2008.
(© Getty Images)

Martin Fidler told the press recently. 'They are not high profile but are much liked.'

It was in their current home, a red-brick house with climbing vines and wisteria, that Michael and Carole brought up the girl who is expected to one day become Queen.

CHAPTER 13

At Marlborough

I t was three months after her fourteenth birthday when Kate Middleton drove with her parents past the porter's lodge and the arched entrance of renowned public school Marlborough College to the all-girl house where she would spend the next four years of her life.

The school is set in extensive grounds in the quaint market town of Marlborough, 33 miles from Kate's home in Bucklebury. Wearing her new uniform, a blue blazer and tartan skirt, the shy teenager arrived at the boarding school, where fees today are more than £27,000 a year, in April 1996 – midway through the academic year and at the start of the summer term.

It was a daunting experience for Kate. She had left St Andrew's the previous summer after passing her Common Entrance examination and had spent two terms at Downe House, a boarding school a few miles from her home in Bucklebury, before her parents decided to remove her.

Now the retiring schoolgirl was once again facing with

trepidation the prospect of starting a new school – her fourth in a decade. This always nerve-racking situation was no doubt made even more intimidating because her fellow pupils were drawn from the upper echelons of society.

It was a sign that everything Kate's grandmother Dorothy had aspired to had been achieved by her daughter Carole. She had become solidly middle class, living in a traditional Home Counties manor house and educating her children at a very exclusive school.

Carole's aspirations would prove to be the making of her daughter. Kate may have felt out of her depth when she joined Marlborough, but within a decade she had blossomed into a confident young woman, taking the world in her stride and dating the next but one in line to the throne.

Marlborough College, which has the motto *'Deus Dat Incrementum'* – 'God Giveth the Increase', or 'God Gives Growth' – from 1 Corinthians 3:6, was founded in 1843 for the sons of Church of England clergymen and within a few decades it had become one of the country's leading boys' public schools. Although it now attracts the children of peers and socialites, former pupils, known as Old Marlburians, are an eclectic bunch, including Poet Laureate Sir John Betjeman, art historian and Soviet spy Anthony Blunt, round-the-world yachtsman Francis Chichester, actor James Mason, war poet Siegfried Sassoon, Conservative politician Rab Butler and singer Chris de Burgh.

Built beside the Marlborough Mound, an ancient man-made knoll thought once to have formed part of a Norman motte-and-bailey castle, the college is centred round a courtyard dominated by a Victorian Gothic chapel with stained-glass windows by William Morris. But the school campus, bordered by the River

Kennet, is sprawled across the town. Today, the college has its own trout ponds and an observatory as well as extensive playing fields. There are eleven rugby pitches, seven soccer pitches, eight cricket squares, six grass hockey pitches, three lacrosse pitches, two volleyball courts, twelve tennis courts and a driving range.

It was in that sporty atmosphere that Kate would thrive. A keen sportswoman, she joined Marlborough six years after it became co-educational – although the school began admitting girls to the sixth form in 1968 – and moved into the girls' boarding house Elmhurst, once a nineteenth-century private house. It had its own garden and purpose-built sixth-form wing and was a short walk from the central courtyard.

One of the first girls Kate met on her arrival was Jessica Hay, five months her senior, who showed her up to their dormitory, helped her to unpack her trunk and went with her to the dining hall for supper. Jessica remembers Kate as a shy and gawky teenager, and told the *News of the World* that her nerves would have been worsened by the older boys' habit of publicly marking new girls out of ten, writing the figures on a napkin at dinner. Jessica recounted that Kate received only ones and twos.

Kate's lack of confidence was also picked up on by another school friend, Gemma Williamson, who was in Mill Mead House, on the other side of the school grounds. 'Catherine arrived suddenly during the middle of the year,' she told the *Daily Mail* in an interview about their friendship. 'She had very little confidence.'

Initially, Kate was terribly homesick at Marlborough and did not spend time with the other girls after eating her supper at Norwood Hall, instead hiding away in her boarding house studying and doing her homework, all the while missing her family.

Many of Kate's fellow pupils were the offspring of earls, dukes and barons. One student, for example, was Sebastian Seymour, the son of the Duke and Duchess of Somerset, who went on to Cirencester Agricultural College, the traditional stamping-ground of upper-class farmers. The atmosphere of privilege must have been somewhat overwhelming, but the well-behaved schoolgirl gradually made friends – despite her unwillingness to rebel. Nicknamed 'Middlebum', a play on her name, she became known for her fun-loving behaviour, loyalty and reliability – although she rarely joined in the wilder antics. Jessica recalled that when her dorm mates held parties, getting drunk on bottles of wine and vodka that they'd sneaked in, Kate would watch from the sidelines. She did not drink or smoke but kept a clear head, maintaining a vigil for the house matron in case her friends were caught. Jessica told the *News of the World*: 'I never once saw her drunk. Even after our GCSEs finished, she only drank a couple of glugs of vodka.'

Kate's confidence would have been boosted in 1997 when her sister Pippa arrived at the school, but instead of rebelling and exploring ways to break the rules, she concentrated on studying for her 11 subjects. Kathryn Solari, who was in her biology set, remembers: 'Catherine was always really sweet and lovely. She treated everybody alike. She was a good girl and quite preppy – she always did the right thing – and she was very, very sporty. I wouldn't say she was the brightest button, but she was very hard-working. I don't think you would find anyone to say a bad word about her.'

Virginia Fowler, a former pupil who had a friend in Elmhurst, recalls her as always being kind to new arrivals. 'She was always quite welcoming. She didn't look down on the new girls like some of the other girls.'

The diligent teenager played hockey for the school, was in the

first pair at tennis, was a keen netball player and cross-country runner and used to beat the boys at high jump, as she had done before at primary school. She was apparently awarded so many honours at speech day that she barely had a chance to return to her seat between presentations.

Charlie Leslie, a keen sportsman a few years above Kate, has described her to reporters as 'an absolutely phenomenal girl'. She was 'really popular, talented, creative and sporty', he remembered. 'She was captain of the school hockey team and played in the first pair at tennis,' but despite her achievements, she was 'very level-headed and down-to-earth'.

After taking her GCSEs, which she passed with flying colours, Kate returned home to Bucklebury for the summer holidays. It was there that she underwent a miraculous transformation.

It was on the first day of the autumn term in 1998, when she returned to Marlborough as a sixth-former, wearing the long skirt that was the uniform of the upper school, that Kate finally showed the steely determination to improve herself that had become a family trait. Gone were the wan cheeks, lanky hair and nerdy image. She had blossomed into one of the most attractive girls in the school.

'It happened quite suddenly,' Gemma recounted to the *Daily Mail*. 'Catherine came back after the long summer break the following year an absolute beauty . . . She never wore particularly fashionable or revealing clothes – just jeans and jumpers – but she had an innate sense of style.'

It was that sense of style, as well as the transformation in her appearance, that would attract the boys in the school. But unlike her wilder classmates, she remained discreet and maintained her dignity, showing the good judgement and reserve that would

make her an ideal consort for a prince. 'It's fair to say that Catherine wasn't much of a party animal,' Gemma said, adding that she believed Kate's parents had ensured she had 'a strong moral compass'. She recalled: 'A group of us used to sneak off out to Reading to go out drinking but she would never join us. She used to giggle when we would tell her what we got up to, but it just wasn't her thing.'

By this time, Kate's friend Jessica was dating Nicholas Knatchbull, one of Prince Charles's godsons, who was Prince William's 'shepherd', or mentor, at Eton. She had met the heir to the Mountbatten fortune at the wedding of Tim Knatchbull, Nicholas's cousin, and Isabella Norman, a friend of Jessica's family. In another interview, with *The Mail on Sunday*, she delighted in talking about being introduced to the Queen and other members of the royal family, including Prince William, at her boyfriend's family seat Broadlands, a Palladian mansion in the Hampshire countryside.

Unlike her school friend, Kate had yet to meet Britain's most eligible schoolboy, but it seems she still dreamed of capturing the heart of her prince. Even in those days, Kate was nicknamed 'Princess in Waiting' – not then by an impatient press but by her giggly school friends as a joke. According to Jessica, she, Kate and another girl, Hannah Gillingham, who was in the same sports teams, used to hang out in the kitchen of the boarding house eating microwaved Marmite sandwiches, a favourite of Kate's, and joking about the possibility of her marrying the prince.

'We would sit around talking about all the boys at school we fancied,' revealed Jessica to *The Mail on Sunday*, 'but Catherine would always say, "I don't like any of them. They're all a bit of rough." Then she would joke, "There's no one quite like William." . . . She always used to say, "I bet he's really kind. You can just tell by looking at him."'

Jessica was not the only girl in Kate's year to mix in royal circles. Emilia d'Erlanger, niece of the 10th Viscount Exmouth, was one of Prince William's closest girlfriends. The youngest of five children of Robin d'Erlanger, a chartered accountant and commercial pilot like Kate's grandfather, and his wife Elizabeth, a regional director of Sotheby's in Devon, Emilia, who was in Kate's history of art class at Marlborough, was once touted as a possible bride for the prince. In the summer holidays after the lower sixth, she was invited by William on a ten-day cruise, hosted by Prince Charles and Camilla Parker Bowles, aboard a 400-ft luxury yacht, the *Alexander*, owned by the billionaire Greek shipping tycoon John Latsis.

While Emilia holidayed with the prince, Kate had to make do with the more prosaic company of her parents. She returned to school the following autumn and was made a prefect. 'Catherine was a very hard-working, responsible girl,' recalls former pupil William Garthwaite, who was in the same year. 'She arrived late [at the school] and became a prefect. That says a lot. She did very well.'

Like most teenagers, the girls at Marlborough would spend hours gossiping about the opposite sex. But while some of the other girls lost their virginity, Kate was apparently made of sterner stuff. 'She is very good-looking and a lot of the boys liked her,' Jessica remembered in *The Mail on Sunday*, 'but it just used to go over her head. She wasn't really interested and she had very high morals.'

'I got the distinct impression that Catherine wanted to save herself for someone special,' Gemma told the *Mail*. 'It was quite an old-fashioned approach . . . Not that anyone ever said anything to her, though . . . she was such a genuinely nice person that all the girls liked her as much as the boys.'

Although Kate stood out from the crowd as being a model

of propriety, she reportedly had several admirers at school, with whom she may or may not have been romantically involved. One of the names in the frame was Charlie Von Mol, whom former pupils describe as 'the school legend'. He was two years above Kate and shared her passion for sport – he was in the first rugby team. Jessica recalled an evening when Kate, after much deliberation, slipped off to the woods for a snog with Charles, but said that it seemed to her that 'she just did it because of peer pressure'.

Two other boys at Marlborough have been named as former boyfriends of Kate, but in fact they may well have been platonic friends. There has been speculation that Willem Marx, the son of a Dutch father and English mother, who was a mathematics genius, may have been her first love. The two have remained friends and Willem, an Oxford graduate who works as a journalist, has since squired Kate when Prince William is not around. She was photographed with him in May 2008 leaving the nightclub Boujis, where they had been drinking Crack Daddies – a champagne cocktail – and dancing until the early hours.

Another possible former boyfriend is rugby player Oliver Bowen, who was in the year above her, although Jessica, talking to the *News of the World*, remembered the pair as being close, she thought the relationship seemed more platonic than romantic.

All this might make Kate sound like an over-serious ice queen, but old school friends have described her as 'goofy', and she clearly enjoyed a joke and had the same anxieties and preoccupations as any teenage girl. One schoolmate wrote in the leavers' yearbook for 2000: 'Catherine's perfect looks are renowned but her obsessions with her tits are not. She is often found squinting down her top screaming: "They're growing."'

However, Kate's demure behaviour and hard work at

Marlborough certainly paid off, as she gained three A levels – A grades in mathematics and art and a B in English – meaning that she could go to the university of her choice. The question was which university to choose.

CHAPTER 14

A Florentine Interlude

Wandering along the cobbled streets of the medieval city of Florence, exploring its renowned art galleries, piazzas and churches, Kate Middleton marvelled at the beauty of the city that was the birthplace of the Italian Renaissance and inspired E.M. Forster to write his novel *A Room with a View*. Following in the footsteps of the book's beautiful young heroine Lucy Honeychurch and her chaperone Charlotte Bartlett, the 18-year-old, who was a keen photographer, captured on film some of the architectural jewels of the Renaissance era.

A promising artist as well as a talented photographer, Kate had left Marlborough College that summer with an A grade in art at A level under her belt and a thirst to learn more about her favourite subject. Now, two months later, the teenage ingénue was living in one of the most beautiful cities in the world, roaming the streets and studying the paintings and sculptures she loved.

———— ∞∞∞ ————

With its pink, green and white marble Duomo, or cathedral, dominating the Tuscan skyline, famous medieval bridge, the Ponte Vecchio, spanning the River Arno and wealth of treasures such as Michelangelo's *David* and Botticelli's *Birth of Venus*, Florence is a haven for art lovers and tourists. Known as 'the cradle of the Renaissance', it has become a traditional place of pilgrimage for public-school boys and girls hoping to study history of art at one of Britain's top universities. A trip to the city, once ruled by the Medici family and now home to some of the greatest treasures in the art world, has become a rite of passage for well-heeled teenagers in the same manner as the Grand Tour was a prerequisite for privileged aristocrats during the nineteenth century. Kate had applied to study art history at several universities and it was almost a given that she would spend a portion of her gap year in Italy before she knuckled down to the everyday rigours of student life.

Kate arrived in Florence at the beginning of September 2000 to do a 12-week course in Italian at the world-renowned British Institute. She was one of about a dozen girls in her class at the Institute, which had been founded at the turn of the century to foster cultural relations between Italy and the English-speaking world, and was based in the Palazzo Strozzino, in the heart of the city.

More than 5,500 miles away, on the other side of the world, Prince William was spending a month working on a scientific and ecological research programme, the Shoals of Capricorn Project, for the Royal Geographical Society on the tiny island of Rodrigues, 400 miles north-east of Mauritius in the Indian Ocean. Registering as Mr Brian Woods, he arrived on the island on 28 August and worked on the project for a month. Initially, he stayed in le Domaine de Décidé, a tin-roofed guesthouse with whitewashed walls and dark shutters, located down a track half an hour from the capital, Port Mathurin. Afterwards, he moved into a private house in Anse aux Anglais – English Bay – which was closer to civilisation.

Like Kate, he had received his A level results (an A in geography, a B in history of art and a C in biology) on 17 August, when Prince Charles had sent his first-ever email to pass them on to his son, who was on an army survival exercise deep in the Belize jungle. But unlike Kate, he had already chosen which university he was going to attend: St Andrews.

A fellow student at the British Institute remembers that when Kate arrived in Florence she had not decided where she would be studying. 'She hadn't confirmed where she was going,' she says. 'She certainly wasn't going to St Andrews at that point.'

It was a formative time for Kate, on the cusp of adulthood. Although she had already been away from home at boarding school, it was the first time she had lived independently from her parents. Having not yet developed the fashion sense that has more recently seen her compared to the late Princess Diana, she looked much like a typical Sloane Ranger, with her long curly hair, Ralph Lauren shirts and V-neck jumpers. Her only concession to student style was the ethnic jewellery she wore.

On arriving in the city, Kate began sharing a flat with a number of different girls, including the singer Chris Rea's niece Alice Whitaker. They lived above an Italian delicatessen on the top floor of a traditional stone building that had been converted into several flats, reached by a stone staircase. The flat was in a tiny street between Piazza degli Strozzi and Piazza della Repubblica, within walking distance of the Institute. Over the next three months, Kate would immerse herself in the life of a student in Italy, shopping for delicacies at the covered food market opposite the historic San Lorenzo church, which houses the Medici family vault, and meeting friends in quaint cafés and lively bars.

It was in one of these bars, the trendy Antico Caffè del Moro – known as the Art Bar or Café des Artistes – that rumours about the possibility of Prince William spending time in the Tuscan

capital after leaving Rodrigues first reached the British students in Italy. Prince Charles had lunched at Highgrove with the Mayor of Florence, inadvertently sparking rumours that his son would soon be joining seven other Old Etonians on the prestigious £5,000 John Hall Pre-University Course in Venice, Florence and Rome. It was only when William flew out to the remote Chilean mountains of Patagonia on 1 October – to embark on seven weeks' voluntary work with the charity Raleigh International – that the rumours were dispelled.

That night in the Café des Artistes, a tiny bohemian backstreet bar run by two brothers who had become renowned for their spectacular cocktails, Kate was sipping a glass of wine when the conversation turned to speculation that the prince would be joining them in the city. Despite the crush on the prince that Kate supposedly had at Marlborough, friends say that she seemed blasé about the news.

It transpires that she had set her sights on a more attainable target, an Old Marlburian called Harry, who was studying in Florence on the John Hall course. One student who met Kate during her gap year reported that by the time she arrived in Florence, Harry had surpassed William in her affections. 'The only time I ever remember her talking about William was when we found out that he was coming over to study in Florence,' the unnamed friend reported. 'We would speculate about hanging out with him, but to be honest Kate never really showed any interest in him, or talked about him that much. She certainly wasn't going to St Andrews with the intention to snare him or anything like that. In fact, she was more hung up on a guy called Harry . . . They had been seeing each other, but he messed her around quite a bit and strung her along.'

Although during her time in the city Kate attracted a great deal of attention from Italian men, notorious for chatting up

British girls, she steered clear of any romantic entanglements, maintaining the modesty for which she had become known at Marlborough. 'We were all pretty well-behaved girls,' a friend remembers. 'She was rather shy around boys. She never seemed really comfortable with the attention. She would get embarrassed if they approached.'

While some of the other students took advantage of their new-found freedom, dating boys, drinking heavily and experimenting with drugs, Kate gained a reputation amongst the other students as a demure English rose. 'Kate would like a glass of wine – and always had a few glasses with dinner – but she couldn't really handle her drink,' one fellow student recalled in an interview with *The Mail on Sunday*. 'She would get giggly and silly after a few glasses, so then she would stop. She was never interested in getting really drunk or letting herself lose control. While others were doing drugs around her, she wouldn't be judgemental – in fact she was quite interested in what they did to you. It was simply that she did not want to try them. I never saw her smoke either.'

When Kate was halfway through her course, her devoted parents, Michael and Carole, flew over to the city for a long weekend, staying in a nearby hotel. But while her father melted into the crowd – a trait his daughter appears to have inherited – Carole made much more of an impression. 'Kate was never someone who sought the limelight,' one fellow student recalled in *The Mail on Sunday*. 'She was sociable and fun but a bit of a wallflower.' She went on to say: 'Her mother was very different to Kate. I think Kate very much takes after her dad.'

Towards the end of the course, before she returned home for Christmas, Kate attended a fashion show held by the American Johns Hopkins University. While the other students revelled in the opportunity to drink themselves into oblivion, Kate nursed one glass of wine all night. 'It was held in a small club and everyone

sat on the floor on cushions,' her friend reported in *The Mail on Sunday*. 'It was quite a drunken affair with everyone downing shots, cocktails and all sorts of concoctions. This was a typical example of when Kate made a glass of wine last the whole evening. It was clearly most people's intention to get hammered, but not Kate's. She didn't like getting out of control, but this didn't mean she wasn't sociable. She would mingle and she loved to dance.'

Over the next eight months, Kate did some more travelling. Some reports indicate that she had been in Chile during her gap year, although when or what she was doing there is not known – and nor is whether this was definitely the case. She did go on a summer holiday with her family, to Barbados, staying at the exclusive Sandpiper Hotel in Holetown, halfway along the west coast of the island. The hotel, which has its own sandy beach, is surrounded by lush gardens brimming with tropical flowers, where Kate spent many hours sunbathing and reading.

'They went to Barbados on holiday pretty much every summer,' a friend reported, 'but interestingly they would go at the beginning of the season – the end of July or the beginning of August – which is when it is cheaper. The seriously wealthy do not go at that time of year – they tend to go around Christmas.'

It may have been to Barbados that Kate went on holiday with Ian Henry. That summer, Kate, who loved sailing, had crewed a yacht around the Solent. It was while she was in Southampton that she met fellow deckhand Ian, from Taunton in Somerset, with whom one tabloid claimed she had conducted a brief romance, going on a secret holiday to the Caribbean. 'We are very good friends,' he admitted to the *Daily Mirror* after news of her relationship with Prince William broke, 'but I have not spoken to her for a while. We met a couple of years ago through sailing. I was crewing on a boat at Southampton and Kate was on another. Occasionally, we would sail together. She is a fun girl. I would call her bubbly,

outgoing and down-to-earth. I did not know that she and William were an item. She is very reserved and does not like being in the spotlight.'

After their summer romance, the two were headed in different directions, Ian to Oxford and Kate to St Andrews. It was there that she would meet her prince.

CHAPTER 15

A Catwalk Queen

Wearing a sheer black lace dress over a black bandeau bra and black knickers, Kate Middleton sashayed down the catwalk in the university town of St Andrews in Fife, revealing her lissom figure.

Under the watchful gaze of Prince William, who paid £200 for a front-row VIP seat, the 20-year-old brunette, towards the end of her first year at university, was taking part in a charity fashion show sponsored by the designer Yves St Laurent. The annual Don't Walk show proved to be a turning point in the life of the English rose, who had arrived at Scotland's oldest seat of learning the previous autumn. Now, just seven months later, she found herself in the prince's inner circle and had attracted the attention of the most eligible bachelor in the Western world.

'I was over the moon when Kate first wore my dress on the catwalk because she has got a fabulous figure and she looked absolutely brilliant in it,' said designer Charlotte Todd, a fashion and textiles graduate. Speaking after it had been confirmed that

Kate and William were an item, she added: 'It is fantastic to think that one of my designs has been modelled by a woman who might one day become the Queen.'

Set in the tiny seaside town of St Andrews on the east coast of Scotland, once the ecclesiastical capital of Scotland and now renowned as the home of golf, the University of St Andrews is overlooked by the ruins of an eleventh-century cathedral tower and of St Andrews Castle. Founded in 1413, it is the oldest university in Scotland and one of the most prestigious in the British Isles, consistently achieving high rankings in the *Sunday Times* university guide. Boasting alumni such as King James II of Scotland, Nobel Prize winner Sir James Black, Edward Jenner, who discovered the smallpox vaccine, First Minister of Scotland Alex Salmond and novelist Fay Weldon, it is a university favoured by bright, affluent students.

The town is overrun by students, who make up a third of its population, wandering around the town on foot, cycling between lectures or frequenting its many pubs and bars, often wearing the distinctive red undergraduate gowns. Prominent in the town's newsagents is the student paper *The Saint*, one of only four in Britain to retain its independence from both the students' union and the university. *The Saint* had contributed to the university's growing reputation for a wild social life when it conducted a survey, picked up by the national press, revealing that students had very active sex lives and had been known to make love in the laundry rooms in their halls of residence and even in the ruined cathedral.

Kate almost certainly went up to St Andrews before the start of the Martinmas Semester on 24 September 2001 for freshers' week. She moved into St Salvator's Hall – deemed by most students to be the best hall of residence because it is set on the quadrangle in the

heart of the old university buildings – for which she paid £2,000 for a year's rent. Although her room was modest – it was furnished with a wooden bed and desk and had a tiny basin – the rest of the hall of residence was more impressive, boasting a wood-panelled dining room and a common room with a stone fireplace, parquet floor, red rugs and comfortable armchairs.

Outside the gates of St Salvator's College, also on the quadrangle, the initials PH are spelled out in cobblestones, marking the spot where Protestant martyr Patrick Hamilton was burned at the stake. Legend has it that a student who steps on those cobblestones will be cursed to fail their degree. Traditionally, the only way for a student who has stepped on the stones to lift the curse is to take a May Day dip in the North Sea.

It was at St Salvator's Hall, nicknamed Sally's, that Kate first encountered the prince, an inevitability considering he was studying for the same degree, history of art, and living in the same hall of residence.

William Wales, as the student prince styled himself, arrived at the university after freshers' week, claiming he did not want to disrupt the lives of ordinary students. Greeted by a battery of photographers and thousands of curious residents and students, he drove down from Balmoral, announcing that the Queen Mother had sent him off with the words: 'If there are any good parties, invite me down.' In an interview before the start of term, he quipped: 'I knew full well she would dance me under the table.'

The Queen Mother had links with the university herself. She had visited several times, receiving an honorary degree of Doctor of Laws in 1929, when she opened its Younger Hall, and having Queen's College named in her honour. On the surface, St Andrews was the perfect place for the prince to study, quieter than most university towns, near Balmoral and far from the London paparazzi. It was a choice that delighted the Queen, whose cousin James

Ogilvy had also studied art history at St Andrews, and she hoped
that the arrival of her grandson would give a boost to the image
of the monarchy in Scotland.

However, ever mindful of his role in life, the prudent prince
decided that the best way to avoid adverse publicity was to create
a barrier between himself and the other students, closeting himself
in his room or the university library, spurning invitations to join
clubs and societies, and avoiding student parties. It was a decision
that blighted his first term at St Andrews, as his self-imposed exile
made it impossible for him to integrate into normal student life. 'I
thought I would probably end up in a gutter completely wrecked,'
he admitted in a candid moment, when asked in interview why
he had not attended freshers' week, 'and the people I had met
that week wouldn't end up being my friends anyway.'

Nonetheless, the prince was able to make some new friends, as
well as catching up with a few fellow students whom he already
knew. Although William and Kate lived on different floors at
the hall of residence, as it was organised into single-sex storeys,
they gradually bonded over shared interests as they worked and
played together. Kate's lineage might not have been as blue-
blooded as the prince's, but they had an enormous amount in
common, both having been brought up in rural surroundings
– Kate in the village of Bucklebury and William on his father's
Highgrove estate in Gloucestershire – and sharing a love of the
countryside (a prerequisite for fitting into the royal family, where
hunting, shooting and fishing, watching polo and going to the
races are the norm). The two teenagers had both been to exclusive
public schools, in neighbouring counties, where pupils socialised
with one another both in and out of school and played against
each other in sports tournaments – another interest they had in
common. While Kate was good at hockey and netball, William
had an aptitude for rugby, soccer and polo, and they were both

keen skiers and tennis players. After school, they had spent their gap years broadening their horizons and travelling around the world. Some reports suggest they had both been to Chile.

Slowly, Kate became a member of the prince's St Andrews set, which included Bryony Daniels, the daughter of a wealthy landowner, Virginia Fraser, whose father is Lloyd's of London underwriter Lord Strathalmond, and army officer's daughter Olivia Bleasdale.

It is not known how Virginia and Olivia first met William, but Bryony, who was brought up in Paines Manor, a Jacobean farmhouse in Pentlow, Suffolk, by her parents David and Pauline, met the prince during her first week at St Andrews when they began studying geography together. Olivia, the daughter of Royal Artillery officer Lieutenant Colonel Jeremy Bleasdale, may have met the prince during her schooldays at the exclusive Westonbirt School, which is only a mile from Highgrove, and Ginny might have been introduced to him by Kate, who would have met her during her brief time at Downe House, former pupils of which include Prince Michael of Kent's daughter Lady Gabriella Windsor.

However, although Kate and the other girls were all spotted as potential girlfriends of the prince, at that stage there was no romance. Kate threw herself into university life while William kept a low profile for fear of tarnishing the royal name. That meant no drinking excessively, taking drugs or kissing in public.

Despite his determination to keep a low profile, within weeks William was dating Carly Massy-Birch, a pretty, fresh-faced brunette who has been working as an actress since graduating, appearing in a few stage and radio plays. She too had a lot in common with William, having been brought up in Axminster in the Devon countryside, where her parents, Mimi and Hugh, ran a farm. She, William and Kate were close friends, remaining so

even after the relationship between Carly and Will disintegrated and he began seeing Kate.

'She went out with William for six or seven weeks when they first arrived at St Andrews,' her mother later confirmed to newspapers. 'All three of them are best friends . . . She really wants Kate to marry Wills so that she can be sure of going to the wedding. If he falls for someone else, she's worried that she might miss out . . . Carly has always been very close to Kate and William, and that has never changed.'

Kate, too, met someone who would win her heart during her first year at university. Rupert Finch was a 22-year-old law student in his final year at St Andrews when he first met Kate. Unsurprisingly, he was a keen sportsman. A gifted cricket player, not only was he a member of the university team, but he also managed the squad during a summer trip to South Africa. Rupert was brought up by his parents, John and Prudence, in a large farmhouse in Fakenham, Norfolk, on land owned by Prince William's uncle Earl Spencer. While his father farmed the land, his mother ran horse-riding excursions. It is not known when Kate and Rupert's friendship turned to romance or whether it continued after he left university the following summer to join the law firm Mills & Reeve as a trainee. Showing great discretion, he has never spoken about their relationship and says that he intends never to do so.

William and Carly split up around the time of Raisin Weekend, an annual time of hedonism and celebration held on the last weekend of November. Freshers are entertained by their academic 'parents', or mentors, a tradition that supposedly dates back centuries. Typically, freshers attend a tea party thrown by their mothers, go on a pub crawl with their fathers and then put on fancy dress for the traditional foam fight. Although this event, the culmination of the weekend's revelries, takes place in St Salvator's

Quadrangle, outside Kate and William's hall of residence, there was no sign of William during the festivities, and if Kate was there, she stayed under the radar.

The break-up with Carly was perhaps the catalyst for some soul-searching on the prince's part. Although he had made some good friends by the time he returned to Highgrove on 15 December for the Christmas vacation, he was having second thoughts about his choice of university and was thinking of switching to a campus closer to home. Feeling lonely and, in the small, relatively remote town, isolated from his old friends nearer home, William was finding it difficult truly to settle in. He was also frustrated by the attention from American students, who gawped at him and followed him around like sheep. Prince Charles pointed out to his son how detrimental giving up on St Andrews would be for his public image but it is Kate who is generally credited with being the person who persuaded him to stay at St Andrews in the long term after his 'wobble', as it was dubbed by royal aides. Next term, she suggested that he might feel happier if he changed to a geography degree instead of continuing with history of art, and he did so at the end of his second year.

'Living in a hall of residence for the first year was a good move,' he later commented. 'That's where I met most of my friends. Immediately, you are all put together – a whole load of people in similar positions – and it was a lot of fun.'

Despite William's doubts about his choice, both he and Kate returned to university on 9 January – her 20th birthday – for the remainder of their freshers' year. By the time she sauntered down the catwalk that April, they had both found their feet and settled into the student lifestyle, albeit in slightly different ways.

While William's first public appearance since arriving at the university, having declined to attend high-profile events such as the freshers' ball, signalled his intention to become more involved in

student life, Kate's stroll down the catwalk revealed a more daring and adventurous side to the hitherto demure young lady.

Her increasing confidence was also revealed by her bullish approach to the controversial Kate Kennedy Club, an elite organisation for male students along the lines of Oxford's Bullingdon Club. The club has been criticised for being sexist and generally chauvinistic. William, ever cautious, initially turned down membership, but Kate co-founded a rival organisation, the Lumsden Club, for female students only. The club aimed to forge better 'town and gown' relations. Named after Louisa Lumsden – a prominent nineteenth-century figure in St Andrews, who was made a dame in recognition of her services to female education – the club aimed to promote the arts and raise money for women's charities by holding a series of fundraising social events, such as a Red-Hot Martini cocktail party and a Pimms party, throughout the year.

Gradually, William followed Kate's lead and began to immerse himself in student life. They were often to be spotted drinking and chatting at Ma Bells, the bar in the basement of the St Andrews Golf Hotel, which is close to the university and overlooks the seafront. Known as 'Yah Yah Bells' because of its reputation as a hangout for the university's Sloane Rangers, it was often heaving in the evenings with students dancing to the resident DJ. Other favourite haunts were The Gin House, a few streets away in South Street, and Broons, which was close to the halls of residence in North Street. Occasionally, he and his friends would head to the Byre Theatre in Abbey Street, on the other side of town, which was the perfect haven for an anonymous night out. 'Everybody thinks I drink beer, but I actually like cider,' Prince William commented in one of the official interviews he gave during his time as a student – part of a strategy to keep the press at bay.

William also took up sport again, joining the university's athletics club, playing rugby and Sunday league football, and becoming a

member of the St Andrews water polo team. A keen waterskier and surfer, he could often be spotted in the North Sea riding the waves, being towed on skis or, if the weather was rough, being dragged on a giant yellow inflatable tube shaped like a banana. He began going on early-morning runs along the sea wall in order to keep fit and work off the adverse effects of his student diet. Not only had he developed a fondness for takeaways and fast food, but he was regularly spotted buying treats from the Burns Sweet Shop in Market Street or pick 'n' mix in Woolworths.

By the end of their first year, Kate had become close enough friends with the next but one in line to the throne to be invited to share a flat the following year with him and two of their closest friends in the heart of town. It was a new, confident Kate who left St Andrews for the summer holidays.

But despite her elevation into royal circles, the 20-year-old undergraduate still had to pay off her student debt. She was hired by upmarket catering firm Snatch to serve drinks at one of the social events of the season, the Henley Regatta, and was paid £5.25 an hour. 'Kate's a superb barmaid,' owner Rory Laing told newspapers. 'We hired her at the Henley Regatta and hopefully she'll be coming down to Cowes to work at our Snatch bar here. As we only employ former public-school pupils, she fits our profile brilliantly. She's a pretty girl, so she takes home plenty in tips.'

That summer, Kate revealed a unique ability to balance two very different aspects of her life – those of royal playmate and hard-up student – showing the combination of sophistication and girl-next-door ordinariness that would be the making of her.

CHAPTER 16

A Royal Flatmate

Kate Middleton looked the belle of the ball in a stunning flapper-style dress as she stood in a marquee in the grounds of her parents' grand red-brick house at a party to celebrate her 21st birthday. Sipping champagne and greeting guests, she chatted to friends from Marlborough College and St Andrews University, all dressed, like her, in '20s costume, and kept an eye out for Prince William, who was guest of honour.

Although the couple had been sharing a flat in the university town during the previous academic year, William's appearance at Kate's party in June 2003 – five months after her actual birthday – underlined how close they had become. He arrived late and left soon after the sit-down dinner, before dancing got under way, returning home to Highgrove to prepare for his own coming-of-age party the following week.

Royal commentators have speculated that Kate's birthday party saw the beginning of a romance that has gripped the nation over the past few years. But only a handful of the couple's close friends really know when their friendship turned to love.

Rumours about the nature of William and Kate's relationship first began to emerge after the spring vacation in 2002, towards the end of their first year at St Andrews, when William announced that he was planning to move out of the hall of residence and into a flat with three friends, one of them Kate. At that stage, Kate and William laughed off suggestions that they were dating, insisting that they were 'just good friends', although William was young, free and single, and Kate on the verge of becoming so. Her relationship with Rupert Finch was on the wane – and her love affair with William was on the horizon.

William and Kate teamed up with Fergus Boyd, the son of a country solicitor from the village of Broughton Gifford in Wiltshire, and one other student, who has never been identified, and found a flat in one of the most sought-after streets in the town.

Fergus, who was William's closest friend at university, had bonded with the prince on the rugby pitches of Eton and was now studying the same geography module as him at St Andrews. He had modelled with Kate in the university's charity fashion show and been on a cricket tour that summer with her boyfriend Rupert in South Africa. Now a financial advisor at Smith & Williamson, he has always remained protective of the royal couple; he is one of the few people who know whether their friendship turned to romance during their second year at university. Certainly, when Kate and William moved in together there were persistent rumours that they were more than friends, prompting the palace to deny that they 'lived together', meaning they did not share a bedroom.

William's presence in St Andrews had a marked effect on the rental market as wealthy American students arrived in the seaside town, willing to pay over the odds to catch a glimpse of their hero. Prices began to rival those in London and students were known to camp on the pavement outside letting agents in their sleeping bags in order to be first in the queue for a flat.

With their connections, the well-heeled trio managed to secure a maisonette in a traditional Georgian terraced house. The friends moved into the apartment in the heart of St Andrews' old town before the start of the Martinmas term on 23 September 2002. It was the perfect venue for the four students to relax in after spending the day at lectures. The new flatmates took turns preparing supper, a task that William found difficult, despite having had cookery classes at Eton. 'I cook quite regularly for them and they cook for me,' he said, in an interview at the end of the academic year, 'although we haven't had a house supper for quite a while because everyone's been doing exams and working quite hard. I've got some very good cooks in my house, but I'm absolutely useless, as my paella experience, which was filmed at Eton a while ago, proved. We tend to have chicken, curries and pasta. But we go out to eat quite a lot – whatever we feel like at the time.'

On the whole, the four students kept a low profile, walking or cycling to lectures, shopping at Safeway and spending the evenings at home, listening to William's R&B music or Fergus's jazz thumping from their stereos. The prince rarely ventured out during the week – unless it was to attend lectures or visit the university library – apart from on Wednesday afternoons, when he played sport. Both William, who had been voted the university's water polo captain, and Fergus trained for two hours on Thursday nights in the pool of St Leonards School.

Speaking about living in a communal house, he said: 'I do a lot of shopping – I enjoy the shopping, actually. I get very carried away, you know, just food shopping. I buy lots of things and then go back to the house and see the fridge is full of all the stuff I've just bought . . .We all get on very well and started off having rotas, but, of course, it just broke down into complete chaos. Everyone helps out when they can. I try to help out when

I can and they do the same for me, but usually you just fend for yourself.'

The only signs of the town's most famous resident and his flatmates were the round-the-clock presence of a blacked-out people carrier outside the property, police patrols up and down the street and increased security cameras overlooking the flat, leading locals to describe it as the second most protected street after Downing Street. Security officers would follow William to university, waiting for him in the kebab shop down the road from the lecture hall.

Not long after Kate moved in with William, in late November 2002, her parents bought a flat in the heart of Chelsea. The timing may simply have been coincidental, but it meant that their daughter had a base in London for society parties.

Less than a week later, Kate was spending her first weekend at a shooting party, hosted by William at Wood Farm in Sandringham, Norfolk. She was one of six girls and ten boys, including the prince, who crammed into the six-bedroom cottage. What the sleeping arrangements were was unclear, leading to more speculation about William and Kate's friendship. That weekend, guests included Olivia Bleasdale and Virginia Fraser – who lived in the same street as Kate and William during term time – and Natalie Hicks-Lobbecke, called 'Nats' by her friends, an army officer's daughter who was studying at Bristol University. There had been speculation at various points linking each of the girls romantically to the prince.

A mile down the road, at Sandringham House, William's father was hosting an altogether more sedate event in the Queen's Edwardian mansion. Prince Charles's guests included the Queen of Denmark, who left early because she was suffering from back pain, the Queen's godson Sir Nicholas Bacon, a barrister who owns thousands of acres of land in Norfolk and shares with Charles an

interest in gardening, Conservative MP Nicholas Soames, Jolyon Connell, editor of news digest *The Week* and landowner Lord Cavendish.

There is no suggestion that Kate – or indeed any of William's guests that weekend – met Prince Charles, although he did arrange for the catering staff at Sandringham to organise a deluxe takeaway service for his son's guests. It would not be long, though, before she was introduced to her flatmate's father.

Five months later, on 3 May 2003, the relationship between William and Kate appeared to have stepped up a pace when they attended the annual May Ball organised by the notorious Kate Kennedy Club, of which William was now a member. Having splashed out on VIP tickets for the charity event, they spent the majority of the ball, held at Kinkell Farm in the Fife countryside, huddled in a corner with their closest friends, sparking rumours that they only had eyes for each other.

A few weeks later, Kate went to watch William playing in a rugby sevens tournament sponsored by The Gin House. Cheering on his team – rival pub the West Port Bar – from the sidelines, Kate seemed more like a girlfriend in waiting than a flatmate. During breaks in the game, when William was not playing, the couple lay side by side in the spring sunshine, deep in conversation, and appeared so comfortable in each other's company that they yet again created speculation that their relationship had moved on to a different level. Following the match, after which the runners-up – William and his team – took home a consolation prize of three crates of lager, they headed for the West Port Bar, where they downed shots and partied. Known for his generosity, William often bought a round for everyone.

Within a month, the Candlemas Semester was drawing to a close, ending Kate and William's second year at the prestigious university. Having finished their exams, the two moved out of their

flat, looking forward to the long summer ahead. But they would not be apart for long.

Although Kate had turned 21 at the beginning of the year, both she and William celebrated their birthdays during that idyllic summer in 2003. But while Kate's birthday party was a private affair, attended by the prince and her closest friends, William's celebration a few weeks later was, naturally, a grander and more public event, attended by most of the royal family as well as a smattering of celebrities. Organised by the Prince of Wales's valet Michael Fawcett, it was held on 21 June 2003 – William's actual birthday – at Windsor Castle. The oldest and largest occupied castle in the world was converted into an African jungle, with two giant model elephants towering over guests, their trunks intertwined to form an archway to the dance floor. Animal skins decorated the walls, a giant giraffe's head took pride of place over the long golden bar, which snaked the length of the room, and a tribal mask stood out from the opposite wall. Three hundred guests, all in fancy dress, danced to the sounds of the band Shakarimba, a six-piece group from Botswana, and William got into the vibe by jumping on stage and playing the drums. Guests included his uncles Earl Spencer and Prince Andrew, who were both dressed as big-game hunters in safari outfits, comedian Rowan Atkinson and polo player Luke Tomlinson. William's grandmother looked stunning as the Queen of Swaziland, in a white gown, tribal headdress and giant fur wrap, while his father wore a safari suit and hunting hat and his cousins Beatrice and Eugenie dressed in matching leopard-skin costumes.

The St Andrews set arrived in a battered white van decorated with balloons and tinsel. But Kate's appearance barely merited a mention in the media, being overshadowed by two events. The first was the arrest of intruder Aaron Barschak, a self-styled 'comedy terrorist', who managed, dressed as Osama bin Laden, to gatecrash the party and stumble onto the stage in the Great Hall, grabbing

the microphone from the prince, who was thanking the Queen and Prince Charles for his party. While William maintained his calm, Barschak was hauled out of the hall and arrested, although he was not prosecuted.

The second was the attendance of Jessica 'Jecca' Craig, the daughter of a wealthy conservationist, and generally believed at the time to have been William's first serious girlfriend. He had grown close to Jecca when he visited her family's 45,000-acre wildlife reserve in the foothills of Kenya during his gap year, two years earlier – there were even reports that they had had a 'pretend engagement' – but only they know whether they still had feelings for one another when she flew into Britain for his Out of Africa party.

Either way, the Prince seemed at pains to quash rumours about their involvement and prove he was single, releasing a public statement, approved by Prince Charles, denying any romance with Jecca – the first and only time that such a step has been taken. The statement was generally deemed to be a shot across the bows intended to stem the intense media speculation that surrounded their relationship, which intensified when her boyfriend, Henry Ropner, received only a last-minute invitation to the party.

But not only did William deny having a relationship with Jecca – he denied having a girlfriend at all. In an interview to mark his birthday, he said: 'There's been a lot of speculation about every single girl I'm with, and it actually does quite irritate me after a while, more so because it's a complete pain for the girls. These poor girls, whom I've either just met or are friends of mine, suddenly get thrown into the limelight and their parents get rung up and so on. I think it's a little unfair on them, really. I'm used to it, because it happens quite a lot now. But it's very difficult for them and I don't like that at all.

'If I fancy a girl and she fancies me back, which is rare, I ask

her out. But at the same time, I don't want to put them in an awkward situation, because a lot of people don't understand what comes with knowing me, for one – and secondly, if they were my girlfriend, the excitement it would probably cause.'

That summer, then, the prince was telling the world that he was single, but it would not be long before the glare of the media's attention shifted to Kate and it became clear that a new royal romance had begun in earnest.

CHAPTER 17

Cold Hands, Warm Hearts

W earing a red bodywarmer and black salopettes, Kate Middleton shared a T-bar lift with Prince William on the slopes in Klosters, the exclusive skiing resort in the Swiss Alps, which has become a favourite with the royal family, revealing that she had captured the heart of Britain's most eligible bachelor.

After months of speculation about their romance, the couple, both 21, were finally snapped by paparazzo photographer Jason Fraser, the man, ironically, who caught on film the famous kiss between Princess Diana and Dodi Fayed on a Mediterranean yacht. That tender moment between William and Kate on 31 March 2004 was photographed and the pictures published in *The Sun* newspaper, infuriating aides at Clarence House, the private office of the Prince of Wales, which had brokered a gentlemen's agreement with the media to allow the prince privacy while he was at university.

The pair, in their third year at St Andrews, had flown from Heathrow to Zurich four days earlier, at the beginning of the spring vacation, to spend a week on the slopes with their most trusted and intimate friends. Amongst their coterie were Harry Legge-Bourke, the elder brother of Tiggy, the former royal nanny, Guy Pelly, a former student at Cirencester Agricultural College, and friend of the royal family William van Cutsem and his girlfriend Katie James, all of whom could be trusted to keep a secret.

By day, the group took to the pistes; by night, they explored the après-ski options, spending one evening at a karaoke bar, where William took the microphone, and another dining at a mountain restaurant overlooking the village, with Prince Charles and his regular skiing companions Charlie and Patty Palmer-Tomkinson.

William and Kate's skiing holiday brought to a conclusion the increasing speculation about the intimacy of their friendship, conjecture that had begun eighteen months earlier when they moved into a flat with two other students at the start of their second year and had gathered pace ever since.

The beginning of the third year must have been a difficult time for Kate, who was grieving over the death of her maternal grandfather, Ronald Goldsmith, who had been in a wheelchair for some time, suffering a narrowed outlet valve to his heart. The first of her grandparents to die, his heart gave out on 10 September 2003, at the age of 72, at the cottage he shared with his wife Dorothy in Pangbourne, Berkshire.

That autumn, when they returned to Scotland, Kate, William and Fergus decided to move away from the centre of town and into a farmhouse on the outskirts of St Andrews, where William and Kate, who both loved the countryside, felt more comfortable. When Martinmas Semester began on 29 September 2003, the four

flatmates moved into Balgove House on the Strathtyrum estate. They would remain there until they left university.

In advance of the move, William said: 'Most people tend to move houses and that was always my intention. In my third year, I have fewer lectures and have to spend less time in the university and so I thought: how about moving somewhere different? I do think I am a country boy at heart. I love the buzz of towns and going out with friends and sitting with them drinking and whatever – it's fun. But, at the same time, I like space and freedom.'

The cottage, set in rolling grounds brimming with orchids and fuschia bushes, was an idyllic venue for the prince to woo his girl. Not only was the house discreet, but it was also totally secure. By the time the royal party moved in, a £1.5 million operation had swung into action in order to prevent another humiliating breach of security in the aftermath of the gatecrashing of William's 21st birthday. A neighbouring cottage was chosen as the centre of a security operation, and squads of officers were drafted in to keep 24-hour surveillance on the farmhouse. The cottage was also bombproofed and CCTV cameras and panic buttons installed, linked to both local police stations and Buckingham Palace in case of an emergency.

The increased privacy and freedom of their new, more rural home gave William and Kate the opportunity to begin their burgeoning relationship away from prying eyes, a rarity for members of the royal family, especially the young prince. When confirmation that they were a couple came, initial reports claimed that they had been going out since Christmas, although there have since been suggestions that they began dating the previous summer, around the time of their birthday celebrations.

Either way, the young couple behaved with the utmost care in their public dealings with one another in an elaborate effort to keep their romance secret. Apparently, they had a pact not to show any affection towards each other in public, leaving the house separately

in the mornings and never holding hands if they were out and about. They kept the nature of their relationship completely hidden from the outside world by having romantic evenings at home, trysts at Birkhall (a 14-bedroom mansion on the banks of the River Muick near Balmoral, inherited from the Queen Mother by Prince Charles) and weekends at Highgrove, where Kate met her boyfriend's father for the first time. The couple would drive down in his black VW Golf for weekends hunting and shooting.

The first hint that their relationship had changed pace came a few weeks before their skiing holiday, when they went riding with the Middleton Hunt in North Yorkshire, and William introduced Kate to his friends as his 'girlfriend'. Within weeks, it was common knowledge that they were together.

When William and Kate returned from Switzerland, it was business as usual, despite the fact that their relationship was now in the public eye. True to form, they remained holed up in their country farmhouse, rarely venturing out unless they could ensure their privacy.

Indeed, they were more cautious than ever. Whereas the previous year Kate had watched from the touchline as William played in the town's annual seven-a-side rugby tournament, in 2004 she kept a lower profile and did not turn out to watch him play for their old local, the West Port Bar, one of a dozen sides competing in the tournament. Hundreds of students and members of the public had come to see the matches, organised by St Andrews publicans, and no doubt more particularly to watch the prince, in his number 4 shirt, limber up and play alongside his housemate Fergus Boyd. Brought on as a substitute, he took a couple of hard tackles and dragged down one of his opponents in pursuit of the ball, but the team still lost two of their three matches. It was only during the evening, at the post-tournament party in the St Andrews Golf Hotel, that Kate turned up to commiserate with her boyfriend.

The couple kissed in public for the first time, but there wasn't a photographer in sight.

A few weeks later, William and Kate donned evening attire for the annual May Ball, held again at Kinkell Farm, which that year had a Saints and Sinners theme. As in the previous year, the royal couple had a VIP pass for the charity do so that they could avoid the riff-raff. 'William was given an access-all-areas pass for security reasons,' the Kate Kennedy Club president, Alex Walsh, admitted.

The couple's discretion was quite extraordinary. Society photographer Zygmunt Sikorski-Mazur, a former solicitor, shot William's inner circle for society magazines such as *Tatler* and *Harpers & Queen*. He snapped their flatmate Fergus Boyd and close friends Olivia Bleasdale and Bryony Daniels but never managed to photograph the couple. 'They were an engaging bunch,' reveals Zygmunt, 60. 'They were always very friendly and helpful to me in my photographic work. As with any young people in the same situation, there were plenty of high jinks, but they always seemed to know when there was a line which should not be crossed. They were almost without exception very well-brought-up children from some of the most well-to-do families in the country.

'It's amazing when I think back that I was never able to photograph Kate, let alone William. It wasn't that they were deliberately obstructive. I just think they had a very good intelligence network and wanted to keep their lives at the university behind a veil of discretion for the most part.

'To get permission to shoot some of the events, like the big balls, would take weeks of negotiating and it was obviously no secret that the press would be at these events. That meant William and Kate would give them a wide berth. But I often heard that they would appear at events that I didn't go to or they'd turn up quite late, after I had left the scene.

'I did see the pair of them once, together with Fergus, enjoying a drink in one of the town-centre pubs, ironically where I had arranged to meet a reporter before the pair of us went on to the autumn ball in 2004. The three of them looked just like any other students, as they sat quietly sipping away, deeply engrossed in a discussion, no doubt about their coursework. Not surprisingly they didn't show at the evening event.'

Jules Knight, who studied history and moral philosophy with William and lived next door to Kate and William in the second year, was a member of that inner circle. 'Will and I weren't known for being studious,' he said later in an interview with the *Daily Mail*. 'We were the only ones on the moral philosophy course and would play noughts and crosses during lectures and take the mickey out of each other.

'I remember he threw a party at his house and the fire alarm went off. Will had to switch off the power to stop it and in doing so he switched off the secret cameras. Suddenly, we were surrounded by security guards.'

Jules, who is now a member of the classical-music group Blake, helped organise that year's May Ball, and was also a friend of Kate's. 'Kate's a sweet, unassuming kind of girl,' he added. 'I don't think any of us knew she would become one of the most photographed women in the world . . . Kate never claimed to be royalty – she was just a normal girl.' He also pointed out: 'We were all in a safe bubble at St Andrews. There was no intrusion. Kate and Will could go for a drink and hold hands and no one batted an eyelid.'

The May Ball was the final hurrah before the students had to knuckle down to their exams, which began on 17 May 2004. Within weeks, it was the summer holidays, which were kicked off when the love-struck couple dressed up as Rhett Butler and Scarlett O'Hara, the star-crossed lovers in *Gone with the Wind*, for a fancy-dress party thrown by a fellow student.

Hardly had William and Kate's relationship begun to flourish, before speculation began to mount that it was on the rocks, sparked by rumours in royal circles that the prince was planning to spend the summer in Africa visiting his teenage sweetheart Jecca Craig rather than going on a romantic break with his girlfriend. In the end, Kate apparently won what the tabloids christened 'the Battle of the Babes' when William decided not to visit Lewa Downs, the Craigs' game reserve in the foothills of northern Kenya, for the first time in three years. Whether he had ever been seriously planning to take the trip we cannot know. Certainly, William, like his father, usually does what he wants and would be unlikely to change his mind due to pressure from either the media or his girlfriend.

Towards the end of July, William and Kate flew out in a party of eight friends to the sun-kissed island of Rodrigues. Known as the Cinderella of the Mascarene Islands, the tiny, peaceful volcanic island is surrounded by beautiful coral reefs and charming lagoons. Only 11 miles by 5 miles across, it has many deserted beaches and forests that are home to the rare golden bat. The prince had first visited it during his gap year. Now, four years later, he returned with the girl who had captured his heart. The couple stayed in a £25-a-night guesthouse, where they retired early and got up early. While Kate lapped up the sunshine, William donned a wetsuit to go scuba diving in the sea and snorkelling in the clear blue waters and rode a hired motorbike along the coastline.

It was the first time that William and Kate had spent a summer holiday together, a rite of passage in any new relationship. The fact that they chose to go away in a group, rather than as a twosome, led to suggestions that William was not as keen on Kate as she was on him. However, it is not uncommon for students – especially those who can afford more than one holiday – to go away in groups.

Within days of arriving back home, the two were separated

Kate

when William flew out to Nashville to stay with American heiress Anna Sloan, who is supposedly the only girl ever to have turned down a date with the second in line to the throne. Whether he went with Kate's blessing can only be guessed at, but certainly she put a brave face on increasing speculation that their relationship was in trouble.

Anna, who was studying at Edinburgh University, is the daughter of the late lawyer and businessman George Sloan. A champion amateur jockey who competed in the Grand National in 1969, he died in 2001 at the age of 62 after shooting himself in a tragic accident on the family's 360-acre estate. A keen horsewoman herself, Anna is believed to have bonded with the prince over their shared experience of losing a parent. She had invited him to visit the sprawling family home, complete with swimming pool, set in the rolling hills of Tennessee. William was amongst 15 companions who spent a week in the village of Leipers Fork, but Kate is not believed to have been invited.

During the holiday, William became something of a tourist attraction, despite the region being known as the Hollywood of the South and William's zeal for guarding his privacy. Locals spotted him everywhere he went: shopping in the trendy store Abercrombie & Fitch, having pancakes, bacon and eggs for breakfast at the Country Boy diner and buying beer from Puckett's Grocery Store. 'He had a couple of friends with him and just looked like an ordinary fellow,' owner Billy Raynor told reporters. 'I said to him, "Are you sure you're going to drink all that?" They just laughed and said they'd be all right. There was a young kid working here who was wearing the same shirt as him and William commented on that. He paid his bill in cash and then they just drove off.'

The group of friends also dined at Sperry's, a restaurant in Nashville decorated with prints of English fox hunts and coats

of arms, where they got through more than 12 bottles of house wine, splitting the £330 bill at the end of the meal. The prince caused quite a stir and diners gawped as he munched his way through a filet mignon wrapped in bacon and stuffed with blue cheese, accompanied by creamed spinach. 'There was a constant stream of people going to the bathroom so they could walk by him,' recalled barmaid LuAnn Reid. 'Patrons were phoning their daughters and granddaughters so they could come in and see him. So many girls started coming in that Sperry's turned into a teen scene for a bit.'

While her boyfriend was enjoying himself in America, Kate kept her head down and ignored the gossip about his flirtations with other women. She didn't have much choice if she wanted to date the globetrotting prince.

When William returned from the States, he is reported to have whisked his long-suffering girlfriend off on a romantic break to the Birkhall estate. They had spent many weekends there before, but this is believed to have been the first time that Prince Charles and Camilla Parker Bowles were also in residence.

The Highland break was deemed to be Kate's compensation for yet another enforced separation before the couple returned to St Andrews. She was reported to have been unhappy when her boyfriend jetted off again with six of his male friends for a break in the Mediterranean, staying on a luxury yacht owned by the Latsis family. It was William's fourth summer holiday in as many months, but, needless to say, Kate had little choice in the matter. She was not invited on the five-day boys-only cruise around the Ionian islands, for which William reputedly hired an all-female crew, a move that could be seen as calculated to put Kate's nose out of joint. However, the prince may simply have been creating a smokescreen, being careful to keep his relationship with Kate out of the public eye.

Chapter 18

Graduates at Last

Sitting casually on Prince William's knee during lunch on holiday in Klosters, Kate Middleton could not have found a more effective way of dispelling rumours that their romance was foundering. Engaging in friendly, relaxed conversation with Prince Charles – and laughing and joking with Prince Harry – she effectively showed the world that her relationship with his elder son had his family's all-important approval.

It was 30 March 2005, almost a year since Kate and William had inadvertently allowed themselves to be photographed together on a ski lift in the Swiss resort, exposing their love affair to public scrutiny for the first time. Now, after a mountain of speculation about their future had accumulated, the publicity-shy couple were being openly affectionate, proving at a stroke that their relationship was still on course.

Kate's presence on the family holiday seemed to be a sign that their relationship was becoming more serious and the strongest indication yet that they were not planning to go their separate ways after university.

The pretty Swiss village of Klosters, five miles from Davos and an hour-and-a-half's drive from Zurich airport, is the ski resort of choice for the royal family. Its main cable car, which runs to the top of Gotschnagrat, has been christened 'the Prince of Wales'. Charles has been skiing at the resort since his marriage to Princess Diana in 1981. The resort holds sad memories for the royal family. It was there that the Queen's equerry Major Hugh Lindsay lost his life in March 1988, after being buried by an avalanche. On that holiday, Prince Charles was also accompanied by Charles Palmer-Tomkinson, a former Olympic skier who had coached him in his younger days, and his wife Patty, who was airlifted to hospital in Davos with Major Lindsay after sustaining leg injuries.

On this trip, though, Charles was surely looking to the future rather than the past as he spent his final week as a bachelor skiing with his two sons, having chosen to visit the resort before his marriage to Camilla Parker Bowles. The future Duchess of Cornwall, who is scared of heights and has never learned to ski, remained in England, putting the final touches to their wedding plans.

While Kate was in the royal party, Harry's girlfriend Chelsy Davy had turned down the chance to join them, preferring to stay in South Africa. In her place, Harry invited close friend Guy Pelly, who had been unfairly pilloried in the past for supposedly leading the young royal astray. On the first day of the trip, Kate, then 23, proved just how comfortable she was with the royal family, sitting next to Prince Charles at lunch, chatting happily with him throughout the day and sharing a cable-car carriage with him. It was the first time the history of art student had been photographed with the heir to the throne, but she seemed to take it all in her stride, showing a maturity beyond her years.

Despite their obvious ease in each other's company, Kate and William, who had made great efforts to hide their romance during

their third year at university, tried to keep their distance in public. At one point, William was seen walking some distance ahead of his girlfriend, who followed behind with other members of their party, the couple perhaps deliberately avoiding spending every minute together in front of the press and paparazzi.

That night, the group spent the evening at the Casa Antica, Princess Diana's favourite nightclub. It was there that the Princess of Wales had earned the nickname 'the Disco Queen of Klosters'. While William and Harry drank bottles of beer and danced, their exhibitionist friend Guy stripped down to his silk boxer shorts and ran around the room. The atmosphere was so relaxed that William gave an impromptu interview to the royal correspondent of *The Sun*, uttering words that have haunted him ever since. When asked about marriage to his long-term girlfriend, the blushing prince retorted: 'Look, I'm only 22, for God's sake. I'm too young to marry at my age. I don't want to get married until I'm at least 28 or maybe 30.'

However, both William's and Guy's actions were overshadowed the following day by a photocall on the slopes during which Prince Charles showed that he could be every bit as gaffe-prone as his father. Without realising that he could be heard through the microphones at their feet in the snow, he moaned to his sons: 'I hate doing this,' before insulting the BBC's royal correspondent Nicholas Witchell, saying: 'I can't bear that man. I mean, he's so awful, he really is.'

His comments proved a PR nightmare for the prince's aides. The forthcoming wedding had already been dogged by a series of criticisms and controversies over the choice of venue, the legality of the civil ceremony, the decision by the Queen not to attend and the role of Camilla when Charles succeeded as King. They had called a press conference in order to redress the balance of adverse publicity, and Witchell had asked an innocuous question about how

the princes felt about the marriage. Unfortunately, William's reply – 'Very happy, very pleased. It will be a good day.' – was followed by his father's comments about the BBC reporter. The journalists who witnessed the heir to the throne's outburst attributed it to his irritation with the press in general over paparazzi photographs of Kate and William taken the day before, which he saw as a breach of their agreement to give the prince privacy during his university years. Charles is also believed to have a dislike of Witchell stemming from a broadcast in which he compared the Prince of Wales's extravagant holidays to those of his great-uncle Edward, Duke of Windsor, an obituary of Princess Margaret written by him and a report on Prince Harry taking drugs.

By the time Kate and William went on their skiing trip to Klosters – six weeks before their final exams – the two St Andrews undergraduates had endured endless speculation, both in the newspapers and on the Internet, about their romance. But, ironically, whilst before their first trip to Klosters everybody had wanted to know whether they were a couple, after it there was constant conjecture about whether they were breaking up.

The rumours began when William went on two holidays without his girlfriend during their three-month summer vacation and reached fever pitch on 25 September 2004, two days before they were due to return to St Andrews for their final year, when Kate failed to appear at the wedding of former debutante Davina Duckworth-Chad, 25, and baronet's son and Old Etonian Tom Barber, 31.

Davina, a distant cousin of the princes, who once posed for *Country Life* magazine's website in a revealing rubber dress, earning herself the nickname 'the Deb on the Web', is the daughter of landowner Anthony Duckworth-Chad, former High Sheriff of

Norfolk, and his wife Elizabeth. She was brought up with her two older brothers, James, later a Coldstream Guards officer and equerry to the Queen, and William, at their country seat Pynkney Hall in Norfolk. Her name was romantically linked to William's when she was invited on a ten-day Mediterranean cruise with the royals during the summer of 1999, alongside Kate's former Marlborough colleague Emilia d'Erlanger. Davina, a history of art graduate, kept in touch with the princes after she left Bristol University and went to work at the West End art gallery owned by Lady Helen Taylor's husband Tim. Now she had invited William and Harry to her wedding, at St Mary's Church in West Raynham, Norfolk. The two princes arrived in a minibus and were joined by their uncle Earl Spencer, a cousin of Davina's mother Elizabeth, who had chosen the boys' mother Princess Diana to be her own bridesmaid 35 years earlier.

Five weeks later, on 6 November, there was yet more conjecture over the state of Kate and William's relationship when Kate failed to arrive on the prince's arm at the society wedding of the year – between Prince Charles's godson Edward van Cutsem, 31, and the Duke of Westminster's daughter Lady Tamara Grosvenor, 23. Unfortunately for Kate and William, the prince's old flame Jecca Craig, by then a student at London's University College, was spotted slipping into Chester Cathedral in a striking brown suede coat scattered with turquoise ribbons, which she teamed with an Australian-style bush hat. Kate, meanwhile, was nowhere to be seen. Although Jecca was an old friend of the groom, having once dated his younger brother Nicholas, and kept a low profile at the wedding – keeping her distance as the royal guests left with the bridal party for the reception, held at Eaton Hall, the Duke of Westminster's grand country house – her presence reignited conjecture that William was still enamoured with her.

What onlookers failed to realise, however, was that protocol would in any case have prevented Kate from arriving with her

royal beau and the numbers might have prohibited inviting her. The etiquette of the seating plan for the society wedding, attended by the Queen and Prince Philip, had already proved a headache for Natalia, Duchess of Westminster, who compared it to 'wading through treacle'. While William and Harry, who are close friends of the four van Cutsem brothers – Edward, Hugh, 30, Nicholas, 27, and William, 25 – had agreed to be ushers, wearing tails and pink rosebuds in their buttonholes, Prince Charles, who met the boys' father at Cambridge, was officially reported to be absent because he was visiting the families of soldiers serving with the Black Watch in Iraq. Many newspapers rumoured, however, that he boycotted the event after it emerged that his consort, Camilla Parker Bowles, was not to be included in the royal party. Instead, she was to have been seated several rows behind Charles, and unlike the other VIPs, who would walk to the cathedral through the grand West Gate, she was expected to enter the cathedral through a side entrance like the rest of the guests. Charles was reported to have deemed it an unacceptable slight.

His son, however, was happy to party, with or without his girlfriend, chatting to other guests, watching the stunning fireworks display and dining on scallops and prawns, fillet of beef and petits fours, before leaving the reception – alone – at 5.30 a.m., the same time as the bride and groom.

As a result of Kate's absence from the two weddings – the most important in the social calendar – the gossips had a field day, speculating that William was feeling claustrophobic, that there were cracks in their relationship and that the couple were talking of a trial separation. But things in the world of this complex young man, who believes that his private life is not for public consumption, can never be taken at face value, and some royal commentators speculated that Kate might have stayed away from the high-profile weddings in order to throw people off the scent.

Certainly, three days earlier the couple had been together at a private dinner party in Scotland, where friends noticed nothing amiss, and two weeks later, on 14 November, after William had for the first time joined the Queen at the Cenotaph for the Remembrance Day service, the couple spent the evening at Highgrove, celebrating Prince Charles's 56th birthday – hardly a sign of a relationship on the rocks.

Indeed, the new year saw the beginning of a period of togetherness that would send out signals to the world that their romance was firmly back on track. On 22 January 2005, they headed for a weekend in the privacy of Birkhall, and towards the end of February the couple spent another long weekend together, in the Swiss mountain resort of Verbier, once the preferred resort of Prince Andrew, the Duchess of York and their friend the playboy and motor-racing millionaire Paddy McNally. They rented a chalet with six friends, skiing during the daytime, dining out in the evenings and watching the Carling Cup final in the local pub. On the Saturday night, they paid a visit to the renowned Farm nightclub, where during its flashy heyday the bar was lined with expensive bottles of vodka, each marked with the name of a regular. Although they largely avoided overt displays of affection in public, the two students barely left each other's side, skiing together and stealing the odd kiss when they thought nobody was looking. Kate's gallant boyfriend even carried her skis over his shoulders for her.

The royal couple showed the same modesty a month later – the night before they flew to Klosters – when they joined Prince Harry and some other friends at the Sugar Hut nightclub in Fulham, south-west London, billed as a 'romantic hotspot for lovers' and located in a dimly lit converted church in the North End Road. In those days, the club, with its award-winning Thai restaurant and bar, where guests lounged on lavish beds and sipped cocktails, was a favourite haunt of celebrities and the royals, although it no

longer has the same cachet. The paparazzi would gather outside to photograph the stars, and William and Kate went to great lengths to avoid being snapped together. First, William was driven away with Prince Harry. Then Kate emerged ten minutes later, arm in arm with a friend, and climbed into another car. It was an extraordinary display of caution, bearing in mind that 24 hours later the couple would openly show their affection for each other in front of Prince Charles at Klosters.

Although Kate joined the royals on their skiing holiday, commonly described as Prince Charles's stag week, she was not invited to the royal wedding on 9 April 2005, because of protocol. Instead, she revised for her finals, which began five weeks later. It would be a testing time for the 23-year-old student, who had been living with the prince for nearly three years. Within a couple of months, they would be graduating and their lives would never be the same again.

Kate and William finished their exams on 25 May and, with their flatmate Fergus, walked down to the beach at Castle Sands to reminisce about their experiences at university. It was the first night of a month of celebrations that would culminate with their long-awaited graduation ball on 24 June, three days after Prince William's 23rd birthday. But before then, Kate and William had a very important date in their diaries.

The wedding of Hugh van Cutsem, 30, to landowner's daughter Rose Astor, 25, on 4 June, was the first society event that Kate and William would attend together, showing how far their relationship had blossomed since the groom's elder brother Edward's marriage seven months earlier. The wedding was held in the idyllic setting of the Church of St John the Baptist in the Cotswold village of Burford – described by Simon Jenkins in his *England's Thousand Best Churches* as 'the Queen of Oxfordshire'.

Kate, who wore a cream jacket, black skirt and black hat, was

confident enough to stroll into the church alone, while her royal boyfriend, who was an usher, showed guests, including Jecca Craig, in a poncho and cowboy hat, into the pews. There was some speculation about the two love rivals coming face to face, but in fact it was not the first time they had been in the same room, as they had both been guests at William's 21st and had met before.

Afterwards, when the newly-weds retired to their 12-ft teepee in the grounds of the Astor estate at nearby Bruern, William and Kate joined friends at the King's Head Inn, four miles away in the village of Bledington, for a post-reception drink. They stayed the night at the sixteenth-century inn, where, according to local legend, William was following in the footsteps of Prince Rupert of the Rhine, who is said to have stayed there in 1646 before fighting in the Battle of Stow. After an English breakfast, the couple, both casually dressed in jeans, left by a side door and drove off in William's black VW Golf, trailed by two protection officers.

The next social event in the diary, on 18 June, was the Argentine Cup, one of the highlights of the polo season, at which Kate showed a rare moment of public affection towards her boyfriend, holding his hand and stroking his leg. It was five days before their graduation ceremony, when the eyes of the world would be upon them.

Kate and William graduated from St Andrews University on 23 June 2005, in the most high-profile ceremony the institution had ever witnessed, having spent four years studying alongside each other and three years living together. At the ceremony, witnessed by the Queen and Prince Philip – who had never before attended a family graduation ceremony – as well as Kate's parents and William's father and stepmother, they were the centre of attention as they both received their 2:1 degrees.

Wearing black gowns, believed to have been hired for £29.50 each, they entered the Younger Hall together, looking every inch the regal couple, but sat five rows apart. Kate, who was wearing a

short black skirt and high heels under her gown, graduated first, 80 students ahead of William. Then it was the prince's turn.

Too nervous to walk through the auditorium, William walked onto the stage through a side door, his head bowed, and approached the pulpit, where he was capped by chancellor Sir Kenneth Dover, who tapped his head with a seventeenth-century scarlet cloth cap bearing a fragment from the trousers of the religious reformer John Knox. The university's bedellus, or beadle, James Douglas, then lifted the hood of his gown over his head.

Afterwards, William kissed his grandmother, who was dressed in primrose yellow, and was congratulated by his father before he went off to find his girlfriend. She was amongst a select few who were invited to mingle with the royal family on the university lawns after the ceremony, but she did not talk to the royals in public, discreetly keeping her distance from them on the edge of St Salvator's Quadrangle with Carole and Michael.

In a speech to the graduates of 2005, Dr Brian Lang, the university's vice chancellor, said: 'You will have made lifelong friends. I say this every year to all new graduates: "You may have met your husband or wife." Our title as the top matchmaking university in Britain signifies so much that is good about St Andrews, so we rely on you to go forth and multiply – but in the positive sense that I earlier urged you to adopt.'

It was a sentiment that echoed the thoughts of the nation as they willed William and Kate towards giving Britain a royal wedding.

CHAPTER 19

The Real World

Sitting on the veranda of a remote African hideaway, 15 miles north of the equator on land owned by the Masai warrior tribe in the foothills of snow-capped Mount Kenya, Prince William and his girlfriend Kate Middleton sipped their cocktails and took in the magnificent view.

Together for the first time since leaving university, the couple shared a romantic moment watching the sunset in the exclusive Il Ngwesi, an award-winning eco-lodge. That night, 17 July 2005 – three weeks after William had flown out for his first solo overseas tour, a brief trip to New Zealand – ended speculation that the couple would drift apart when they had left St Andrews and were living in the 'real world', as William had referred to life after university.

Kate was in a party of William's closest friends, including Old Etonian Thomas van Straubenzee, the nephew of Princess Diana's childhood friend Willie, who had known the prince since their days at Ludgrove, the exclusive prep school in Berkshire. The group

joined William towards the start of his time at the Lewa Wildlife Conservancy, run by Jecca Craig's parents, where he was spending a month helping out.

That morning, while William had been working on the estate, his friends had trekked for hours, exploring the bush as they made their way to the lodge, perched 5,600 ft up the Mukogodo Hills, on the edge of the Ngare Ndare River, looking down over northern Kenya. William and Jecca joined the group before nightfall for cocktails and a barbecue.

It was the third time that William had been to stay on the estate, but it was the first time he had taken Kate to visit the country he had fallen in love with during his gap year in 2001. The fact that he had invited his girlfriend to stay at Lewa Downs finally put an end to conjecture about his feelings for his childhood sweetheart. Both he and Kate were now friends with Jecca and her new boyfriend, financier Hugh Crossley, the son of a Norfolk landowner whom she had been dating since he had recuperated at her family's ranch following a climbing accident on Mount Kenya.

Jecca is descended from a wealthy British family who emigrated to Kenya after the First World War, settling on a cattle ranch in Lewa Downs in 1922, where eventually they began offering tourists luxury safari holidays. Keen conservationists, the Craig family set up the Ngare Sergoi rhino sanctuary in 1983 to protect the black rhino from poachers. This would evolve into the Lewa Wildlife Conservancy, a not-for-profit wildlife sanctuary. Housed inside a 70-mile solar-powered electric fence, it is patrolled by armed rangers and teems with rare species, including the highly endangered Grevy's zebra.

Jecca's parents, Ian and Jane, who played host to the prince during his gap year and whom he regards as a 'second family', and her uncle William and aunt Emma live in the grounds of the ranch, enjoying a colonial lifestyle fit for a prince. Under the name Lewa

Wilderness Trails, they rent out eight luxury cottages, complete with fireplaces and verandas, in the gardens of their home. Guests can use a saltwater swimming pool, a clay tennis court and riding stables; they can choose to go on drives around the estate, bush walks with a professional tracker, jogs with a Masai warrior, or horse or camel rides.

William, however, was not there just for a holiday but to learn about conservation from Jecca's family. The prince spent the majority of his African trip working on the ranch, but also took the opportunity for a long-awaited post-graduation holiday with his friends. He spent around £2,000 to hire the lodge for his friends to stay in, complete with a glorious swimming pool that looks as if it is overflowing into the wilderness below. Kate and William's cottage had its own balcony and a double bed on castors, meaning that the royal lovebirds could sleep outside, protected by a mosquito net, under the stars. It would have been a wonderful experience for the group, who were spoiled for choice of what to do. They could have followed the river with local guides, toured the estate in a 4x4 looking for game, visited the baboon troop and the black rhinos, or simply relaxed at the lodge.

For Kate and William, the African break was the first chance they had had to spend time together since leaving St Andrews, and they must have wanted to enjoy every minute, away from the stresses and strains of their lives in Britain and the storm of speculation over their future.

Kate and William had left the sanctuary of the small university town on Friday, 25 June 2005, after their graduation ball, knowing that their lives would never be the same again. Neither would they have the freedom they had enjoyed over the previous three years nor would they be able to live together as a couple again unless they

became man and wife. It was a pivotal time for the young prince and his girlfriend, who both had to think hard about what they intended to do now that they had completed their degrees.

But before they addressed themselves to that task, there was one more night of carefree, student-style partying to enjoy, at the upper-crust private members' club Boujis, a favourite haunt of the young royals, socialites and aristocrats, as well as the odd sports personality, Eurotrash banker and Hollywood star. It is there that *Starsky & Hutch* stars Ben Stiller and Owen Wilson were smuggled out of a fire exit to avoid the paparazzi only to be spotted when their driver was nowhere to be found, and there too that England cricketers including Freddie Flintoff and Kevin Pietersen ended their 32-hour drinking marathon after the Ashes win in 2005. But its most famous clientele are William and Harry, who are drawn in by its exclusivity and discretion. It is located in Thurloe Street, South Kensington, just a few doors from the flat where Princess Diana lived before her marriage. One doesn't get behind the Boujis rope unless one has serious connections, which gives it the advantage of being a WAG- and soap star-free zone. The doormen never tip off the paparazzi – they have to cruise around until they spot the royal protection officers – and the princes can retreat to the exclusive Brown Room for their own private party. At the club, the motto is 'Rules Are Broken' and the signature drink is the Crack Baby, a cocktail of vodka, passion-fruit juice, Chambord and champagne that arrives in a test tube. Kate has gained a reputation at the club for her demure behaviour. She drinks modestly and always touches up her make-up in the lavatories before leaving the venue and facing the waiting paparazzi.

Jake Parkinson-Smith, the grandson of the flamboyant fashion photographer Norman Parkinson, ran the club in 2005. (He has since been sacked after accepting a caution for possessing cocaine.) 'The princes are very ordinary, nice guys,' he said once in a rare

moment of indiscretion. 'They remind me a lot of my friends. They feel very safe because their pals come – Guy Pelly, Freddie Windsor. It's the English aristo set. They all know each other, they all went to Eton together and all play polo together, so it's all very comfortable and happy.'

William and Kate, with Guy Pelly, turned up at the club in the early hours of Monday, 28 June, two days after leaving their graduation ball, and headed straight onto the tiny dance floor beside the neon-orange bar. With typical discretion, they left separately a couple of hours later, Kate disappearing first in a waiting BMW before William and Guy emerged.

Within hours, Kate was back at home while the prince was heading to New Zealand with his recently appointed private secretary, Jamie Lowther-Pinkerton, a former SAS officer, and Thomas van Straubenzee. The trio arrived at Wellington Airport on a scheduled flight and were greeted by New Zealand Prime Minister Helen Clark.

William had first been to the South Pacific country with his parents when he was just nine months old and he was now there 22 years later on an official visit to commemorate the 60th anniversary of the end of the Second World War. Representing the Queen, he met war veterans and laid two wreaths: at the National War Memorial in Wellington on 3 July and at the Cenotaph in Auckland a week later. He also spent time with the British Lions, who were on tour in the country, watching them lose to the All Blacks before flying out to Africa for his reunion with Kate.

Kate Middleton returned from Africa facing one of the hardest challenges of her life: how to adjust to life outside the confines of university and create a role for herself while dating the heir to the throne. Whereas William had his life mapped out – although he

did not like to admit it – Kate had nothing in her diary bar a few social engagements. Not only did she face the logistical nightmare of trying to find a suitable job for a princess in waiting, but she had to conduct herself with decorum outside the protection of 'The Firm'.

It was an extraordinarily difficult path for the 23 year old to negotiate, one that her fellow graduates would never have to experience, but which she managed with typical aplomb. In keeping with her reputation for decorum, she spent most of her time sheltered in the bosom of her family, to whom she is very close. Her sister Pippa, who had just turned 21, was midway through her English degree at Edinburgh, and her brother James, 18, had just left Marlborough. She kept her head down, smiled for photographers and ignored the tittle-tattle implying that her relationship with the prince would never last the course.

Such was Kate's discretion while William was on the other side of the globe that she was rarely seen out and about, unless it was for everyday activities such as shopping in her local Waitrose or browsing with her mother in Peter Jones, the department store that has become a haven for Sloane Rangers and the Chelsea set. Her one trip out, to the Festival of British Eventing, sparked yet more speculation, this time about an imminent engagement, because the horse trials were held on Princess Anne's country estate, Gatcombe Park. However, Kate's appearance, in the Stetson she had worn on safari in Africa, could hardly be deemed especially significant, as the event was open to the public and was a favourite with her country set.

Within a few weeks, she was reunited with William when he flew back from Kenya to take the gruelling selection test for the Royal Military Academy Sandhurst, held at Westbury Barracks in Wiltshire. The 23-year-old prince passed both the physical and technical tests with flying colours.

Then it was back to the social whirl. On 24 August 2005, the couple spent the evening at Purple, a cavernous nightclub with a sunken dance floor and two raised bars at either end, throbbing with house music. Although the club, which has since closed, did not have the exclusivity of Boujis, it had the distinct advantage for the royals of being hidden away in private grounds at Chelsea Football Club, a stumbling block for the paparazzi. William and Harry had first discovered the club in September 2003, when they went there for the birthday party of TV presenter Natalie Pinkham, the daughter of a millionaire Northamptonshire property developer. Photographs taken that evening would later cause a storm of criticism when, three years after the event, a national newspaper published one of Harry kissing Natalie, mistakenly suggesting that he had cheated on Chelsy Davy.

In 2005, it was Kate and William who attracted some attention, although not quite the same level of controversy. They began their evening with friends at The Collection, a striking bar and restaurant housed in an old warehouse in Chelsea's fashionable Brompton Triangle. The building had previously been home to a Porsche garage, a Conran furniture shop and a Katharine Hamnett boutique, and the restaurant was renowned for its entrance – an 80-ft catwalk, designed by the architect Sir Norman Foster – and its long bar. As well as hosting parties for the British Fashion Awards, the exclusive jeweller Cartier and the singers Beyoncé and Prince, it had become a favourite haunt for celebrities and royals.

After having a few drinks – William stuck to red wine while Kate sipped margaritas – it was on to Purple, where the couple, for once, let their hair down. After spending some time in the VIP room, they took to the dance floor, where William drank sambuca, chatted with the DJ and requested a few tracks for his girlfriend, including 'Shakedown' by rapper DMX, dance hit 'I Like the Way You Move' by BodyRockers and Starsailor's 'Fall to

the Floor'. The couple finally emerged at 1.30 a.m. looking slightly the worse for wear. But their carefree student behaviour could not last much longer.

Over the next month, Kate put on a brave face as her boyfriend flitted all over the country, preparing for life as a working royal. His next public engagement, on 3 September, was with the Queen and Prince Philip at the Highland Games in Braemar, a quaint village in Aberdeenshire. William sat in the royal box, chatting with his grandparents as they watched a tug-of-war competition, Highland dancing and a veterans' parade and listened to the pipes and drums of the 1st Battalion The Highlanders and the Gordon Highlanders Regimental Association. Meanwhile, in contrast, his girlfriend busied herself by going shopping on Kensington High Street, where she was spotted popping into Topshop and Miss Sixty.

Four weeks later, on 30 September, William left Kate alone again to celebrate his friend Oliver Hicks' record-breaking solo voyage across the Atlantic at the Chain Locker pub in Falmouth. The Old Harrovian, 23, had spent the previous 124 days out at sea in a 23-ft boat, travelling 4,040 miles from North America to the Isles of Scilly and becoming the first person to row solo eastwards across the Atlantic as well as the youngest person to complete a solo row across an ocean. 'There was masses of scrummage on the pontoon when I rowed in,' said Oliver. 'Richard Branson – one of my sponsors – shook my hand and sprayed me with champagne. Willy came along and pulled my hat down over my eyes and then they carried me off to the pub.'

But, according to Oliver, the only reason that Kate did not turn up with her prince was because William wanted to protect her from the scrum. 'They are together,' he told the press. 'I spent the weekend with them. The reason they never confirm their relationship is because they don't want to make it open season for people to ask questions.'

Indeed, the following night Kate was at William's side for a black-tie charity ball organised by the Institute of Cancer Research for 400 socialites at the Banqueting House in Whitehall. But yet again the couple faced a barrage of speculation, this time because they sat at separate tables for the £80-a-head event, despite the fact that at such a function this would be considered normal etiquette, not a sign of a disintegrating relationship. The prince was also criticised for ignoring Kate – only dancing with her once – and flirting with other girls, but in society circles it is deemed polite to work the room, albeit perhaps in a more thoughtful manner.

In any case, their time together was short-lived. Three days later, William would start the first of three work-experience placements chosen to prepare him for his duties, and Kate would discover just how challenging and contradictory her own role as the girlfriend of a future king could be.

William's first job as a working royal began on 4 October 2005, when he arrived at Chatsworth, seat of the Duke and Duchess of Devonshire and one of Britain's grandest stately homes. He spent the next two weeks in the Peak District learning how to run the 35,000-acre estate, even working behind the scenes in its award-winning butcher's shop. Wearing a traditional apron and straw boater, he joined the other backroom workers weighing the heavy cuts of meat. But he and his two police detectives lived in more luxurious surroundings than his fellow workers, staying in a sixteenth-century hunting tower overlooking Capability Brown's stunning park. Originally built as a summer banqueting house from which ladies could watch their gentlemen hunting, the 400-ft turret with its narrow spiral staircase had been restored earlier that year to accommodate paying guests, although William was let off the £900-a-week rent. It was a plum first job for the prince, who has inherited his father's love of the environment and has always harboured a desire to be a gentleman farmer. In the visitors' book,

which he signed 'Will, Gloucestershire', he wrote: 'A wonderful place to stay but don't try to tackle the stairs once you have a drink!'

After discarding his green wellies, William donned a pinstriped suit for the next stage in his work experience, shadowing bankers at HSBC. He spent a week working with the bank's Charities Investment Services team in St James's Street, just around the corner from Clarence House, before commuting to its investment arm in Canary Wharf. He also spent some time at the Bank of England, learning how it sets interest rates, and visited the London Stock Exchange, Lloyd's of London, the Financial Services Authority and the Queen's lawyers, Farrer & Co.

His final stint before Christmas was with the Royal Air Force Valley Mountain Rescue Team in Anglesey, North Wales, where he spent two weeks learning emergency lifesaving skills. He then took part in a mock rescue, abseiling down a 200-ft cliff while holding one end of a stretcher that had been filled with ballast to simulate an injured climber. But his trip was thrown into controversy, after he was flown from Anglesey to RAF Lyneham, in Wiltshire, on a 622mph Hawk jet to collect the army boots he wanted to break in for Sandhurst.

Meanwhile Kate was struggling rather more to find her niche after university. Reports that she lived with Prince William, had dined with the Queen and was being groomed for life in the family were far wide of the mark. Although palace aides gave her some unofficial advice about dealing with the media, she was still afforded royal protection and VIP treatment only when she was on William's arm. The rest of the time, she had to fend for herself, walking a precarious line between life as a royal and life on the outside.

While William was away, Kate flitted between her parents' wisteria-clad home in Berkshire and their flat in Chelsea, south-west London, showing little sign of getting a full-time job. In

fact, she was working behind the scenes trying to set up her own Internet company designing and selling children's clothes, an idea eventually rejected as she found it too hard to get the business off the ground. However, that work left her plenty of spare time to go to the gym and go shopping, gradually earning her a reputation for being nothing but a princess in waiting.

It was during one of those shopping trips, with her mother Carole, that Kate first encountered a designer who would help bring her out of her shell. Until then, like most well-brought-up Home Counties girls, Kate favoured the wardrobe of the modern Sloane, wearing boot-cut jeans, cowboy boots, country tweeds, floral skirts and dresses, and kitten heels. But after she met Katherine Hooker, a former film-set designer whose clients include models Jerry Hall and her daughter Lizzie Jagger, at the Spirit of Christmas Fair in Olympia, she underwent a subtle transformation. Although she did not become a fashion icon overnight, she began to look slightly more polished. 'Kate saw my stand . . . and approached me,' Katherine said later. 'She has been in and out of the shop since then, sometimes with her mother and sometimes just on her own. She is very self-assured, very down-to-earth and normal.'

However, while Kate was in some ways growing more confident, she still had a long way to go. When she was photographed on a number 19 bus, 'Waity Katy', as she had been dubbed by the tabloid press, was immediately compared to a young Princess Diana going about her life in the capital before she married the Prince of Wales. But there were two significant differences: Diana worked as a kindergarten teacher before she was engaged, and she had a ring on her finger when she emerged into the public eye.

CHAPTER 20

A Look of Love

Wrapped up against the winter wind in a scarlet coat, Kate Middleton made her first official public appearance, attending Prince William's passing-out parade at the Royal Military Academy Sandhurst. Wearing a broad-brimmed black hat and matching boots, the 24-year-old smiled broadly as Second Lieutenant Wales paraded past her and received his commission as an officer, having completed his 44-week course.

Kate's presence at the ceremony on 15 December 2006 marked a significant shift in the couple's relationship since they had left university 18 months earlier. Although she was not sitting in the royal stand with William's father, grandmother and other members of the family, her attendance at such an important event was deemed significant and fuelled speculation that an engagement was imminent. Indeed, the interest in Kate's appearance at the parade was so feverish that ITN went so far as to hire a lip-reader, who reported that the prince's girlfriend had commented afterwards, 'I love the uniform. It's so sexy.'

Kate, with her parents Michael and Carole, and the prince's private secretary Jamie Lowther-Pinkerton, was one of the last to take a seat in the public stands. The quartet sat in the front row, next to Thomas van Straubenzee and two of the prince's godfathers, the exiled King Constantine of Greece and Norton Knatchbull, Baron Bradbourne. Clasping her hands in front of her, Kate then stood for the national anthem as the Queen and the Duke of Edinburgh, the Prince of Wales and the Duchess of Cornwall took their places on the dais.

William's platoon had achieved the coveted honour of being named Sovereign's Platoon, entitling them to carry the Queen's banner during the ceremony. They had come out on top after weeks of intense competition between the nine platoons in the intake, competing over the weeks in a range of activities including shooting to drill and a timed log race. The prince, who was escorting the Queen's banner, and therefore carrying a rifle as opposed to a sword and wearing a red sash over his uniform, stood out from the sea of soldiers. Kate watched as the Queen and the academy's commandant, Major General Peter Pearson, inspected the 233 cadets. Elizabeth stopped for a moment to greet her grandson, who was standing at the end of his platoon.

Afterwards the Queen told William and his fellow cadets: 'I am speaking to every individual one of you when I say you are very special people. A great deal will be expected of you. You must be courageous yet selfless, leaders yet carers, confident yet considerate, and you must be all these things in some of the most challenging environments around the world so that men and women will willingly follow your lead into every possible situation with absolute trust in your judgement. These are very special attributes, but those whom you will command, and your country too, will expect nothing less.'

That night, at the stroke of midnight, as fireworks lit the sky and champagne corks popped, William took part in one final Sandhurst

ritual, ripping off the tape covering the pips on his uniform. It was just days before Christmas and Second Lieutenant Wales had a bright future in front of him. Now the world wanted to know whether that future would include Kate.

The future commander-in-chief of the British Armed Forces arrived at the Royal Military Academy Sandhurst to begin his training on 8 January 2006, the day before Kate's 24th birthday, having bid his girlfriend a fond farewell the previous evening.

It was four days after the lovebirds had thrown their legendary caution to the wind and kissed in public for the first time, revealing how close they had become. That kiss proved to be a turning point in the public perception of the relationship. Before then, they were dogged by rumours that it was on the rocks, but afterwards speculation centred on when they would get married.

The two graduates saw in the New Year in a cottage on the Sandringham estate before flying out the following day to Klosters. Conscious that they would soon be separated for the longest period since they had begun dating, they avoided the resort's hotels, bars and restaurants, staying discreetly in a friend's chalet and spending their time alone together. The public display of affection came during an off-guard moment on their third day, after they had spent the morning tackling the black runs. As they made their way off-piste down Casanna Alp, they stopped momentarily for a touching embrace.

The following day they flew home for William to prepare for his military cadetship. But Kate had a surprise in store for him: a farewell party. She had invited 40 of his closest friends to send the prince off in style, sipping champagne at the prince's London apartment at Clarence House before going on to the Kilo Kitchen & Bar, a French bistro in Mayfair. There were only three days

to go until William went to Sandhurst and the couple would be separated for five weeks.

Officer Cadet Wales was following in the royal family's military tradition: in recent years, Prince Charles had been in the RAF and the Navy, while Prince Andrew saw active service as a helicopter pilot in the Falklands. William arrived at the academy with his father in the pouring rain and was greeted by Major General Andrew Ritchie, then commandant of Sandhurst. After enrolling, he emerged from the Old College building wearing a red badge with his surname on it and waved goodbye to Prince Charles. The new cadet then joined his colleagues in his dormitory, unpacking his kit, which included a blue drill uniform, olive barrack uniform and physical training kit.

Founded in the wake of the Second World War, the elite military academy was set up to train regular army officers, replacing two outmoded establishments, the Royal Military College in Sandhurst and the Royal Military Academy in Woolwich, both of which had trained gentlemen cadets. William joined a long list of illustrious recruits to the academy, including the late King Hussein of Jordan, the sultans of Brunei and Oman, Prince Michael of Kent and Sir Winston Churchill, as well as his younger brother Harry, who was about to enter his third term at Sandhurst.

One of 270 cadets, including Alexander Perkins, great-grandson of Sir Winston Churchill, William spent the next five weeks sleeping in a small dormitory, sharing communal washing facilities and surviving what new recruits describe as 'hell on earth'. Thirty-seven dropped out in the first year. Banned from leaving the base and allowed only limited use of the telephone, the cadets, who were expected to do their own laundry, iron their shirts and polish their black military boots, rose each day at dawn for a series of intensive drills and endless inspections. They were trained in handling weapons, initially SA80 5.56-mm rifles,

later 51-mm light mortars, light support weapons and Browning 9-mm pistols.

Insisting that the second in line to the throne would not be granted any special privileges, Major General Ritchie said: 'I can assure you that he will be treated the same as every other cadet. Everyone is judged on merit. There are no exceptions made. He will be up early tomorrow morning and will then get stuck into military training. The fitness regime and tactics will begin in earnest. They need to know what it's like to be tired and to be hungry, to lead their soldiers in demanding situations around the world.'

Kate and William were reunited the weekend before Valentine's Day, when they met up at Prince Charles's Highgrove estate, but unfortunately their romantic getaway was spoiled by a drugs scandal at one of their regular haunts.

The young couple were drinking with William's cousins Zara and Peter Phillips and the prince's close friend Guy Pelly in the Tunnel House Inn, a rural pub nestled in the Cotswold village of Coates, when Pelly, a former student at Cirencester Agricultural College, was secretly filmed smoking cannabis. Pelly, who had previously been falsely accused of introducing Prince Harry to the drug, claimed he had been deliberately set up, having been passed what he thought was a cigarette by a pretty girl. There was no suggestion that either Kate or William had taken drugs, but questions were raised over the company they kept. They left Gloucestershire on Sunday evening, William returning to Sandhurst for kit inspection the following day, and Kate going back to the sanctuary of her parents' home.

A month later, on 17 March, Kate showed just how serious their relationship had grown when she turned up at the Cheltenham Gold Cup for one of the highlights of the racing calendar without Prince William, who was confined to barracks at Sandhurst. Wearing a Katherine Hooker coat, controversially accessorised

with a mink hat, she was slowly beginning to look like a royal princess. After spending the morning wandering around the paddock looking at the form of the racehorses, she joined Prince Charles and the Duchess of Cornwall for a family lunch in the royal box.

It was the first time Kate had appeared in public with the couple who are widely expected to become her in-laws without the comforting presence of her soldier boyfriend, yet she looked totally at ease in their company. After lunch, she joined Camilla's children, Tom, with his wife Sara, and Laura, with her fiancé Harry Lopes, as they watched the afternoon's racing and saw their mother presenting the Gold Cup for the first time to the winner, War of Attrition, ridden by Conor O'Dwyer.

The outing was a spectacular PR coup for Kate, who hadn't been invited to the races by the royal family but had turned up independently. After being hounded by photographers, however, she was invited into the royal box.

The following day, Kate caught up with William at Eton College after he took a weekend's leave to play in an old boys' Eton Field Game match (the sport is a cross between rugby and football) at his former school. She and a friend turned up at the ground to watch the match, and the prince's girlfriend casually strolled up to embrace him, in full view of all the spectators. After giving him a kiss, Kate playfully ruffled his thinning hair, a sore point with the prince, who had managed to hide his bald patch under a long, floppy style until he had been forced to crop it at Sandhurst. William did not seem to have any objection to his girlfriend showing affection towards him in public, and within a month the couple would be on holiday together on the Caribbean island of Mustique, sparking speculation that they would soon get engaged.

After three months' training, Prince William began his Easter holidays on 12 April, the day his younger brother Harry passed out from Sandhurst as a fully fledged officer, meaning that the future king would have to salute his younger brother in public for the next eight months, until he himself graduated.

That night, the brothers enjoyed a double celebration, but it was William who was reportedly the party animal, not his younger brother. While Harry spent the evening with Chelsy, who had flown over from South Africa for her first royal engagement, William was unable to invite Kate to the party, as he himself was a guest, not the host.

Instead he was reported to have got 'merry' at the bar, swearing and being rowdy, before retiring early to his barracks, where he spent the remainder of the evening drinking. The following night, he was reunited with his girlfriend at Boujis, where the royal party ran up an estimated £2,500 bill, raising concerns about what some saw as their excessive partying.

However, two weeks later, William was on his best behaviour, flying out to Mustique to join his girlfriend for a week's holiday, sparking the inevitable rumours that he was on the verge of popping the question. The tiny 1,400-acre island on the northern tip of the Grenadines, 18 miles south of St Vincent, has been a favourite royal hideaway since Princess Margaret first travelled to the island during the '60s. Colin Tennant, now Lord Glenconner, had given her a plot of land on her marriage to Lord Snowdon. Margaret commissioned the legendary theatrical designer Oliver Messel to create a lavish villa, Les Jolies Eaux. It was there that the princess had a notorious affair with garden designer Roddy Llewellyn, who was 17 years younger than her, and it is there that her son Viscount Linley proposed to Serena Stanhope. Since the '60s, the island has become a playground for the seriously rich and famous; rock legends Mick Jagger and David Bowie both have homes there,

and Noel Gallagher and Kate Moss are regulars at its legendary nightspot Basil's Bar.

Prince William and his girlfriend stayed in a villa belonging to the multimillionaire owners of the Jigsaw and Kew fashion chains, Belle and John Robinson, who live with their five children in a former hunting lodge, once owned by Sir Walter Raleigh, in the Wiltshire countryside. They count actors Natasha McElhone and Richard E. Grant as personal friends. The Robinsons did not know the young lovebirds but lent their £8,000-a-week luxury mansion to them in return for a donation to the hospital on St Vincent.

The stone-built clifftop villa, high above Macaroni Beach, had everything the couple could desire, with five bedrooms, a swimming pool, a maid, gardener and cook, not to mention spectacular views over the island's picture-perfect Caribbean beaches, azure sea and volcanic peaks. Kate arrived at the house on 26 April, flying from Heathrow (where she was given VIP treatment) to Barbados before taking a private jet to the island. William, who was on a sailing course at Sandhurst, flew out two days later.

The couple spent the week playing volleyball with friends and challenging locals to a Frisbee match, drinking pina coladas and vodka and cranberry juice at Basil's Bar and Firefly, cruising on a luxury catamaran and playing tennis with its owner, multimillionaire Sir Richard Branson (his daughter Holly is a friend of William). They returned home on 6 May for the wedding of William's stepsister Laura Parker Bowles the following day.

Although the couple had attended a society wedding together, Laura's wedding to Harry Lopes, an Old Etonian and former Calvin Klein model who is the grandson of the late Lord Astor of Hever, was the first time that Kate had been invited to a family wedding, showing the extent to which she had been assimilated into the royal family. She had turned down an invitation the previous year to attend the wedding of Laura's brother Tom to *Harpers & Queen*

fashion journalist Sara Buys for fear that the media interest in her would disrupt the couple's big day.

Now, as Kate and William arrived by coach for the wedding at St Cyriac's Church in Lacock, Wiltshire, and went on to the reception afterwards at Camilla's former home Ray Mill House, the talk was that they had taken another step towards a royal engagement.

While William returned to Sandhurst after the wedding for his second term at the academy, Kate remained a fixture on the social scene, showing little inclination to get a job. One of her first engagements, the week after the wedding, was the launch of The Shop at Bluebird, a boutique below Terence Conran's exclusive eaterie, in the former garage that once housed Donald Campbell's land speed record-breaking Bluebird car. Kate attended the event with her younger sister Pippa, chatting to the fashion crowd and supporting the shop's owners, the couple who had lent her and William their villa, Belle and John Robinson. The fashion crowd who attended the party would soon be taking notice of a young pretender.

It was at the Boodles Boxing Ball, held at the Royal Lancaster Hotel on 3 June and organised by Charlie Gilkes, an Edinburgh University student and friend of Kate and William, in aid of the paediatric medical research charity Sparks, that Kate first unveiled her true potential as a designer clothes-horse. Wearing a stunning turquoise gown by American designer BCBG Max Azria, which she bought from Harvey Nichols for £354, she really sparked the interest of the fashion press for the first time. Kate attended the £100-a-night champagne reception, dinner and amateur boxing event with William to support their friend Hugh 'Hunter' van Cutsem, who was fighting a chartered surveyor and Cambridge boxing blue, Huw 'The Welsh Whirlwind' Williams.

After that glamorous evening, William returned to Sandhurst and she was back to the social whirl alone. On 23 June, when he

was on a military training exercise in Wales, she attended a party at The Roof Gardens in Kensington hosted by Sir Richard Branson to celebrate the start of Wimbledon. Arriving in a group that included Sir Richard's daughter Holly, she spent the night dancing with Guy Pelly and chatting to tennis player Maria Sharapova. It was around this time that Kate first caught the eye of the American celebrity magazine *People*, which compared her wardrobe in favourable terms with Princess Diana's under the subheading 'Kate steps up her style to royal heights'. In fashion terms, she had arrived.

Sadly, however, during the same period both Kate's grandmothers were suffering from cancer and did not have long to live. Carole's widowed mother Dorothy was the first to die, on 21 July, three years after her beloved husband. Carole was at her 71-year-old mother's bedside in the Royal Marsden Hospital in Reading when she lost her four-month battle against lung cancer.

To try to cheer his girlfriend up, William whisked her away at the beginning of September to the holiday island of Ibiza. They chartered a yacht with friends on the Balearic island and spent a week partying in the sunshine.

After their seven-day break, the couple enjoyed one final night on the tiles before William returned to Sandhurst for his third and final term. But that night, Friday, 8 September 2006, would send the media into a frenzy of speculation about a royal wedding. The evening began normally enough when William and Kate arrived at their favourite club, Boujis, walking through the doorway separately in order not to be photographed together by the waiting press. But, at 3.30 a.m., when the couple left the club, they abandoned their normal cat-and-mouse behaviour. Instead, William ushered his girlfriend through a crowd of paparazzi before they collapsed giggling into the back of their chauffeured Range Rover. The resulting photograph of the couple smiling at each other is perhaps the most candid ever taken of them. Their tender gaze at

one another was described as 'the look of love', and their obvious affection noted with some relief by commentators who pointed out that here was a real love match. William's evident happiness and natural air were contrasted with his father's response when asked on his engagement to Diana whether he was in love, to which he replied that he was, 'whatever love means'.

But another cloud was looming on the horizon. Just two days after William had returned to Sandhurst, Kate's paternal grandmother, Valerie Middleton, succumbed to lymphoma at the age of 82 at the Countess of Brecknock House Memorial Hospital in Andover, Hampshire. The date was 13 September 2006. Kate had now lost three of her grandparents.

By now, Kate's brother James had followed Pippa up to Edinburgh University. Kate, meanwhile, had still not found work. In a last-ditch attempt to find a job that suited her circumstances, she contacted Belle Robinson. Recognising Kate's potential, she jumped at the chance to offer her a job as an accessories buyer at Jigsaw, working four days a week to enable her to juggle her commitments to William.

'As a thank you to us,' Belle said in a recent interview with the *Evening Standard*, 'Kate supported a couple of Jigsaw events we did. Then she rang me up one day and said, "Could I come and talk to you about work?" She genuinely wanted a job but she needed an element of flexibility to continue the relationship with a very high-profile man and a life that she can't dictate.' In another interview, with *The Times*, she said: 'People assumed it was a mercy act on our part, but Kate's a bright girl. She set up the website for her parents' business so we thought those skills would be useful.'

Kate apparently fitted in well at the company and became a popular member of the team. Talking to the *Standard*, Belle gave an insight into how Kate's position as girlfriend to the prince affected her day-to-day life: 'There were days when there were TV

crews at the end of the drive. We'd say, "Listen, do you want to go out the back way?" And she'd say, "To be honest, they're going to hound us until they've got the picture. So why don't I just go, get the picture done, and then they'll leave us alone." I thought she was very mature for a 26-year-old, and I think she's been quite good at neither courting the press nor sticking two fingers in the air at them.'

A couple of weeks after arriving at Jigsaw, Kate must have realised just how fortunate it was that she was working a four-day week when William requested her presence at a shooting party in Sandringham on the first weekend in December. That Sunday – two weeks before William's passing out – Kate threw caution to the wind and allowed herself to be photographed for the first time on the Queen's 20,000-acre Norfolk estate, watching William shooting pheasants and bagging dead birds. The pictures might have angered animal-rights protestors, but they also showed just how naturally Kate fitted into the royal family's world.

By the end of a year that the couple had begun with a kiss on the ski slopes of Klosters and ended with a dance at the Sandhurst Ball, bookies William Hill had slashed the odds on a possible royal engagement from 5–1 to 2–1. For the first time since they had left university amidst a storm of speculation over their future, they both had jobs – William as an officer in the Household Cavalry and Kate in the fashion world. Yet dark clouds were looming on the horizon and the next year would be crunch time for Kate and William.

CHAPTER 21

The Break-Up

Hidden away behind the red-brick walls of her parents' substantial house in the Home Counties village of Chapel Row in Berkshire, Kate Middleton spent the evening of Friday, 13 April 2007 mourning the end of her love affair with Prince William.

While her former boyfriend drowned his sorrows in the nightclub Mahiki, Mayfair's latest celebrity haunt, quaffing champagne and drinking its legendary Treasure Chest cocktails, Kate, then 25 years old, spent a quieter and more subdued evening with her family.

It was barely a week since Britain's most famous romance had drawn to a close – and hours before their separation hit the news-stands – yet the couple's behaviour could not have been more different, underlining just how far apart they had grown since leaving university. Whereas Kate was looking for more commitment from William, the 24-year-old army officer, who had just left Sandhurst, was not ready to settle down.

News of the couple's split came as a shock to the public, who had been following every twist and turn in their relationship since they had begun dating at St Andrews University four years earlier. An engagement announcement had been widely expected and few had noticed signs that the relationship was on its way out.

It had all seemed so different four months earlier in mid-December, when Kate and her parents had been invited to watch the prince pass out from the Royal Military Academy Sandhurst, a ceremony that must have been heart-warming for the Middletons, who had grown close to their daughter's boyfriend. A regular visitor to their home, William would drive the 33-mile journey around the M25 to visit his girlfriend after training exercises and must have relished the time he spent with her tight-knit family, something he had missed out on to an extent during his own childhood. But everything changed the moment he left Sandhurst and embarked on the next stage of his army career.

For those who looked closely, the cracks began appearing over the festive season, when Kate's parents decided to rent a £4,800-a-week mansion in Scotland for their extended family. Despite speculation that she might be, Kate had not been invited to spend Christmas with the royal family at Sandringham – only fiancées are afforded that honour, not girlfriends. Instead, the Middletons decided to invite William to spend Hogmanay with them at the Georgian mansion Jordanstone House on the outskirts of Alyth in Perthshire. Set in rambling grounds, the eighteenth-century mansion, which had belonged to the Conservative politician Sir James Duncan and his second wife Lady Beatrice (an actress known in her heyday for being the voice of Larry the Lamb in the Children's Hour series *Toytown*), was certainly fit for a prince. Crammed with antiques and old masters, the house still has its original two staircases (one for staff), a vast kitchen and laundry downstairs, a library of rare books and wood-panelled reception rooms with vast fireplaces

upstairs, and thirteen bedrooms furnished with four-poster beds. But William, who spent Christmas at Sandringham, 400 miles away, failed to make an appearance.

It would not be until the following weekend that Kate was reunited with her boyfriend, at Highgrove, but even then it was more of a farewell party for William than a birthday celebration for Kate. The future king was about to follow his younger brother into the Blues and Royals, a regiment with one of the longest histories of any in the British Army. He would wholeheartedly embrace his new role, teasing Harry that he would rise faster through the ranks because he had a university degree.

One of two regiments that make up the Household Cavalry (the other is the Life Guards), the Blues and Royals were formed in 1969 when the Royal Horse Guards (known as the Blues for the colour of their tunics) and the Royal Dragoons, both of whom could trace their origins back to the seventeenth century, were amalgamated. The only mounted cavalry unit in the British Army, the regiment has the unique role of guarding the Queen on ceremonial occasions as well as serving around the world. Its regimental emblem – an eagle worn on the left sleeve of the blue tunic – commemorates the occasion on which it seized an eagle standard from one of Napoleon's infantry battalions at Waterloo. Now stationed at Combermere Barracks in Windsor, its Colonel of the Regiment is the Princess Royal.

Kate was working at Jigsaw on the morning of 8 January 2007, when Second Lieutenant Wales reported for duty. Little did she realise how much their lives would change in just a few months.

Stepping alone out of her front door 24 hours later to go to work on her 25th birthday, wearing a £40 black-and-white dress from Topshop (which subsequently sold out within days), she was greeted by a barrage of photographers fired up by the conviction that she and her royal boyfriend would soon be announcing their

engagement. For the first time, she showed that the pressure was getting to her and she scowled.

The unprecedented paparazzi turnout provoked comparisons with the treatment of Princess Diana in the final years of her life and led the royal family to swing into action. While Kate's lawyers Harbottle & Lewis, who also count Prince Charles among their clients, tried to work out a compromise with the media, Prince William authorised his press officer to make a statement on his behalf. 'Prince William is very unhappy at the paparazzi harassment of his girlfriend,' he said. 'He wants more than anything for it to stop. Miss Middleton should, like any other private individual, be able to go about her everyday business without this kind of intrusion. The situation is proving unbearable for all those concerned.'

It was a terrible day for Kate to have to face the overwhelming attention. Now working in London, she could no longer escape the limelight by retreating to the sanctuary of her parents' home and she had to leave her flat each morning to go to work. Without William by her side, there was little that the royal family could do to help her, as she was not entitled to Scotland Yard protection until they became engaged. The pressure would soon prove too much.

At first, William remained the gallant boyfriend, driving up to London to visit his girlfriend and party in the capital, and Kate put on a brave front, donning a stunning £800 silver dress by BCBG Max Azria to attend a party at Mahiki with the prince on 1 February. Run by nightclub impresario Piers Adam and club promoter Nick House, and designed to resemble a Polynesian beach bar, it had become a firm favourite with the couple after they spent a night there before Christmas with Tom Parker Bowles and his wife, Sara. William's party-loving friend Guy Pelly was the club's marketing director, and Henry Conway, the son of the now disgraced MP

Derek Conway and flamboyant self-styled 'Queen of Sloanes', ran Thursday-night parties there.

During his first few weeks at the barracks, William managed to make another two trips to the capital, for a night out at Boujis – when he reportedly gave his girlfriend an antique Van Cleef & Arpels diamond-framed compact as an early Valentine's Day gift – and a trip to Twickenham on 10 February to watch England beat Italy in the Six Nations Championship. He and Kate cheered on rugby hero Jonny Wilkinson's record-breaking comeback: he scored 15 points in the team's 20–7 victory.

However, William's nights out with his girlfriend gradually dwindled as he threw himself into the life of a Household Cavalry officer, enjoying the feeling of being young, free and single. Torn between spending time with his girlfriend and partying with his fellow officers, it seemed there was no contest. It was a testing period for their relationship.

Kate put on a brave face, clubbing with her girlfriends at Mamilanji on Monday, 26 February, but the writing was on the wall for the relationship as she slowly tired of having an absent boyfriend.

On 4 March, in a last-ditch attempt to shore up their romance, William whisked Kate off on a make-or-break holiday to Zermatt, a village at the base of the Matterhorn in the Swiss Alps, where they stayed in an exclusive £1,500-a-week chalet. But instead of going alone with Kate, he invited some friends along, including Thomas van Straubenzee and Guy Pelly, the man often described as the princes' 'court jester'. From the outside, it appeared as if William and Kate – who missed out on a family holiday in Barbados in order to spend quality time with her boyfriend – were on the verge of an engagement announcement, staying in their chalet while their friends hit the nightclubs, and embracing and kissing on the slopes. In reality, however, things were far from

rosy, and an engagement must surely have been the last thing on their minds.

Their last public appearance together was on 13 March 2007, the opening day of the National Hunt Festival in Cheltenham, which had been a favourite with the late Queen Mother, who rarely missed a festival, attending latterly in a buggy painted in her racing colours. Arriving in William's black Audi saloon, Kate looked comfortable chatting with Zara Phillips and drinking champagne in a box belonging to racehorse owner Trevor Hemmings. But William and Kate's body language was strained, and fashion writers criticised the pair for looking like 'lamb dressed as mutton'. It was the first fashion faux pas by Kate, and possibly an indication of her unhappy mood.

Three days later, William was off to the depths of Dorset to begin a ten-week tank-commander course at the army's training camp at Bovington. But that did not deter Kate from attending the Cheltenham Gold Cup without him. Wearing a sky-blue jacket, brown skirt and matching beret, she looked much more relaxed – and more fashionable – than on her previous visit with her prince. Met on arrival by two plain-clothes police officers, she was escorted to the royal enclosure for a lunch hosted by the Queen's Master of the Horse, Lord Vestey. There she laughed and joked with guests including van Straubenzee, jumping up and down when she picked a winner and covering her mouth with her hand when she lost. Her appearance that day in the same box as William's aunt Princess Anne and Camilla's former husband Andrew Parker Bowles seemed just another confirmation that Kate was on the verge of becoming an official member of the family. But some commentators thought she might have overplayed her hand by appearing in the royal enclosure, a move that was rumoured to have rankled with William.

In any case, it was while William was in Dorset that the

couple's relationship began to fall apart, strained by their constant separation. Instead of making the 130-mile journey to London at weekends, William seemed to prefer to spend his down time with his fellow officers.

During his first night out with the Blues and Royals – nicknamed the 'Booze and Royals' in Bournemouth, the nearest large town to the barracks – William pushed Kate beyond her limits. She had always ignored rumours of his roving eye and put up with his flirtatious behaviour towards the girls who threw themselves at him, but his cavalier behaviour at the Elements nightclub on 22 March had unfortunate consequences. Although there is no suggestion that the future king cheated on his girlfriend, two of the girls he encountered that night sold their stories to the tabloid newspapers, which must have been humiliating for Kate. That Thursday night, William and his friends painted the town red as they downed lager and sambuca chasers and flirted with girls in the nightclub, unbothered that they were taking photographs of the prince on their mobile phones.

Ana Ferreira, 18, an international relations student, was in the club when she heard that William was dancing in another room. After going to watch the commotion, she posed for a picture with him, only realising afterwards that the prince had touched one of her breasts. 'Word went round that William was in a section playing cheesy '80s music,' she told *The Sun*, 'so we went to look . . . There were a lot of girls hanging around him and he was posing for pictures. He had me on one arm and my friend Cecilia on the other. I was a little bit drunk myself, but I felt something brush my breast. I thought it couldn't be the future king but now I've seen the picture it's no wonder he's got a smile on his face.'

Another girl, Lisa Agar, a 19-year-old performing-arts student with a lip ring, claimed that William pulled her onto a podium to

dance with him. 'He said something like, "Come on. Show us how it's done. You're too good for this place,"' she told the *Sunday Mirror*. 'He was being very flirty and I was quite taken aback but just went for it. He was laughing his head off and waving his hands in the air.' Lisa, who was dressed in a tight pink top, leggings and heels, claimed that William was following pints with shots of sambuca. 'I call that stuff rocket fuel,' she added, 'because it does give you a huge hit very quickly and gets you rolling drunk.'

In the early hours, William's friend invited her back to the barracks to continue the party. 'When I said I wasn't sure,' she recounted, 'Wills came over and said, "Are you coming back? It'll be a laugh. Come on. We need to go." I followed them all back to their base in a friend's car and then we all went into a lounge area in the barracks, lying about on a leather chair and sofas. In the end, I only stayed about 20 minutes. Strangely, I felt a bit sorry for William and I thought maybe he was cheering himself up.'

William's behaviour that night was by no means unusual for a serving soldier in his 20s, even one who is a member of the royal family. Two days later, Prince Harry showed his own excessive streak when he fell out of Boujis, having downed too many Crack Baby cocktails. The Blues and Royals officer had been in the club after spending a week on exercise with his regiment and was unwinding with friends, including former flame Natalie Pinkham, when he decided to try to avoid photographers by sneaking out the back. Angered that he had been spotted, he was reported to have lunged at one of the paparazzi, before falling over and landing in the gutter, although royal aides claimed he had simply lost his footing and stumbled.

Kate and William spent one last night together on 31 March, when they dined at the King's Head, Bledington, with their friends Hugh and Rose van Cutsem, whose wedding they had attended the previous summer. However, at this point, the heart and soul had

gone out of their relationship and it was drawing to a close.

A few days later, Kate popped over to Ireland with her mother Carole for the private view of an exhibition by a close family friend, Gemma Billington. Mother and daughter slummed it, staying in Dublin's cut-price three-star Quality Hotel. After looking at Gemma's paintings, Kate chatted to drummer Ben Carrigan and guitarist Daniel Ryan of Irish indie rock band The Thrills. The following day, she went to the National Gallery of Ireland.

Her appearance at the exhibition of paintings, which took place at the Urban Retreat Gallery in the city's Hanover Quay, brought in a flurry of publicity for Gemma, the 53-year-old daughter of a Garda sergeant from County Kerry. She and her husband Tim, 63, a farmer and racehorse breeder, are close family friends of the Middletons. They live just down the road, on a 320-acre farm in the village of Stanford Dingley, where William and Kate have become familiar faces in the local pub, the Boot Inn. Their seven children grew up alongside the Middleton siblings and went to the same school, while Carole and Gemma play tennis together.

'Kate is a lovely girl who is just one of our kids who happens to be going out with a boy called William who happens to be a prince,' she said in an interview with the *Sunday Independent* to publicise the exhibition. 'He is just a normal boy, really. I think it's tough on her, but she handles it well. The Middletons are a very close family who have meals together, watch movies, play sports and go on holidays together. It's funny how you think people are different, but we are all just muddling our way through life. Whoever you happen to be going out with, you have to take the rough with the smooth.'

While Kate was having a cultured time in Ireland, William was leading an altogether different existence. He spent the evening of 4 April at Bournemouth's late-night wine bar Bliss with a group of his fellow officers from the Household Cavalry. That night, the

place was packed with 200 fans watching acoustic guitarist Dan Baker playing a gig. But halfway through the two-hour set, one of William's rowdy friends leapt on stage, saying: 'Please stop playing these crap songs. The prince wants dance music.' The singer, who halted the gig for ten minutes until the officers had left the room, told a newspaper: 'I was staggered when this drunken man scaled the stage and ran up to me mid-song. It was the rudest thing I've ever experienced. This gig was the pinnacle of my career. I've practised for years in the hope of a chance to perform like this.'

Meanwhile, for William and Kate, it was the beginning of the end. The couple's final showdown came when they met up a few days later over the Easter weekend. William had turned down an invitation to spend the holiday with Kate's family but the couple managed to get together for a face-to-face conversation and realised they wanted different things out of life. While Kate was looking for some form of commitment from her boyfriend, William felt he was being pressurised to propose. It seemed as if there was only one way forward, but Kate still hoped that William would change his mind.

At midday the following Wednesday, any hopes she might have had of a reconciliation were dashed. It was reported that she had a lengthy conversation with William on her mobile, after which she left work early and disappeared for the rest of the week. Meanwhile, William was said to have phoned the Queen at Windsor Castle, shortly before she left to visit the Earl of Carnarvon at Highclere Castle, to tell her that his and Kate's relationship had drawn to a close.

By the time William turned up at Mahiki on Friday the 13th, news of the couple's break-up had not yet emerged. But the prince was aware that he would be on the front pages the following morning

and it seemed he was going to ensure he was seen to be having a good time.

Arriving with friends at 11.30 p.m., he was shown to a private table next to the dance floor, where the party downed £450 bottles of 1998 Dom Pérignon champagne before working their way through the cocktail menu, called the Mahiki Trail because it is devised around a treasure map. If guests finish all 18 concoctions, they are rewarded with the club's infamous Treasure Chest, a mixture of brandy and peach liqueur, lime, sugar and champagne.

At one point during the evening, William is supposed to have yelled, 'I'm free!', before performing his own version of the robot dance goal celebration that Liverpool striker Peter Crouch had shown him during a World Cup training session. As the opening chords of the Rolling Stones' 'You Can't Always Get What You Want' rang out, his friends dragged him onto the dance floor. But the prince's high spirits slowly turned maudlin, and at 3.30 a.m. he staggered out of the VIP exit to the club and got into his chauffeur-driven car. A royal-protection-squad officer settled the £4,700 bill and the prince went home. Within hours, the world would find out that Britain's most eligible bachelor was back on the market . . . but for just how long?

CHAPTER 22

The Reconciliation

Their arms entwined around each other, Prince William and Kate Middleton seemed oblivious to the world as they danced seductively to their favourite song, the BodyRockers' 'I Like the Way You Move'.

Throwing caution to the wind, the couple kissed passionately on the Perspex dance floor backstage at Wembley Stadium, leaving VIP guests at the Concert for Diana without any doubt that they had rekindled their romance. After their floorshow, they retired to a discreet corner of the room, lit by candles and scattered with rose petals, where they spent the remainder of the evening sitting on a white leather sofa, hidden by drapes, holding hands, whispering in each other's ears and sipping mojitos.

That public display of affection, in the dwindling hours of 1 July 2007 – so out of character for the prince – marked a new beginning for the young couple, who had broken up 12 weeks earlier over William's failure to commit. Hours earlier, William, 25, gave no hint that the romance was back on track as he strolled

onto the stage with his brother Harry, 22, to introduce the concert, a tribute to their late mother on what would have been her 46th birthday. 'This evening is about all that our mother loved in life: her music, her dancing, her charities, and her family and friends,' he said, before introducing Duran Duran, one of Diana's favourite bands, telling the crowd to 'have an awesome time'.

It was the first time that William and Kate had been seen together in public since their romance had disintegrated, sparking speculation that they had settled their differences. But although they were both in the royal box, they sat separately, two rows apart, and did not look at each other once.

The Concert for Diana, which raised £1.6 million for charity, was organised by Princes William and Harry as a tribute to their mother on the tenth anniversary of her death in a car crash in the Pont de l'Alma tunnel in Paris. They invited 23 acts, spanning their own and their mother's generation, including the English National Ballet, to perform at the gig, which was beamed to an audience of 15 million in Britain and 500 million worldwide. It was an unusual combination of acts, but that did not seem to deter a crowd of 63,000 people paying £45 for tickets to watch Diana's favourites Tom Jones, Bryan Ferry and Duran Duran on stage alongside American hip hop artists Kanye West and P Diddy and British soul singer Joss Stone.

Sir Elton John, who wrote the Princess Diana tribute song 'Candle in the Wind 1997', opened the gig with a rendition of his classic 'Your Song' before introducing the two princes to the audience. To a standing ovation, William and Harry took to the stage. 'Hello, Wembley!' shouted Harry. After paying tribute to their mother and introducing the next act, the princes took their places in the royal box alongside other royals of their generation: their cousins Beatrice and Eugenie, Zara Phillips and her boyfriend Mike Tindall, the England rugby player. While William carefully

avoided Kate, who was wearing a white Issa trench coat, Harry sat next to his girlfriend Chelsy, 21, and gave her a kiss. The trio danced and clapped as Nelly Furtado belted out her song 'Say It Right'. The only hint that the couple's relationship was back on course was when the television cameras panned to Kate happily singing along to Take That's 'Back for Good'.

However, afterwards, at the £250,000 after-show extravaganza, at which guests downed raspberry or cappuccino vodka jellies and dined on oysters, lobster and crab, while acrobats and dancers writhed in cages around the room and tropical fish swam below the dance floor, it was a different matter. William and Kate arrived and left separately, but inside they could not be torn apart.

Studiedly ignoring Kate while he chatted to Joss Stone, William made a beeline for her the moment she took to the dance floor, clasping her from behind and planting a kiss on her lips. They were together for the rest of the evening, announcing to the world that they had revived their relationship.

News of the royal break-up had first leaked out on Saturday, 14 April 2007, three days after Kate and William's last phone conversation, following which she had fled the capital for the sanctuary of her parents' home in Berkshire with a pile of paperwork and a mission to keep her head down. Both her siblings were at home that weekend – it was James's 20th birthday on the Sunday – and the family rallied around. In an ironic twist, Pippa, 23, who was about to sit her finals at Edinburgh University, had separated from her own aristocratic boyfriend, J.J. Jardine Patterson, the wealthy heir of a Hong Kong banking family, because of his refusal to commit, and the two sisters comforted each other.

But on James's birthday, the family awoke to a series of anonymous attacks in the Sunday newspapers suggesting that

Kate would never be accepted by the royal family – and William's aristocratic circle – because of her mother Carole's middle-class upbringing and lack of breeding. It was a cruel character assassination of a family that epitomises Middle England and a woman who, like many others in the countryside, enjoys a game of tennis, riding her horse and walking the family's golden Labrador. Harking back to Nancy Mitford's 1954 essay 'The English Aristocracy', the reports suggested that William's upper-crust friends apparently sneered at her non-U (U meaning upper class) use of 'toilet' and 'pardon' (as opposed to 'lavatory' and 'what') and cringed at her chewing gum during William's passing-out ceremony at Sandhurst. It was later revealed that she was chewing a nicotine substitute, although, of course, to those who wished to criticise her for it, this was no excuse for the breach of etiquette. Another faux pas was supposedly greeting the Queen with the words 'Pleased to meet you' instead of 'Hello, Ma'am', but Carole had never been introduced to the monarch.

Sensing a public-relations disaster, the palace immediately distanced itself from the stories, blaming Fleet Street for the furore. But the royals have not always been above snobbery – the Queen's confidant Lord Charteris once memorably described the Duchess of York as 'vulgar, vulgar, vulgar, and that is that', and Prince Charles has been known to despair that people no longer 'know their place' – so it is impossible to judge where the stories came from.

In any case, Prince William was so horrified by the vitriol levelled at Carole that he telephoned his former girlfriend to reassure her that his friends were not behind the attack. That telephone conversation, four days after they had broken up, would be the first tentative step towards a reunion.

Within 24 hours, when William had returned to his barracks in Bovington, Kate decided that she too had to brave the world. Her eyes hidden behind dark glasses, she finally emerged from the

comforting walls of her parents' house at 10.15 a.m. to be driven up to London by James. Dressed in jeans – and wearing a brave face – she popped into her flat in Chelsea to pick up her tennis racquet, a symbol that proved her life would not be grinding to a halt. The accessories buyer then dashed into her office in Kew, south-west London, to collect some paperwork before heading back to her parents' home. Her defiant appearance that day sent a message to the world that she refused to wallow in self-pity.

Kate spent another few days in Berkshire, ignoring the crescendo of speculation over the break-up, nursing her broken heart and reading letters of support – she is estimated to have received more than 300 from as far afield as Australia – while the world waited to see what she would do next. The public-relations supremo Max Clifford estimated that, as the only girlfriend ever to have lived with a future king, she could earn more than £5 million from her story – but Kate was far too dignified to kiss and tell.

By Thursday, after a week of compassionate leave, Kate felt confident enough to return to London and resume her old lifestyle, determined to show the prince just what he was missing. That evening, after spending the day at work, she met some friends at La Bouchée, a restaurant in Fulham, before turning up at Mahiki, where William had been drowning his sorrows six days before. It was a spectacular PR stunt – the first in a series of textbook manoeuvres that could have been designed to attract the prince's attention and show him that she was quite capable of coping very well alone. Wearing a £45 minidress from Lipsy with long boots, and flashing some thigh and cleavage, her appearance at the bar, where she drank a Jack Daniel's and Coke with the club's marketing director and William's close friend Guy Pelly, could hardly have gone unnoticed. She spent most of the evening on the dance floor before leaving the club at 2.30 a.m.

One of the men she danced with that night, architect Alex

Shirley-Smith, was smitten. 'She flicked her hair and looked over her shoulder at me,' he told the *Daily Mail* afterwards. 'The next thing I knew she had twirled backwards towards me so her back was up against me. She started doing some very sexy moves and she was absolutely gorgeous. She was a great dancer. Then she was snatched away by a really drunk guy, who I think was one of her friends. He probably thought he was trying to rescue her, but as he pulled her away, she winked at me and I knew she was flirting.' He went on to recount that later that night, as the song 'Unbelievable' by EMF came on: 'We naturally gravitated towards each other and Kate stepped forward and looked at me cheekily, put her hands on my shoulders and we both sang the rest of the song to each other while we danced.'

A week later, on 26 May, Kate was out on the town again, at William's old favourite Boujis, well and truly embracing the life of a singleton. Wearing a black minidress and boots, she joined friends at a Thai restaurant in Chelsea, before going on to the club. William could not have failed to notice.

In the aftermath of a break-up, another clichéd response is to get fit and lose weight, and Kate was no exception. But instead of spending hours in the gym, she joined The Sisterhood, a female rowing crew who were planning to cross the English Channel in a dragon boat to raise money for charity. They had challenged their male rivals The Brotherhood to race the 21 miles across the Channel from Dover to Cap Griz Nez, near Calais, and had been training since the previous November. Kate was one of two helmswomen.

Led by Emma Sayle, 29, who had gained a reputation for being 'the poshest swinger in town', the group was never going to fade into obscurity. She had invited a motley crew, many of whom had controversial backgrounds, to join The Sisterhood.

Emma, whose father is former diplomat Colonel Guy Sayle OBE,

had been four years above Kate at Downe House. She had attracted notoriety as director of operations at swingers' club Fever and founder of Killing Kittens, a company that organises sex parties. Her best friend Amanda Cherry, 29, another member of the team, caused a huge scandal at Downe House when, shortly after leaving, she had an affair with her former politics tutor Ian Goodridge, more than 20 years her senior. He left his wife for the 19 year old and the two married.

Billing themselves as 'an elite group of female athletes, talented in many ways, toned to perfection, with killer looks, on a mission to keep boldly going where no girl has gone before', The Sisterhood's training sessions on the River Thames near Chiswick and Putney became a magnet for the paparazzi.

Kate had been invited to join the group by Alicia Fox-Pitt, 26, the sister of Olympic three-day eventer William Fox-Pitt, and one of her oldest friends. Alicia's older sister Laurella was also in the team. The Fox-Pitt sisters, who had been at Marlborough with Kate, had been brought up on the family estate, Knowlton Court, on the outskirts of Canterbury in the Kent countryside. Like their brother, they are both talented riders, but while Alicia juggles private tutoring with studying to become a vet, Laurella is a keen kickboxer and aspiring actress.

The fourth Old Marlburian in the crew was Bean Sopwith, 26, who had studied archaeology at Oxford. A trainee stuntwoman, she had appeared in Jack Osbourne's television series *Adrenaline Junkie*. Bean had had a serious climbing accident four years earlier, falling 30 ft down a Welsh cliff face. She nearly lost her hand, but not only did she make a full recovery, she went on to take up freefall skydiving.

Kate's involvement with the team raised eyebrows at the palace, but at that stage she was revelling in her new freedom. 'We've been training three times a week,' commented Emma. 'Kate is extremely

fit and very strong, so as long as she can commit to the rest of the training sessions, she'll be in the boat.'

Around the same time as she began toning up her body, Kate's look began to grow ever more polished and she revealed a sense of style that would not have been out of place in fashion bible *Vogue*. Now a sample size eight, and getting regular haircuts at the salon of celebrity stylist Richard Ward – a favourite of Tara Palmer-Tomkinson, Isabella Hervey and Lisa Snowdon – she was ranked number eight in the society magazine *Tatler*'s list of best-dressed women. Geordie Greig, its editor at the time, said of the placing: 'Kate has not put a foot wrong. She appears modest and beautiful, and is liked by the press. There is a breezy unpretentiousness about how she looks and what she wears. The perfect princess in waiting.'

Kate also discovered her designer label of choice, Issa, whose jersey wrap dresses have clad the figures of the Hollywood starlets Scarlett Johanssen and Keira Knightley. It was in designer Daniella Issa Helayel's top-floor studio in Fulham that she first spotted the Lucky dress, inspired by a vintage baby gown, with puff sleeves and a short skirt, which she apparently has in every colour, and it was there that she bought her outfit for the Concert for Diana. Daniella has maintained that Kate has no official connection with the company, although she brings invaluable publicity. 'She is not an ambassador for Issa,' she said discreetly, 'and it's not that she gets all these freebies. We have friends in common, and we're fortunate that the dresses suit her so well.'

By the end of May, Kate's younger sister Pippa, considered the racier of the two, had finished her finals and moved down to London, where the two girls became some of the most sought-after guests on the social scene.

While Kate had climbed the social ladder because of her royal

connections, Pippa had become a member of the elite country-house set, dating heir J.J. Jardine Patterson and sharing a student flat with the Duke of Roxburghe's son Ted Innes-Ker and George Percy, heir to the Duke of Northumberland. Already snobbishly known in some circles as 'the Wisteria Sisters', Kate and Pippa were soon dubbed 'the Sizzler Sisters' by *Tatler*, which described them as 'very determined' young women.

The sisters' first appearance together was at the society jewellers Asprey on 15 May, when award-winning author Simon Sebag Montefiore invited them to the launch of his book *Young Stalin*. There they mixed with an elevated crowd that included Simon's sister-in-law Tara Palmer-Tomkinson, the writers Plum Sykes and William Shawcross, newscaster Emily Maitlis and Conservative MP (and friend of Prince Charles) Nicholas Soames. Two days later, Kate was back on the dance floor at Boujis, with her younger sister in tow. After partying with actresses Anna Friel and Mischa Barton, they left the club hand in hand at 3 a.m., walking part of the way home, which ensured that they were photographed together.

Although friends rallying around William suggested that his ex's high profile was 'driving him up the wall', Kate's armoury of tactics appeared to be working, as he made the first tentative steps towards a reconciliation. Missing his former girlfriend and realising that he had made a mistake, he persuaded Kate to meet him at his apartment in Clarence House on 26 May, the first in a series of trysts during which they talked over the separation.

However, enjoying her new-found freedom, Kate kept William guessing, being spotted at Mahiki four days later with several eligible men. Wearing a flimsy red top and white trousers, she arrived at the club's Johnny Cash theme night on the arm of Henry Ropner, son of the shipping tycoon Sir John, who lived in a £1 million flat in Chelsea. Henry, who had gone to school with William and dated his old flame Jecca Craig, had known Kate since he was a

geography student at Edinburgh University. Inside the club, she sipped the aptly named cocktail Good-Time Girl and danced with Jamie Murray Wells, the millionaire founder of Glasses Direct. She left the club with estate agent Charles Morshead, who bore a remarkable similarity to William.

But, although Kate was said to be keen to 'live life to the max', she was not looking for romance – because she already had her sights elsewhere. She finally succumbed to William's charms once again on 9 June – ten weeks after they had broken up and two weeks after they had their first tentative drink – accompanying her former boyfriend to a raucous mess party in his barracks to celebrate the end of his gruelling course as a troop leader. Entitled 'Freakin' Naughty', the party, complete with bouncy castle and paddling pool, was packed with guests dressed up as naughty nuns, doctors and nurses, but William could not take his eyes off Kate. After chatting to her all night, he danced intimately with her before kissing her in the middle of the crowded throng. He took her back to his private quarters in the early hours of the morning.

Even then, Kate did not stop partying, going five days later to Raffles nightclub, which describes itself as 'one of the last bastions of decadence and debauchery' and was founded by an Old Etonian friend of Princess Margaret. Three days later, on 17 June, while William was at the Trooping of the Colour with his family, Kate flew out to Ibiza for a holiday from the social whirl. She stayed in a five-bedroom villa on the south-west of the island with a party of friends including her brother James and her school friend Emilia d'Erlanger, also a close friend of Prince William. After they arrived, the group headed straight for the Blue Marlin bar, an exclusive venue overlooking the Cala Jondal bay in San José. During the trip, Kate topped up her tan in preparation for what would turn out to be the highlight of her social season.

It was 30 June 2007, the day before the Concert for Diana, and speculation was mounting over William and Kate's first public appearance since they had broken up. Maintaining her legendary cool, Kate ignored the gossip and donned an Issa dress to spend the afternoon at Wimbledon, where – when rain did not stop play – she watched the 2004 champion Maria Sharapova annihilate her Japanese opponent in straight sets. That night, under cover of darkness, she sneaked into Clarence House for one last secret tryst, going to extraordinary lengths not to be spotted. Leaving her home in Kensington around 9 p.m., she parked her Audi in the car park of a Mayfair hotel around midnight, walking into the palace on foot so as not to be seen. An hour and three quarters later, one of the palace aides picked the car up and drove it into the grounds. The following day, she sat in the royal box, cool as a cucumber, as if nothing had happened. It was only at the after-show party that the couple gave the game away.

CHAPTER 23

Back in the Royal Fold

*L*ooking elegant in an ivory doubled-breasted coat and black boots, Kate Middleton congratulated her dashing boyfriend, Flying Officer William Wales, after he was presented with his wings by his father in a ceremony at the oldest air force college in the world.

In their first official appearance since they had got back together – and the most prominent ever – Kate strolled side by side with her boyfriend, who was wearing full dress uniform, down the corridor at the Royal Air Force College Cranwell on their way to a drinks reception with Charles and Camilla. The couple's public show of togetherness, on 11 April 2008, a year after they had broken up, once again fuelled speculation that they were on the verge of getting engaged. Although Kate had attended William's graduation ceremony at Sandhurst with her parents in December 2007, she had not on that occasion been photographed with the prince.

Arriving with Princess Diana's sister Lady Sarah McCorquodale, Kate, then 26, was ushered into RAF Cranwell, near Sleaford in

Lincolnshire, through a back entrance. Sitting with William's aunt, she watched, smiling broadly, as her boyfriend and 25 other officers received insignias from Prince Charles, who himself had graduated from RAF Cranwell in the early '70s.

Afterwards, William joined his father and stepmother as, despite rainy weather, they ventured onto the runway to look at a display of planes, among them the very Chipmunk T10 trainer plane in which Charles had learned to fly. Little did they realise how big a storm was brewing.

By the time Kate Middleton had been reunited with her prince at the Concert for Diana, in July 2007, she had become one of the season's most in-demand party guests – a coup for a girl who had been dismissed as a social climber. *Tatler* had placed her eighth on a list of the world's best-dressed women and named her as their 'most-wanted' guest, describing her as a 'sexy siren' made 'super-in-demand' now that she was single. Suddenly, Kate Middleton was cool.

Three weeks after the concert, her status was assured when she received a sought-after gilt-embossed invitation to one of the parties of the season, the Duchess of Cornwall's 60th birthday banquet. Her attendance at the formal black-tie ball, organised by Prince Charles's aide Michael Fawcett and Camilla's sister Annabel Elliot, an interior designer, showed that her newly rekindled relationship with Prince William was as strong as ever. Although she had not initially been invited to the party, she was put on the guest list the moment that she and William got back together.

Wearing a long white gown, Kate looked totally relaxed and happy as she sipped champagne and cocktails in the gardens of Highgrove with Zara Phillips and Mike Tindall. Prince Harry and Chelsy Davy were unable to make the party as they were on holiday,

but there were plenty of celebrity guests, including the comedians Joan Rivers and Stephen Fry, TV presenter Jools Holland, actors Dame Judi Dench and Edward Fox, actress Joanna Lumley and her conductor husband Stephen Barlow and actor Timothy West, with his wife Prunella Scales. After dinner – a three-course organic meal – Kate and William made their way onto the dance floor, where the prince mouthed the lyrics of the Frank Sinatra song 'It Had to Be You' to his girlfriend.

Having returned to the royal fold, it was only a matter of time before Kate would pull out of The Sisterhood's dragon-boat team, which had attracted so much publicity when she was single. Unfortunately, she dropped out of the race, which took place on 24 August, at the last minute, meaning that the girls could not find a replacement, although that did not stop them crossing in record time and raising £100,000 for charity.

Apparently totally enamoured with his girlfriend, William whisked Kate away on 16 August for a romantic holiday on the paradise island of Desroches in the Indian Ocean. It was the first time that the couple had been away together since their skiing trip to Zermatt in January 2006, before William started at Sandhurst, and only the second time they had ever been on holiday *à deux*. Desroches was the perfect venue for a couple seeking privacy. With a tiny population of only 50 people, the island, which is 144 miles south-west of Mahe, the main island in the Seychelles, is ideal for divers and holidaymakers looking for sandy beaches, coconut plantations, endless coral and luscious vegetation, and it caters for only a handful of tourists. William and Kate stayed in a £500-a-night suite in one of ten double chalets in the Desroches Island Resort, overlooking a lagoon, where they spent their days scuba diving, snorkelling and sunbathing. At night, they dined in the resort's restaurant, with a view of the ocean, or ate under the stars. After having dinner with members of staff on the last night of the

holiday, William told them, 'We will definitely return. We have had the most fantastic break.'

After they returned from their holiday – a week before the tenth anniversary of Princess Diana's death – the couple went to great lengths to avoid being seen together. Kate did not attend the thanksgiving service for the late princess and they gave their usual haunts a wide berth. However, on 5 October they finally let their guard down during a night out at Boujis and were photographed together for the first time since they had broken up six months earlier. In a change from their usual paparazzi-avoidance tactics, they came out of the club together and drove off in William's Range Rover.

On 11 October, the couple were spotted together again when they flew up to the Birkhall estate for a long weekend to spend the last few days of the deerstalking season with Prince Charles and the Duchess of Cornwall. Dressed in camouflage gear, Kate was seen two days later, lying in the heather and being coached by ghillies on how to use a hunting rifle. Her presence on the stag hunt that day may have endeared her to Prince William, but it outraged animal-rights protestors. She looked well on the way to becoming a fully fledged member of the royal family.

As the girlfriend of Prince William, Kate had grown accustomed to coming second to royal duties, but now it was brought home to her that she would have to come second to the military as well, as William missed her birthday, on 9 January, for the second year in a row. As the future commander-in-chief of the British Armed Forces, the prince had little choice in the matter; the previous year, he had been on duty with the Household Cavalry and this year he had just signed up to the RAF.

Kate celebrated her 26th with her parents, Michael and Carole,

and sister Pippa at Tom Aikens restaurant in Elystan Street, Chelsea. Afterwards, she and Pippa dropped in at Kitts, a swanky new nightclub in Sloane Square, the heart of Sloane Ranger territory. For the next few months, she would see little of her man. He was based 126 miles from London at RAF Cranwell.

Built on land requisitioned by the Admiralty from the Earl of Bristol, RAF Cranwell was commissioned on 1 April 1916 as a training college for the Royal Naval Air Service, which merged with the Army's Royal Flying Corps to form the RAF two years later. The Royal Air Force College opened in 1920 under the command of Air Commodore C.A.H. Longcroft. Fourteen years later, the future Edward VIII opened its current brick and Portland stone building, with its central portico of six Corinthian columns.

In a message to the first entry of cadets, the Chief of the Air Staff, Sir Hugh Trenchard, said: 'We have to learn by experience how to organise and administer a great service, both in peace and war, and you, who are present at the college in its first year, will, in future, be at the helm. Therefore, you will have to work your hardest, both as cadets at the college and subsequently as officers, in order to be capable of guiding this great service through its early days and maintaining its traditions and efficiency in the years to come.'

Eighty-eight years later, on 7 January 2008, William arrived at the base on a four-month attachment to its Central Flying School, fulfilling a desire to follow in the footsteps of his forefathers. Men of four successive generations of his family have become RAF pilots: his great-grandfather Prince Albert, later King George VI, was the first member of the royal family to serve in the RAF, immediately after its formation. Both Prince Philip and Prince Charles graduated as flight lieutenants, in 1953 and 1971 respectively, and, like William, Prince Charles received his wings from his father. He has since been promoted and now holds the rank of air chief marshal. Kate's family also have links to the RAF. Her grandfather

Peter Middleton joined the service during the Second World War and got his wings in Canada.

Central Flying School Commandant Nick Seward commented on William's arrival: 'During his time with us, Flying Officer Wales will be realising a personal ambition to learn how to fly and this will be the beginning of a lifelong relationship with the Royal Air Force. Throughout his attachment, whilst also training alongside fellow officers, we are very keen to make sure that Flying Officer Wales will have the opportunity to meet airmen of all ranks to enable him to have as broad as possible an idea of the RAF and how it differs from what he has seen in the army. Following his training, Flying Officer Wales will be attached to several front-line units, including support helicopter, search and rescue, air transport and fighter aircraft, which the Royal Air Force operates.'

For the three-month course, tailored specifically to his needs and intended to make him a competent rather than an operational flyer, William donned the RAF's instantly recognisable olive-green flying jumpsuit, with zips and name tag, to learn to fly solo and perform basic aerobatics. He was one of the first in his class at 1 Squadron of 1 Elementary Flying Training School to make a solo flight, eight days after his arrival, in a propeller-driven Grob G 115E light aircraft.

After a month in Lincolnshire, William was transferred to RAF Linton-on-Ouse in North Yorkshire, where he trained on the faster propeller-driven aircraft the Tucano T1, which can travel at speeds of up to 345 mph. Although he was now even further from London, he did manage to drive the 225-mile trip on the odd weekend, when he and Kate would enjoy a leisurely Sunday lunch at the Builders Arms, a gastropub on the Kings Road.

On 14 March, Kate made her third trip in as many years to watch the Cheltenham Gold Cup, turning up with Thomas van Straubenzee as an escort. They cheered home Denman as he beat

his stablemate and reigning champion Kauto Star in the prestigious race. It was a year since Kate had last been seen at Cheltenham, shortly before her split with Prince William, and the contrast could not have been more different. This year, she had ditched the tweeds for a thigh-skimming navy-blue raincoat and trilby.

Two days later, William and Kate were on their fourth skiing trip to the Alpine village of Klosters. In a break with royal tradition – Prince Charles usually stays in the royal suite at the five-star Hotel Walserhof – the party of friends rented an apartment high in the mountains. Prince Charles joined them later on in the week. Wearing a chic white skiing jacket and confidently tackling the off-piste runs, Kate looked relaxed as she was photographed poking William with a ski pole. Her appearance with one of William's bodyguards invoked memories of Princess Diana, who was often seen skiing with a Metropolitan police guard while on holiday with Charles. The sight caused a group of photographers to gather on a ridge overlooking the terminus of the Gotschna cable car waiting to catch a picture of her arrival, enabling the press to compare the images of Princess William's mother with those of his girlfriend.

After their holiday, William was stationed at RAF Shawbury, near Shrewsbury, Shropshire – and 170 miles from London – where he flew a helicopter for the first time. He then undertook his final test to gain his wings. 'William was very good,' said instructor Wing Commander Andy Lovell. 'I was very impressed by his flying skills. He had a natural handling ability and was very quick to learn. He responded well to instructions and demonstrated plenty of spare capacity.' Flight Lieutenant Simon Berry, 26, who was on the same course, added: 'William was socialising with everyone. He was just a normal bloke, a normal guy and very sociable. He was working really hard, flying in the morning, coming down and doing two hours of flight school, and then working all hours in the evenings like everyone else.'

However, it later emerged that William, codenamed 'Golden Kestrel', was not quite as 'normal' as the other RAF officers. Stationed at RAF Odiham, west of Basingstoke in Hampshire, he spent his final week training with 7 Squadron, learning how to fly a £10-million twin-rotor Chinook helicopter. It was during his time there that the 25-year-old officer let his youth and enthusiasm get the better of him, taking five 'joyrides' at a cost of £86,434 to the taxpayer. Although he was accompanied at all times by a senior instructor and experienced crew, and three of the flights could have been a legitimate part of his training – using family residences as navigational marker points to plot his course – two others involved using the helicopter as transport to social events, causing a public-relations nightmare that threatened to overshadow his graduation ceremony.

Having drawn up the flight plans himself, William decided that his first training exercise, on Wednesday, 2 April, should be a trip to his family home, Highgrove, where he could 'buzz' his father (it is not known whether Prince Charles was at home at the time). Under tuition, he flew the 106-mile round trip to Gloucestershire. The MoD later claimed that the trip, which cost £11,985 in fuel, maintenance and man hours, was part of a 'general handling exercise'.

The following day, perhaps in a bid to show off to Kate, William suggested practising his take-off and landing skills at her home in Berkshire, as the MoD routinely uses other locations when their two permanent fields in the area surrounding RAF Odiham are busy. After getting permission from the police and the Middleton family, he flew the 12 miles from his base and circled over the house at 300 ft, before landing in a paddock in their grounds. He did not get out of the helicopter but took off 20 seconds later. The trip cost £8,716, but was defended on the grounds that 'battlefield helicopter crews routinely practise landing in fields and confined

spaces away from their airfields as a vital part of their training for operations'.

However, on Friday, 4 April, William bent the rules even further, travelling 260 miles to Hexham, Northumberland. While another pilot flew back to base, he travelled on to the Scottish border town of Kelso, to join Kate at the wedding of their close friend Lady Iona Douglas-Home (granddaughter of Sir Alec Douglas-Home and daughter of the chairman of Coutts, she had met the couple at St Andrews) and banker Thomas Hewitt. The most expensive of William's jaunts, at £18,522, the 'general training' flight took 4 hours and 15 minutes but was defended by the MoD as 'a legitimate training sortie'.

After returning to base from the wedding, William had to conduct low-level flying training. Having buzzed his father and girlfriend, the obvious choice was his grandmother. He made the 256-mile round trip to the Sandringham estate in Norfolk on Wednesday, 9 April, at a cost of £4,358, although the Queen was not there at the time.

Luckily, news of these trips had not yet emerged when he attended a gala dinner the night before his graduation ceremony to celebrate the 90th anniversary of the RAF. Wearing his No. 5 mess dress for the first time, he joined Charles and Camilla in the officers' mess at Cranwell, after they'd watched a sunset flypast of Spitfires and Hurricanes.

Twenty-four hours later, William used another Chinook training exercise as an excuse to ferry him and Harry to the Isle of Wight. Avoiding the Friday afternoon rush-hour traffic, he picked up Prince Harry at Woolwich Barracks before flying on to RAF Bembridge, on the island, for a drunken weekend. The official reason given for the £8,716, 190-mile trip was 'open-water training', but unofficially the princes were attending the stag party of their cousin Peter Phillips, who was to get married the following month to Autumn

Kelly. The 24-man party, which included Zara Phillips' boyfriend Mike Tindall, was staying in the sailing resort of Cowes, where they spent two days touring the restaurants and bars, starting in a restrained fashion in the Anchor Inn, an eighteenth-century pub, and getting wilder as the weekend went on.

The MoD said that the flight was intended to train William in low-level flying, negotiating busy air traffic over London, crossing water, flying in low cloud and landing at an enclosed helipad, but by the time he took the flight William had already been given his wings, and documents revealed under the Freedom of Information Act showed that he had kept his superiors in the dark over the reason for his trip.

One of the main gripes was that the MoD had allowed William to use one of its 48-strong fleet of Chinooks as his own personal taxi service when the RAF was overstretched in Afghanistan. But once the floodgates opened, the complaints snowballed. Some complained the money the MoD had spent on William's training had been wasted, as he was never likely to fly on the front line, others that he had been fast-tracked through the course in double time.

RAF-trained pilot Jon Lake, an aviation analyst, said at the time: 'This is an absolute waste of training hours on the Chinook helicopter that the military are hard-pressed to afford. No other pilot at Prince William's stage of training would be allowed anywhere near the left-hand seat of a Chinook. It's like a learner driver being given the keys to a Formula One car just because his father owns the racing team.'

Air Chief Marshal Sir Glenn Torpy, head of the RAF, was reported to have been furious about the situation and the 'sheer stupidity' of allowing William to make the Isle of Wight flight, asking for a detailed explanation of how it had come about. Even so, the MoD decided that although 'a degree of naivety' had been involved, there should be no punishments as no rules had been broken.

While William was enjoying his boys' weekend in Cowes, Kate spent some quality time with her family. It was her brother James's 21st birthday on 15 April, and the entire Middleton clan went out to celebrate. They started their evening at Cocoon, a futuristic Pan-Asian restaurant in a former Odeon cinema at the bottom of Regent Street owned by the same team as Boujis, on whose dance floor they ended the night.

By then, Pippa had found a job working for the upmarket event organisers Table Talk, who plan exclusive parties for blue-chip companies such as Merrill Lynch and Morgan Stanley, jewellers Asprey and auction house Christie's. Founded in 1992, the company, which had catered one of Elton John's exclusive White Tie and Tiara balls, jumped at the chance to employ Kate Middleton's sister. With her society contacts and love of the high life, she was to be a natural at the job.

James too had left university – he had dropped out of Edinburgh, where he had been studying environmental geoscience, the previous summer, after his first year – and had set up his own offshoot of the family firm, the Cake Kit Company, which provided the ingredients and accessories for making novelty cakes. While he got on his feet, he was working out of his parents' offices and staying in the family home. 'I knew that that mouthful of academic prescription was not going to do it for me,' he told *Tatler*. 'I wanted to join the workforce. So I quit early and started my own baking business. My parents had planted a gene in me with their business, and for me it was going to be all about baking. I even had a grandfather on my mother's side, Ronald Goldsmith, who had been a baker during the war, so there was a family link too.'

Two weeks after James's birthday, during William's final week in the RAF, he made his first trip to the front line in Afghanistan, from where he was to repatriate the body of the 94th serviceman to be killed in the country since hostilities began in 2001. The

prince joined a group of RAF officers flying into Kandahar airport to bring home the body of Trooper Robert Pearson, 22, a Queen's Royal Lancer, who had been killed when his Viking armoured vehicle hit a landmine in Helmand Province. William took his turn at the controls of the C-17 Globemaster military transporter and spent three hours on the ground meeting servicemen. Back in the UK, he met the family of Trooper Pearson.

Both the Queen and Prince Charles had approved the 30-hour trip, which took place overnight on 27 April and was deemed so risky that a news blackout was imposed until after his return. Cynics claimed that aides had dreamed it up as a public-relations exercise to improve the prince's battered image, but Clarence House insisted it had been planned before his helicopter joyrides had been exposed. Five days later, on 2 May 2008, William bowed out of the RAF and started a month-long break before an attachment to the Royal Navy. During that time, another royal would take the heat off him and spark a crisis within the family.

CHAPTER 24

Out of the Shadows

S itting in a pew in the historic St George's Chapel in the grounds of Windsor Castle, Kate Middleton shared a private joke with Chelsy Davy as they attended their first royal wedding in the presence of the Queen.

Wearing a pale-pink fitted jacket, a black Issa dress and a matching black pillbox hat with net veil, Prince William's girlfriend slipped into the Gothic chapel on 17 May 2008 for the wedding of his cousin Peter Phillips to Autumn Kelly.

Arriving alone, the 26-year-old brunette was representing her boyfriend at the first wedding of a grandchild of the Queen, as William had been forced to turn down the invitation because it clashed with a prior engagement. While she was at the royal wedding, he was 4,000 miles away in the foothills of Mount Kenya, awaiting the traditional Masai marriage ceremony of Batian Craig, the brother of Jecca, to Melissa Duveen.

Kate's solitary appearance on such an important occasion underlined the extent to which she had been accepted by the royal

family and, to many observers, indicated that it was only a matter of time before she became a royal bride. Her role at the wedding lead to flurry of newspaper articles speculating about an imminent engagement, with one friend remarking that they thought there was 'undoubtedly an understanding' between the couple since the relationship's revival that it would lead to marriage.

The wedding also marked a step forward in Harry's girlfriend Chelsy's relationship with the family. She had attended her first official engagement earlier in the month when she had watched her boyfriend being awarded with a medal for his service in Afghanistan. But for Chelsy, who looked unusually demure in a black-and-white floral dress and matching black jacket, this was the first meeting with her boyfriend's grandmother.

However, the two girls' attendance at the event was overshadowed by a storm of controversy over the commercialisation of the royal family, as the newly-weds had made a £500,000 deal to allow their nuptials to be featured in *Hello!* magazine. Both William and Harry were said to be 'deeply unhappy' that their girlfriends were prominently featured in the coverage, splashed across 59 pages of the magazine, which stated: 'Even the two glamorous royal girlfriends couldn't take the spotlight off the bride on her big day.' Despite having slipped in through a side door of the church, rather than entering through the famous West Steps, in order not to upstage the bride, the two girls were photographed 29 times between them, laughing together, letting their hair down on the dance floor and being entertained by Prince Harry. The two princes were not amused.

The marriage of the Queen's grandson Peter Phillips and Autumn Kelly, the Canadian daughter of a hairdresser and electrical retailer, was perhaps the most high-profile royal union since the wedding

of Prince Edward and Sophie Wessex on 19 June 1999. Although Prince Charles and the Duchess of Cornwall had married the previous year, they had had a civil ceremony, which the Queen did not attend.

Organised by Margaret Hammond (a former assistant to Peter's mother, Princess Anne, she came out of retirement for the occasion), the service was attended by all the senior members of the royal family, apart from Prince William. Yet when the couple first met, at the Montreal Grand Prix in 2003, Autumn had no idea the man she was dating was 11th in line to the throne. Peter did not tell her about his royal connections, and she only learned the truth while watching a television programme about Prince William.

Peter, 30, arrived at the chapel at 3.40 p.m., 20 minutes before his bride-to-be, wearing a morning suit and accompanied by his two best men, childhood friend Andrew Tucker and Ben Goss, a friend from Gordonstoun. Wearing a £7,500 Sassi Holford dress, a tiara loaned to her by Princess Anne, and a necklace and earrings given to her by the groom, Autumn walked up the slippery steps and into the church clutching onto her father 'for dear life' to the strains of the 'Prince of Denmark's March' by Jeremiah Clarke. Autumn, who was PA to Sir Michael Parkinson, and a former promotions girl and actress, was attended by six bridesmaids in green Vera Wang dresses, including her childhood best friend Jackie Aubie and her future sister-in-law Zara Phillips.

The couple, who were married by the Dean of Windsor, Bishop David Conner, Autumn having converted from Catholicism to the Church of England to prevent Peter having to renounce his right to the throne, exchanged rings and vows.

Emerging from the chapel at 5 p.m., they left in a carriage for Frogmore House in Windsor Great Park, Queen Victoria's favourite residence, which had been lent to them by the Queen for their

reception, organised by Peregrine Armstrong-Jones, the party-planning younger half-brother of Lord Snowdon.

The couple joined their 300 guests at a wedding breakfast of potted Cornish crab with lobster butter, roasted rack of Welsh lamb and a choice of three puddings: molten chocolate fondant with salted caramel ice cream, coffee and hazelnut mousse with tiny sugared doughnuts or berries encased in a brandy snap. They cut their wedding cake, which had been made at Buckingham Palace and was laden with sugar-crafted lily of the valley and stephanotis, with a military sword belonging to Peter. After the Queen and Prince Philip departed, the wedding party withdrew to a marquee in the grounds, decorated with chrome lanterns, where they danced until the early hours to the sounds of a blues band.

It was a typical society occasion but one with a twist: the couple had sold the rights to coverage of the wedding, for an estimated £500,000, to *Hello!*, more usually home to the shenanigans of footballers' wives and soap stars, raising disturbing questions over the status of minor royals, who do not perform public duties or draw money from the public purse, but do benefit from their connections. The couple had already given a 19-page interview on the eve of the wedding at Aston Farm, a cottage on Peter's father's estate adjoining Gatcombe Park in Gloucestershire, but this was only the first of two articles on the marriage, the second covering the ceremony itself.

The deal, negotiated by the magazine's fixer the Marquesa de Varela, provoked a storm of criticism after it emerged that Peter had discussed it in advance with his mother but failed to consult the monarch, who only learned about the contract – the first in royal history – after it had been signed. Even then, the royal family did not realise the extent of the magazine's coverage, which included candid images of the royal family taken during the reception and evening party. The storm was exacerbated when it emerged that the

newly-weds had final approval of the pictures used in the feature, including around a dozen of the Queen, although it is not known whether they approved these themselves or authorised someone else to do so on their behalf.

Four days after the royal wedding, Kate flew out to Mustique to meet William on the holiday that was widely tipped to prompt a proposal – some bookies had even stopped taking bets on whether an engagement would occur, saying it was a matter of when, not if, the couple sealed their union. The couple arrived on the Caribbean island on 21 May, almost two years to the day since they had spent a romantic week in the Robinsons' villa and a year since they had been reunited. This time, they hired the exclusive £1,785-a-night Villa Alumbrera, set, like the Robinsons' house, in the cliffs above Macaroni Beach on the east coast of the island. Owned by the widow of a Swedish mining tycoon, the glamorous house, which has featured in *Architectural Digest*, is one of the most secluded on the island, with breathtaking views of the sea and its own footpath leading to the beach. The couple stayed in a bedroom with its own private courtyard and outdoor shower. The house also had a luxurious swimming pool, terrace bar, gazebo, tennis court, pavilion and games room – everything a young couple could wish for. However, when they returned to England a week later, there was still no sign of an engagement.

On Monday, 2 June 2008, Sub Lieutenant William Wales arrived at the Britannia Royal Naval College in Darmouth for the first day of a two-month attachment to the Royal Navy. He was the latest in a long line of royals, beginning with his great-great-grandfather George V, to be cadets at the college. His great-grandfather George VI also trained there, as did the Duke of Edinburgh, who fought at sea during the Second World War and is believed to have met

the Queen in Dartmouth. William's uncle Prince Andrew trained at the college before becoming a helicopter pilot in the Falklands War and Charles was there before his service in the Royal Navy, during which he commanded a minehunter.

For the next three weeks, William studied naval history and learned seamanship, trained alongside the Royal Marines on amphibious and mountain-welfare exercises, dived with a nuclear submarine and flew in all of the navy helicopters, including the Sea Harrier, the Lynx, the Sea King and the Merlin. On his first exercise, he was shown how to handle a 15-metre twin-engine picket boat on the River Dart. Wearing No. 4 dress, the navy's version of combats, he took his turn to drop anchor on the harbour training ship *Hindostan*, a former minesweeper moored nearby. When he failed a bet to do it first time, he turned to his seven classmates and two instructors, saying: 'That's a crate of beer, then.'

Now seriously committed to Kate, the prince took every opportunity to travel the 224 miles back to London to visit his girlfriend, in contrast with his time in the Household Cavalry, when he preferred to party with his fellow officers. On his first weekend off, he and Kate joined friends at London's Royal Lancaster Hotel for the Boodles Boxing Ball, where four Old Etonians were trading punches with Cambridge graduates to raise money for the Starlight Foundation, a charity set up by former *Dynasty* actress Emma Samms to grant the wishes of terminally ill children. Wearing black tie, the royal couple met up with Harry and Chelsy for a champagne reception, dinner and auction. Afterwards, they joined Guy Pelly, Thomas van Straubenzee, Jamie Murray Wells and Jecca Craig in ringside seats for the boxing.

The first match featured Jecca's boyfriend Hugh 'The Hitman' Crossley, who lost out to Bear 'The Pain' Maclean. The group then watched William's former classmate James 'The Badger' Meade, the son of the international showjumper Richard Meade, being beaten

by Al 'Bonecrusher' Poulain, a former equerry to Prince Charles. Kate, who was wearing a stunning £1,000 pink Issa gown, floor-length and slashed to the navel, winced and covered her eyes during the fights, while William and Harry punched the air, showing their Help for Heroes wristbands, in support of a charity for wounded servicemen and women. The £100-a-ticket event was organised by their friend Charlie Gilkes, who also owned Kitts, the young royals' new favourite nightclub. It raised £120,000 for the charity and granted the wish of cystic fibrosis sufferer Bianca Nicolas, 19, to sing at the event and meet Harry and William.

Kate was so touched by her encounter with Bianca that she decided she wanted to become involved with the charity, whose patron is Princess Alexandra, a cousin of the Queen. She suggested forging a link with Party Pieces, in order to hold kids' parties and give party bags to 10,000 sick children in hospitals over Christmas. It was the first time Kate had publicly supported a charity, one of the prerequisites for a future princess. 'I find it terribly exciting,' Emma Samms told the *Daily Mail*. 'We are extremely thrilled, as you can imagine. They will be supplying us with all of the decorations and toys to play with, and the children are all going to get party bags. I am looking forward to meeting up with Kate soon to thank her properly for what she has done for Starlight. It is such a huge donation. What a great thing they are doing – and what a great change it will make to these kids.'

The weekend after the Boxing Ball, William was down in London again for his investiture into the Order of the Garter. Kate escorted him to the event, held at Windsor Castle on 16 June in front of the Queen and all his aunts and uncles. It was the first time that she had been to such a formal royal event – another significant milestone on the road to becoming a member of The Firm – but she could not keep a straight face. When William processed past the historic Galilee Porch on his way from the chapel to the castle, wearing a

blue velvet cloak and a hat adorned with ostrich plumes, she and Harry burst into fits of giggles. William, however, managed to keep his composure for the annual Garter Day Service, in which he was awarded the highest honour the monarch can bestow, membership of the order renowned for its motto '*Honi soit qui mal y pense*', which translates as 'Shame on him who thinks ill of it'.

Within two days, William was back at sea, spending 24 hours underwater on the nuclear submarine HMS *Talent*, taking part in an exercise to track down and destroy an enemy sub. Sleeping aboard the submarine, he spent time in the control room, next to the nuclear reactor, and saw the cruise missiles in the torpedo room. At the end of the stint, he was winched off the boat by a Sea King helicopter.

The next weekend spelled the end of the prince's three weeks' training with the navy, perfect timing as he was celebrating his 26th birthday on Saturday, 21 June. He and Kate spent the weekend with Harry and Chelsy at the Beaufort Polo Club near Westonbirt Arboretum in Gloucestershire. After watching England (captained by Luke Tomlinson, an Old Etonian and close friend of the princes whose family owns the club) beat New Zealand in the Williams de Broë International Test Match, the couple danced the night away at the Boujis to Beaufort party in a marquee in the grounds. The following day, William and Harry joined Luke on the polo field with the Apes Hill Club Barbados team. They beat the Stobarts 5–3 in a charity match that raised £50,000 for the Countryside Foundation for Education and the Tusk Trust.

After his birthday weekend off, it was time for William to get serious. On Monday, 23 June, he began a five-week operation at the Type 23 frigate HMS *Iron Duke*, a 4,900-ton warship that was working with American Drug Enforcement Administration agents to track down cocaine smugglers during the hurricane season in the Caribbean. Once again, he was separated from his girlfriend.

After just four days on the warship, armed US coastguards seized £40 million-worth of cocaine from a speedboat north-east of Barbados. William was on board the Lynx helicopter that spotted the 50-ft vessel and apparently played a key 'planning and surveillance' role in the seizure. Later, he took part in a hurricane disaster training exercise off the volcanic island of Montserrat, as one of the forward command team landing on the island.

While her boyfriend was on exercise, Kate went to her second royal wedding of the year without him, confirming her established position in the family. Wearing a floral dress and pale-blue fitted jacket with a black feather fascinator, a hair accessory favoured on recent occasions by the Queen and the Duchess of Cornwall, she joined guests on 19 July at the Queen's Chapel in St James's Palace for the marriage of Lady Rose Windsor, a great-granddaughter of George V and 23rd in line to the throne. The youngest daughter of the Duke and Duchess of Gloucester, and William's second cousin, Rose, 28, who works in the film industry (she is credited on one of the Harry Potter movies as an assistant in the art department), wore a Franka couture wedding gown and a tiara that had belonged to Queen Mary for her wedding to George Gilman, 26, the son of a former director of Leeds United Football Club.

During his five weeks out at sea, William barely spoke to his girlfriend, 4,500 miles away, let alone saw her. He was allowed to use his mobile telephone but reception out at sea was poor. By the time he disembarked on 2 August, he was desperate to see her. It was the longest they had been apart since they began dating at St Andrews five years earlier.

The couple were finally reunited in Mustique, where they had made their fond farewells two months earlier. It was the third time they had holidayed on the island. This time, they stayed on the western coast in the Villa Rocina, created by Oliver Messel, who was also responsible for Princess Margaret's Les Jolies Eaux. The

secluded house, owned by Venezuelan millionairess Violera Alvarez, had a dining gazebo on the veranda overlooking the ocean, a cinema and gym. With its master bedroom suite with steps leading straight onto the beach, it was an ideal getaway for the prince and his girlfriend, especially after his time spent holed up in a tiny cabin at sea. They spent their days relaxing by the pool, water skiing and sharing a ride on an inflatable ring. On their final night, they attended a gala dinner to celebrate the 40th anniversary of the Mustique Company, which runs the island, where they met up with Kate's former bosses Belle and John Robinson.

As soon as they returned to British shores, the couple hit the town, keen to show off their golden suntans. Their first port of call was Raffles, round the corner from Kate's flat in Chelsea. Leaving there at 3.45 a.m. on 15 August, Kate had a momentary lapse in decorum, flashing rather more of her tan than she intended when her multicoloured tunic dress rode up her thighs. William stumbled and almost fell on top of her.

A few weeks later, they flew out to Austria together for the wedding of Chiara Hunt, the doctor granddaughter of the late Baron Hunt of Fawley, who once posed for *Country Life* reclining naked in a bath full of lollipops. Chiara, the sister of their university friend Olivia and of TV presenter Ben Fogle's wife Marina, married Rupert Evetts, a Blues and Royals officer, on 6 September in Salzburg. It was the first time William had been able to attend a wedding with Kate that year, and the event gave the couple the chance to catch up with Lady Davina Windsor, the elder sister of Rose. Davina was there with her husband, Gary Lewis, a former New Zealand sheep shearer, whom she had married in 2004. It was now 16 months since Kate and William had got back together, but still there was no sign of a royal engagement

Soon afterwards, William began the final months of the military service that was intended to prepare him for his future role as head

of the armed forces. Having spent a year in the army, four months with the RAF and two months with the navy, he was going on tour with Britain's elite services – the Special Air Service, the Special Boat Service and the Special Reconnaissance Unit – to learn about unconventional warfare, counter-terrorism and reconnaissance. He also spent time with the Chief of Defence Staff, Air Marshal Sir Jock Stirrup, worked at the MoD and was attached to the Army Air Corps. It was a *Boy's Own* dream for the prince, although he would not be on operational duties.

As the crescendo of conjecture over their future grew ever louder and the country slumped into a recession, William and Kate made a conscious decision to keep a lower profile. Over the next few months, they were seen only at charity events – and even then separately – sparking rumours that their relationship was once again on the rocks. In fact, the couple were as strong as ever but were keeping out of the limelight, socialising at dinner parties and house parties rather than going clubbing.

One of Kate's rare public appearances that autumn was in support of a planned surgical ward at the Children's Hospital, Oxford. Tom's Ward was to be named in memory of the brother of one of her friends, Sam Waley-Cohen, an amateur jockey who has ridden in the Grand National. Tom Waley-Cohen, who was the same age as Prince Harry and went to pre-prep school Wetherby with the princes, died in 2004 at the age of 20 after battling Ewing's sarcoma, a rare form of bone cancer. He was at Marlborough with Kate, where, although he was a few years below her, he was a recognisable figure because he had had his left leg amputated below the knee. 'Thomas was a very remarkable boy and was always upbeat,' says his mother Felicity, daughter of Viscount Bearstead, a member of the Hill Samuel banking dynasty. 'Everybody was aware of him at Marlborough because he only had one leg and he was incredibly naughty. He was definitely not one of life's victims.'

Kate was one of the three organisers of an event called the Day-Glo Midnight Roller Disco to raise money for Tom's Ward, at the new Oxford Children's Hospital, as well as for the charity Place2Be, which provides counselling for schoolchildren in need. She joined fellow organisers Sam Waley-Cohen and Holly Branson on 17 September for the roller disco at the Renaissance Rooms in Vauxhall.

William couldn't make it, and Kate turned up with her sister Pippa. Dressed in yellow hotpants, a green sequinned halterneck top and pink legwarmers, she was captured sprawling on her back, legs akimbo, in what was deemed an undignified pose for a future Queen. But the publicity raised awareness of the charity, which she has long supported behind the scenes. After the event, Sam said: 'We wanted to do something fresh and new, something that would be fun and a bit tongue in cheek, reflecting the lighter side of life, very much like Thomas was himself. Kate has been fantastic in using her contacts to get people along. She has persuaded loads of people to commit. Her involvement has obviously raised the profile.'

Not to be outdone by his girlfriend, Prince William joined his brother Harry in a charity motorcycle rally to raise money for Sentebale, the charity Harry set up to help disadvantaged children in Lesotho. The two brothers set off on 18 October on an eight-day ride through the South African wilderness, sleeping rough as they crossed 1,000 miles of inhospitable terrain. Both passionate bikers, they were believed to have been inspired by Ewan McGregor and Charley Boorman, who rode from John O'Groats to Cape Town for the TV series *Long Way Down*. Despite the fact that the princes' participation in the rally contributed to the success of the fundraising event, questions were raised about the security required and that such costs were supplemented by the British taxpayer, undermining their altruism. Sitting on his Honda CRF 230-cc bike and dressed in body armour and thick protective boots, William

said: 'Harry and I had an idea last November to take part in this rally because it's a mixture of adventure and charity, the key being the money raised today goes towards Nelson Mandela's Children's Fund, Unicef and Sentebale – three absolutely brilliant charities.'

After her successful charitable ventures, Kate decided that she wanted to spread her wings and handed in her notice at Jigsaw. She left on 1 November, with an envelope of Jigsaw vouchers after a low-key finger buffet. The move sparked another round of rumours about her future with William and consternation within the palace over Kate's insubstantial CV. Despite being 82 years old, the Queen has a reputation for being one of the hardest-working royals and is said to have a soft spot for Sophie Wessex, who was a career girl before she married Prince Edward.

But Kate was set on a career in photography and it was rumoured that she flew to New York for a couple of lessons with Mario Testino, a favourite photographer of Princess Diana and the man who took the iconic *Vogue* shots of her. A month later, she curated her first exhibition, by celebrity portrait photographer Alistair Morrison, whom she had met while she was at St Andrews. The exhibition, Time to Reflect – a selection of portraits of stars such as Tom Cruise, Kate Winslet and Ewan McGregor taken in photo booths – was held at The Shop at Bluebird on Kings Road, owned by her former boss, and raised money for the United Nations children's fund Unicef. Kate's family and friends, including Guy Pelly and Laura Parker Bowles, rallied around and William, who had just arrived back from a secret mission with the Special Boat Service, formed during the Second World War to conduct raids behind German lines in North Africa, with the motto 'By Strength and Guile', made a last-minute appearance.

Speaking at the launch, Alistair, 51, who has a gallery in Windsor, said: 'Kate approached me when she was at university to come and do a little bit of work with her and we've kept in touch. She came

to my gallery and we talked through some of her work. She was looking to get a little help. She is very, very good, and it shows. She takes very beautiful, detailed photographs. She has a huge talent and a great eye. I'm sure she will go far.'

However, although the exhibition was deemed a success, Kate still had to earn a living, and by the end of the year she was working for Party Pieces, doing a technology course to learn how to compile digital catalogues, photographing products and setting up its new venture, First Birthdays, which she was going to manage. It was mundane work and can have done little to stretch the brain of the girl who got an upper second at St Andrews; nor did it silence her critics, but it did mean that she was on hand for her prince when he called.

On 13 December, he did just that and they spent a weekend pheasant shooting at Sandringham, showing just how comfortable Kate was with the green-wellie brigade. But while she inevitably attracted more criticism from the animal-rights lobby, it was William's appearance at the shoot that got people talking. The prince had grown a beard during an exercise in the Caribbean with the Special Boat Service the previous month, following a naval tradition, like his father and grandfather before him, of remaining unshaven. Charles grew his facial hair while serving in Alaska in 1975 and Prince Philip grew a beard during his wartime service aboard HMS *Valiant*.

As dictated by royal protocol, the couple spent Christmas apart, Kate on her third holiday to Mustique that year and William at Sandringham. They were reunited for New Year at Birkhall, where they went walking and shooting. Then, for the first time in three years, they spent Kate's birthday together, on 9 January 2009, celebrating with a low-key family dinner at her parents' home. However, any thoughts that the family might have had about a royal wedding had to be put on hold, as William had a new career.

CHAPTER 25

Princess in Waiting

Wearing his olive-green flying suit and regulation goggles under his helmet because of his poor vision, Flying Officer Wales took off on 14 January 2009 for the first of the flights in his training to become an RAF search-and-rescue pilot. With an instructor by his side, the 26-year-old prince – who is rarely seen in public wearing the metal-rimmed glasses he needs for driving – underwent an hour-long lesson on a single-engine Squirrel helicopter at the Defence Helicopter Flying School at RAF Shawbury, where helicopter crews for all the armed services are trained.

It was five days after Kate's 27th birthday and her boyfriend, given the new codename 'Golden Osprey', was on his third day back at the base, near Shrewsbury in Shropshire, where he had first discovered a passion for flying helicopters in the weeks before he got his wings. He had rented a country house in the county, complete with swimming pool and tennis courts, as an alternative to his cramped room on the base.

Yet William's arrival at RAF Shawbury confounded all expectations. Widely expected to leave the military at Christmas and take on the role to which he had been born, he stunned royal analysts by transferring from the British Army into the RAF. His move came after his brother Harry had led his men into battle in Afghanistan. It was deemed too dangerous for the second in line to the throne to follow suit and go into a war zone, but he was allowed as a compromise to sign up with the RAF, learning to fly single-engine Squirrels and twin-engine Griffins. After doing an attachment with the Search and Rescue Training Unit at RAF Valley in Anglesey, where he had spent two weeks on work experience before Sandhurst, he will qualify as a search-and-rescue pilot in 2010, flying its famous yellow Sea King helicopters on hazardous rescue missions across the seas and mountains.

'I now want to build on the experience and training I have received to serve operationally,' he said. 'For good reasons, I was not able to deploy to Afghanistan this year with D Squadron of the Household Cavalry Regiment. The time I spent with the RAF earlier this year made me realise how much I love flying. Joining Search and Rescue is a perfect opportunity for me to serve in the forces operationally, while contributing to a vital part of the country's emergency services.'

William's dramatic turnaround finally dampened speculation that the country would be celebrating a royal wedding in 2009, but it would soon be overshadowed by the breakdown of another royal relationship.

On 15 January, three days after William arrived at RAF Shawbury, Lieutenant Harry Wales walked through the doors of the Army Air Corps at RAF Middle Wallop, south-west of Andover in Hampshire, and enrolled on a 14-month training course to learn

to fly Apache helicopters. Like William, he had put his love of flying before his relationship. But unlike Kate, Chelsy was not prepared to wait. Within days, she had announced on the social networking website Facebook that their five-year romance was over and she was single again. It was the end of a tempestuous relationship between a couple who had seemed genuinely to love each other. But the logistics of carrying on a long-distance love affair had torn them apart. Although the politics, philosophy and economics graduate was prepared to sacrifice her ocean-view apartment in Cape Town for student digs in Leeds, where she was studying for a post-graduate degree, she was not prepared to be constantly at Harry's beck and call. Kate, however, appears to be more persistent and is expected to wait for her man.

The first possible date for a royal wedding between William and Kate is now being touted as 2010, the year when the prince will qualify as a search-and-rescue pilot and get his first posting. If he and Kate formalise their relationship that summer, they will be able to move into married quarters and live together for the first time in five years, this time as man and wife.

William would not be the first member of the royal family to live with his wife while serving in the military: Prince Philip was posted to Malta a year after his marriage to the young Princess Elizabeth, and the couple had one of the most carefree years of their married life there. They lived in Lord Mountbatten's Villa Guardamangia and danced many a night away at Valletta's Hotel Meridien Phoenicia. But, until William proposes to her, Catherine Elizabeth Middleton is officially in limbo, neither a member of the royal family nor an anonymous commoner.

Kate's introduction to royal life has moved forward only very gradually since the day she left university and met the Queen at her graduation ceremony. Palace protocol dictates that until she is engaged to William, she will not be accorded any status within

the royal family. Although she has met the Queen socially on a couple of occasions, stories that she has dined alone with the monarch – or indeed had one-to-one meetings with her – are greatly exaggerated. So are reports that her parents have met the monarch, making a mockery of spurious gossip that her mother Carole breached etiquette by greeting her with the words 'Pleased to meet you'. Neither has Kate been invited to spend Christmas with the royal family at Sandringham; it is just not the done thing for the Queen's grandchildren to romance their partners under her roof. Equally, suggestions that she has moved into Clarence House – and been given a security pass – have been dismissed as nonsense. Although the couple have stayed there, William prefers to spend his weekends at Highgrove.

There has also been much speculation over the grooming for royal life that Kate is supposed to have received since she began dating William and the personal protection she is supposed to have been afforded. But she has received little advice since her relationship with the prince started, apart from the occasional friendly suggestion from Prince Charles's communications secretary, Paddy Harverson, on how to handle the media.

Her main port of call if she has a problem is the legal firm Harbottle & Lewis. Her solicitor, Gerrard Tyrrell, has managed to negotiate an uneasy truce with the press over the level of intrusion into her life, writing warning letters to newspaper and magazine editors and threatening legal action under human-rights legislation. The law firm obtained 'disturbing' footage of the paparazzi outside her Chelsea home in case she ever needs to support a complaint. While photographers have since stopped waiting outside her home, they have begun following her wherever she goes, leading the PCC to investigate, obtaining assurances from the tabloid papers that they would not use photographs taken in circumstances in breach of the industry's anti-harassment code.

Kate's first – and so far only – official complaint to the Press Complaints Commission about harassment was over a photograph published in the *Daily Mirror* a few months after her 25th birthday, showing her walking down the street on her way to work with a cup of coffee and car keys in her hand. The newspaper immediately apologised for using the photograph. Editor Richard Wallace said: 'We published an innocuous picture of Ms Middleton walking down the street with a cup of coffee. It was taken by a freelance photographer in circumstances where we were later told she felt harassed. We got it wrong and we sincerely regret that.'

Until Kate marries her prince, there is little more that can be done. As an ordinary member of the public, she is not entitled to round-the-clock police protection and, despite reports to the contrary, she has neither a formal bodyguard nor a police radio. She was spotted once, at the polo, in possession of a high-tech Airwave radio, but she was carrying it for William. Scotland Yard has stepped in on occasion – notably after her 25th birthday, when they sent two officers to stand outside her home, another couple to patrol the street and a pair to escort her to work – but they cannot assign her an official officer from SO14, Royalty Protection Branch, until she is engaged, because the funding would come from the public purse.

However, there are perks to being a princess in waiting. Kate has negotiated a 'specially enhanced arrangement' on a £23,000 silver Audi A3 hatchback coupé in which to drive around town, a sign that she is worth her weight in publicity. Both William's parents have always driven Audis – Diana used to drive around in an Audi cabriolet, while William has a powerful Audi S4 4.2 litre V8 black saloon – so she will certainly fit in with The Firm.

Down in the Wye Valley in Herefordshire, there is an even more luxurious reward awaiting her: a palace fit for a princess. Built on a former royal hunting forest, which was donated to

the Knights Templar of Garway during the Middle Ages, the 900-acre Harewood Park estate lies in a valley between Hereford and Ross-on-Wye, about 50 miles from Highgrove. After the dissolution of the monasteries during the reign of Henry VIII, it came into private ownership, eventually ending up in the hands of the family of the Civil War lawyer and MP Bennet Hoskyns. Since the late nineteenth century, it has gradually fallen into disrepair. Its Georgian mansion had to be demolished after the SAS used it for target practice. But the land was bought by the Duchy of Cornwall eight years ago and is gradually undergoing a multimillion-pound restoration.

Initially, locals believed that Prince Charles was planning to create a rural version of Poundbury, the model town he built in Dorset during the '90s. But villagers now believe, partly because Prince Charles is taking such a keen interest in the project, that the manor house is being restored as a starter home for Prince William and his bride. Designed by Craig Hamilton, an architect he has worked with in the past, the six-bedroom stately home has been created around an inner courtyard with a portico entrance and has a library, drawing room and dining room, as well as an orangery and stables. It will be built out of reclaimed brick, timber from the Duchy estate and salvaged Welsh slate tiles on the roof and will have every conceivable energy-saving device, including solar power and a reed-bed sewerage system. Coincidentally – or perhaps not – it will be completed in 2010, just as William finishes his RAF training. Then, perhaps, the girl whose story begins in the mining villages of Durham will move into her palace in Herefordshire.

It has been an extraordinary journey for the woman who was christened Catherine Elizabeth Middleton and has become known

in the public perception as Kate. Like a butterfly emerging from a chrysalis, the shy, retiring schoolgirl has transformed into a confident and glamorous young woman with the poise to become a royal bride. *Vogue* editor Alex Shulman has described her as 'a contemporary version' of Princess Diana. 'She has the same mainstream style and will go on, like Diana, to get more glamorous,' she said. But Kate is made from a different mould; Diana had aristocratic connections and was a member of the Establishment. Kate's background is more in line with those of the consorts of European royalty; on the Continent, the wives of princes and kings have degrees and careers. If, or when, as many believe, Kate becomes Queen Catherine, she will be the first wife of a British monarch to have graduated from university, displayed her lingerie on the catwalk and lived with a king out of wedlock.

At some stage in the future, William V will become the 42nd monarch to ascend the throne since his namesake William the Conqueror overthrew Harold in the Battle of Hastings in 1066. Kate could also be the fifth of her name to rule. The first was Catherine of Valois, daughter of the French King Charles VI who married the Plantagenet King Henry V in 1420, after his historic win at Agincourt. Then there were three wives of Henry VIII: Katherine of Aragon, mother of his daughter Mary, whom he divorced; Catherine Howard, whom he beheaded; and Catherine Parr, who outlived him. Finally, there was the Portuguese infanta Catherine of Braganza, who married Charles II by proxy in 1662, two years after the reformation of the monarchy. She, by coincidence, was the sister-in-law of the last commoner to marry a British king, Anne Hyde.

If William does ask Kate to marry him, he could do worse than follow in the footsteps of William Shakespeare's Henry V when he proposed to his Kate:

Kate

A speaker is but a prater; a rhyme is but a ballad. A good leg will fall, a straight back will stoop, a black beard will turn white, a curled pate will grow bald, a fair face will wither, a full eye will wax hollow; but a good heart, Kate, is the sun and the moon, or rather the sun and not the moon, for it shines bright and never changes, but keeps his course truly. If thou would have such a one, take me; and take me, take a soldier; take a soldier, take a king.

Appendix

KATE MIDDLETON'S FAMILY TREE

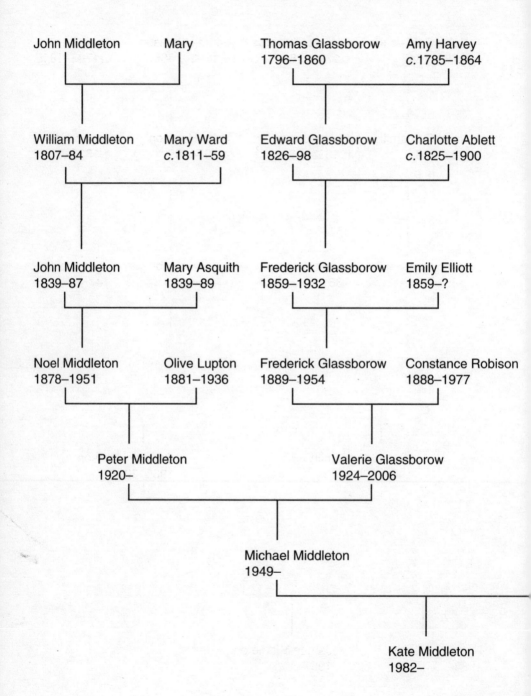

John Middleton   Mary

Thomas Glassborow   Amy Harvey
1796–1860   c.1785–1864

William Middleton   Mary Ward
1807–84   c.1811–59

Edward Glassborow   Charlotte Ablett
1826–98   c.1825–1900

John Middleton   Mary Asquith
1839–87   1839–89

Frederick Glassborow   Emily Elliott
1859–1932   1859–?

Noel Middleton   Olive Lupton
1878–1951   1881–1936

Frederick Glassborow   Constance Robison
1889–1954   1888–1977

Peter Middleton   Valerie Glassborow
1920–   1924–2006

Michael Middleton
1949–

Kate Middleton
1982–

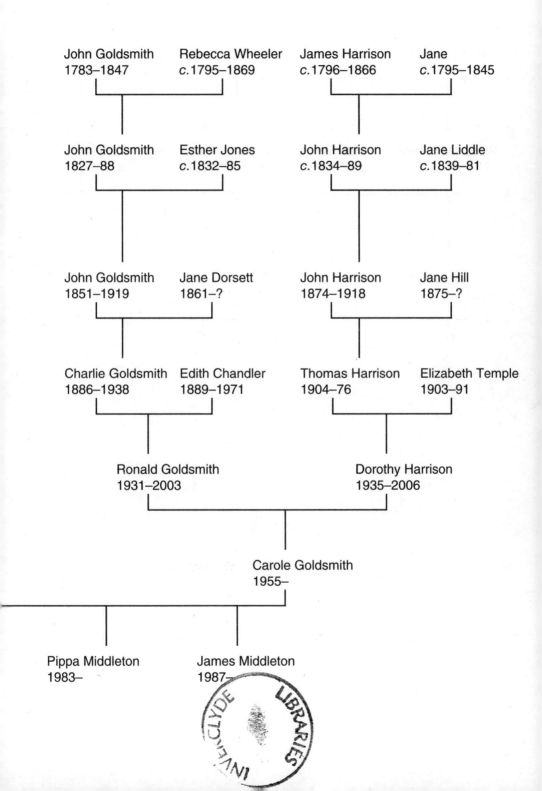

John Goldsmith 1783–1847 — Rebecca Wheeler c.1795–1869

James Harrison c.1796–1866 — Jane c.1795–1845

John Goldsmith 1827–88 — Esther Jones c.1832–85

John Harrison c.1834–89 — Jane Liddle c.1839–81

John Goldsmith 1851–1919 — Jane Dorsett 1861–?

John Harrison 1874–1918 — Jane Hill 1875–?

Charlie Goldsmith 1886–1938 — Edith Chandler 1889–1971

Thomas Harrison 1904–76 — Elizabeth Temple 1903–91

Ronald Goldsmith 1931–2003 — Dorothy Harrison 1935–2006

Carole Goldsmith 1955–

Pippa Middleton 1983–

James Middleton 1987–